ELEPHANTS HAVE THE RIGHT OF WAY

A UNICEF memoir

Horst D. Rüttinger

Edited by J. Steven Lamperti

For privacy reasons, some names, locations, and dates may have been changed.

Revision 1.0 11/2023

ISBN: 979-8-9861501-4-7

Lamprey Publishing
LampreyPublishing@gmail.com

Cover Design by J. Steven Lamperti

Printed in the United States of America

Dedicated to Horst's wife, Doris,
and his three daughters,
Renate, Susanne, and Andrea

CONTENTS

Title Page	
Copyright	
Dedication	
Editor's Preface	3
Early Days	4
How it all began	5
Early Years	7
The postwar years: 1945 to 1964	12
1956	19
Strange places, strange customs	20
1964	23
Unicef Notes:	24
Unicef Beginnings	27
Development	32
Just Independent	36
Nigeria	40
The Great Rift Valley	41
Uganda	46
Uganda II	50
Uganda III	55

Comments on Uganda 60
Focus on Logistics I (Rwanda) 64
Focus on Logistics II 68
1965 71
Rwanda 72
Congo 75
Congo II 80
Toni Nutti 83
1967 86
Zanzibar 87
Emergency Landing 90
1968 94
Safari 95
1970 98
Doris Story 99
Abidjan 101
Abidjan II 106
Colonel Odumegwa Ojukwu 110
The Cannibals 112
Suat 116
Domestique 117
1971 121
Abidjan Eastbound 122
Abidjan Eastbound II 125
Abidjan Eastbound III 128
Citroen 2CV 132
Hans von Sponeck 134
Iraq 138

1972	139
Vaccines in Mali	140
Mali	142
1973	145
Elephants have the right of way (Mali II)	146
Mali III	151
1974	153
Nigeria	154
1975	157
John Bradford	158
1977	161
Bridge in Nouakchott	162
New York	165
New York II	169
Unknown flour	171
1978	173
Afghanistan	174
1979	178
Kampuchea	179
Kampuchea II	183
1980	187
Inside Kampuchea	188
Still inside Kampuchea	193
Kampuchea Aftermath	198
Kampuchea again	205
1982	207
Lebanon Emergency	208
Lebanon II	212

Lebanon III	214
Lebanon-Bekaa	217
Second trip to Beirut	221
1983	228
Supplies and China	229
To Somalia before Christmas	234
1984	239
Cockroaches	240
Andrea in Kenya	241
Afghanistan II	243
1985	244
Ethiopia	245
Ethiopia again	252
The Road to Assab	254
Girl in the elevator	257
Volunteers	260
Band-aid	262
Computers	266
1986	269
Eritrea	270
Personal car	274
Susanne's visit to Addis	279
War and Peace	281
South African Taskforce	285
Sierra Leone	286
Port of Assab	287
1987	289
Zaire	290

Madagascar	293
Madagascar II	297
Madagascar III	299
1988	301
India	302
1989	307
Kamikaze Banana	308
Burundi – Fear	310
Afghanistan III	313
1990	321
Condoms	322
JIU-Mission on Logistics	323
JIU – Mission on Logistics II	326
JIU – Mission on Logistics III	330
JIU-Mission on Logistics IV	335
JIU-Mission on Logistics V	340
JIU-Mission on Logistics, VI	345
JIU-Mission on Logistics – India	348
JIU – Summary	352
EPI and Logistics	357
1991	360
Zaire II	361
1992	367
Cambodia	368
1993	371
Called out of retirement	372
OLS	373
Predja	377

1994	381
Khartoum, Sudan	382
1999	386
Lassa fever	387
Lost People	389
Computers and Y2K and Africa	390
Editor's Afterword	392

AFRICA
POLITICAL DIVISIONS
1 JANUARY 1966
★ Capital
BOUNDARY REPRESENTATION IS
NOT NECESSARILY AUTHORITATIVE
0 500 1000 MILES
0 500 1000 KILOMETERS
1-66
Algiers
Tunis
TUNISIA
Rabat
Tripoli
Benghazi
MOROCCO
Sidi Ifni
IFNI (Sp.)
ALGERIA
LIBYA
Cairo
UNITED ARAB REPUBLIC
El Aiún
SPANISH SAHARA
MAURITANIA
Nouakchott
MALI
NIGER
CHAD
Khartoum
SUDAN
Dakar
SENEGAL
THE GAMBIA
PORT. GUINEA
Bissau
Bamako
Niamey
Ouagadougou
UPPER VOLTA
Fort-Lamy
FRENCH SOMALILAND
Djibouti
Addis Ababa
GUINEA
Conakry
Freetown
SIERRA LEONE
IVORY COAST
GHANA
TOGO
DAHOMEY
NIGERIA
Porto-Novo
ETHIOPIA
CENTRAL AFRICAN REPUBLIC
SOMALIA
Monrovia
LIBERIA
Abidjan
Accra
Lomé
Lagos
CAMEROON
Bangui
Mogadiscio
FERNANDO PO
Santa Isabel
Yaoundé
EQUATORIAL GUINEA (Sp.)
PRÍNCIPE (Port.)
SÃO TOMÉ (Port.)
ANNOBÓN
RIO MUNI
Libreville
GABON
CONGO
DEMOCRATIC REPUBLIC OF THE CONGO
UGANDA
Kampala
KENYA
Nairobi
Kigali
RWANDA
Bujumbura
BURUNDI
Brazzaville
Léopoldville
PEMBA
ZANZIBAR
TANZANIA
Dar es Salaam
Luanda
ANGOLA (Port.)
ZAMBIA
Lusaka
MALAWI
Zomba
Salisbury
SOUTHERN RHODESIA (U.K.)
MOZAMBIQUE (Port.)
Tananarive
MALAGASY REPUBLIC
SOUTH-WEST AFRICA (Rep. of S. Af.)
WALVIS BAY (Rep. of S. Af.)
Windhoek
BECHUANALAND (U.K.)
Gaberones
Pretoria
Mbabane
Lourenço Marques
SWAZILAND (U.K.)
Maseru
BASUTOLAND (U.K.)
REPUBLIC OF SOUTH AFRICA
Cape Town

EDITOR'S PREFACE

Horst Dietrich Rüttinger was born in 1928 in Schweinfurt, Germany. He died in Heidelberg, Germany, in 2020. This book is a collection of stories he wrote describing the world travels and events of his life and his work for Unicef and other organizations.

Horst married Dorothea Elizabeth Tolle in December 1955. They had three daughters: Renate, Susanne, and Andrea, as described in this book.

* * *

I, your humble editor, am Horst's son-in-law. I married Andrea in 1988.

Horst decided late in life to write his memoirs. He corresponded for years with Howard Singer, a writer and a friend of Susanne's, about the book's content. The main consequence of this collaboration was the motivation to write that Horst got from needing to send stories to Howard.

The idea of editing the stories Horst wrote into a book has been with me for a while. In fact, we talked about it a little before he died. That didn't happen then. Now, a few years later, the time seems right.

Horst encouraged me in my desire to become a writer. At one point, he gave me a book entitled "Is there a book inside you?" I hope my editing has helped bring out the book inside him.

* * *

I first met Horst in the early eighties, when I was nineteen or twenty. My first impression, unusual for me, was that this was a man to be respected and admired.

But let's let Horst tell you who he is in his own words.

EARLY DAYS

HOW IT ALL BEGAN

I come from a very ordinary family, nothing special. None of my ancestors were famous. My grandfather had quite a large farm in Bavaria, which he lost during the depression in the twenties, before his oldest son, my father, could take over.

My father and mother married in 1926 during a very critical and difficult time. If I look at their marriage date and my elder brother's birthday, I know they had to marry. The status of a single mother at that time in Germany, surely also in the US, was no fun.

They had another difficulty, my father was a Lutheran protestant, and my mother was catholic. My grandparents on the mother's side were strictly catholic, and to marry a protestant was, to their way of thinking, almost a sin. That did not help my mother at all. I know my mother had a very hard time, but she did not talk about it much.

My parents had four children, and my father was out of work. I spent a lot of time with my mother's parents; there was always food. My grandparents (mother's side) were good people and full of love for us, their grandchildren.

We were baptized catholic; that was a condition when my mother married my father. My grandfather on my mother's side was also a farmer. My grandmother was a schoolteacher. She died in 1942. The grandfather lived until he was 92 years old.

My father did not come back from the war in 1945. We got the news of his death in France from another war veteran and friend who came home in the autumn of 1945. When he heard this, my grandfather said to his daughter, my mother: "This is because you married a protestant!." I can still say that I liked my grandfather, but you can imagine his narrow-mindedness.

My father's family was much more tolerant and open-minded. I have inherited my open-mindedness from my father and his parents. Later in my life, when I met many people from all cultures and religions, I sometimes thought of what my grandfather said to my mother. I wonder what he would have said if my mother had married a Jew. As one knows, there were many mixed marriages in Germany and the rest of Europe.

People have learned and changed in this last part of the millennium, but not all thou' did learn.

Doris and I are proud that our children and ourselves are respectful of other people, cultures, and religions. We had, of course, the good fortune to travel around this world and meet many different people. We have also seen the suffering and misery of intolerance, fanaticism, and ignorance. Fundamentalism, regardless of which religion it comes from, I absolutely can not stand.

When did I first consider leaving Germany and seeking my fortune in foreign countries? I think it was and had to do with that incident when my grandfather told my mother that it was her own fault that she became an early widow because she married a protestant. Born in 1928, I was 17 years old when this took place.

More and more, I became convinced that I must go out and meet other people and see other lands. I had a girlfriend then, but she thought I was crazy. If I had stayed with her, I am sure that we would have only traveled as tourists to foreign countries. My great luck was when I met Doris; she supported my aspiration and was part of it. We met abroad, in Switzerland. For Germans, Switzerland is not really a faraway country. Those came after we were married in 1955 and almost immediately traveled to the Middle East.

EARLY YEARS

My family and I were not Nazis but were not in a resistance movement either. We were, as the vast majority of Germans were, "Mitlaeufer" (hanger-on), meaning, in my case, I did what I was told to do. You must also remember that as a boy in Germany in those days, we were constantly and totally brainwashed. I believed, almost to the end of the war, that we were fighting for a just cause.

We knew there was a concentration camp in Dachau. However, I, speaking just for myself, did not know what was going on there and was not actually interested in it.

Later in the UN, I had a Danish colleague who, as a member of the Danish resistance, was arrested by the Germans and taken to Dachau. He told me he was placed in a special part of the camp where only Scandinavians were held. He said the Scandinavian section at Dachau was not too bad.

I did not know of Auschwitz in Poland, far from where we were. I am not proud of having been a "Mitlauefer." But this is what I was.

I spent a lot of time at my grandparent's farm in Bavaria. I think, but have no proof, that my grandfather, the arch catholic, at an early stage, say 1935-1936, knew what was going on but did not speak out loud. They had 10 children. My mother was one of them.

My uncles were much older than we were, and eventually, they all had to join the military. One of them, the youngest, Raimund, fell in Russia at the age of twenty-five. My uncle Kaspar often spoke of his disapproval of the Nazi regime and predicted where, in his opinion, it would take us to. He was always admonished by his father and other members of the family. The Dachau concentration camp was not far from the farm. This was known, and they told him, Kaspar be quiet, or you will end up in Dachau.

In 1937 we moved to Wuerzburg, in the North of Bavaria, where we lived in the middle of town. Some Jewish families lived in our neighborhood, and some Jewish shops were nearby. Notably, a bakery where people, including us, bought bread. I think it was in 1938 when the Nazis showed their hatred against the Jews, at least in my town, more openly. By then, Jews also had to wear the yellow star with "JUDE" written on it.

In November of 1938 was the "Kristallnacht" when Jewish synagogues, shops, and other properties were smashed and burned. The bakery in our neighborhood was also destroyed and never reopened. But in any case, we would not have been able to buy bread in a Jewish bakery any longer. Local Nazi party watchdogs made sure that there was no contact between Jewish Germans and other Germans.

After the Kristallnacht, my father said, "that was not right," but this was all he ever said about this. Most shops had a sign at the door or window saying "Juden sind hier unerwuenscht", meaning Jews were not welcome. I remember Jews were living in our neighborhood until the war's end. I wondered and never learned where they got their provisions from during this time.

My father was, except for some casual jobs, unemployed between 1927 to 1933. That was the time when my brothers and I were born. Many Germans were in a similar situation. In 1933 the vast majority followed the new "Fuehrer," who promised work for everyone without thinking too much. When they started to think, it was too late.

Surveillance by the state was flawless. One could trust nobody, not your friend and not your neighbor. Those who observed the new rules improved their living conditions. There was plenty of work, but nobody thought this work was actually created by war preparation. The big things that everyone saw were the building of the

"Westwall" (fortification of the border to France) and the Autobahn (highway). The creation of the Volkswagen and the promise that everybody could get a car by saving five marks monthly excited people. The first delivery of a VW never happened; the outbreak of war made things real.

Was I in the "Hitler Jugend" (Hitler-Youth)? Of course, I was; if anybody says he was not, he is a liar. There was a time up to 1942 when it was sort of "voluntary" to be a member of the Hitler Jugend. Still, if you were not, watchdogs in the neighborhood started to ask why you were not joining. As of 1942, it was compulsory to be in the HJ unless you were Jewish or half-Jewish. You had to attend the weekly "Apell" (roll call). If you did not come, you had to have a good excuse, or else you and your parents were in trouble.

I came back from the war in 1945. This would imply that I was in the army. Yes, I was. In a later chapter, "The Postwar Years," this will be mentioned again. While I was a soldier, I was not involved in what could be classified as a "war crime" action. That was not my doing, nor could I have avoided it if I had been at the wrong place at the wrong time. I had been in a regular army unit, later POW of the American army, and was released by the end of May 1945. Those soldiers who had been in special units and the SS, accused of war crimes, were not released. Some were put on trial by a war crime tribunal.

I want to write a book about my international life. My background needs to be described as part of what drove me to become an international civil servant. There is nothing sensitive, from my point of view, nothing I wish to hide. I do not want to write a book on my early years and life during Nazi Germany. There was nothing I could be proud of, and, as a seventeen-year-old brainwashed young fellow at the end of the war, there is also nothing I am ashamed of. Another thing, the war and also the "Third Reich" ended 55 years ago. I am certainly not searching my mind repeatedly to find out what I might have done wrong as a boy.

When the war was over, I opened my eyes and mind

during the period of about a month when I was a prisoner of war. Together with three or four other soldiers, I was taken prisoner by American GIs.

At this point in time, at the end of April 1945, there was no longer any organized resistance by the German army. We were on the Southern bank of the river Danube, German soldiers, each carrying a gun. We had just lost our platoon in the wake of an American tank attack. They had crossed the river (Danube) from the north without having too much resistance. The first tanks went by without even bothering about us. One tank commander, exposed from the waistline on top of the tank, shouted something we did not understand, but I think he shouted, "throw away your guns!" This tank was in a hurry and continued. I can not remember what we did; perhaps we did throw away our guns at this point.

It took half an hour until more US armored vehicles came and took us prisoner. Now that it was the last days of the war, German soldiers surrendered in great numbers. In the end, we were about 100,000 in a big open field. There were no barracks, houses, tents, or even a fence. There was a gate, however, at the entrance to the campground. That gate was largely symbolic, as the fence was not built.

Each morning a big truck arrived and distributed one ration package for each POW. I think the US army had 3 different ration packages for GIs, one for mornings, one for lunch, and one for the evening. Each had a different color. We got only one a day and had no say in which one. As a young lad, that was not enough, but some of the soldiers brought food into the camp when they were taken prisoner. So trading took place. For instance, the US rations included cigarettes. I did not smoke and traded my cigarettes for food.

Then I found out that being near the gate in the morning, there was a chance to get a job. The GIs always needed workers. There was an extra ration for this. For several days I washed military trucks and jeeps with a fire hose from a water hydrant heavily guarded by a GI. That was a good job. I got an extra ration and plenty of cigarettes.

One evening as I had just returned to the camp from my car wash job, a jeep came along, and an officer asked me, in perfect German, whether I wanted a job. Yes, I said. He brought several other comrades and me to a sawmill some miles away. There we worked sawing the poles needed for a fence around our camp. That was priority work. We sawed timber the whole night and manufactured nice and strong poles. In the morning, we were relieved by other POWs. In the evening, I was able to do a second shift. We had good food. I distinctly remember getting my first American coffee, hot and sweet.

Most of the guards were black GIs. Then and later, when I lived in the US-occupied zone of Germany, I found out that officially black and white GIs were equal. However, in practice, blacks were often discriminated against in the army at that time. This was my first lesson in the "new life": discrimination against others, or tribalism, as it is called in Africa, seems inherent in people. I promised myself that I would never again discriminate against anyone different from me.

THE POSTWAR YEARS: 1945 TO 1964

By the end of April 1945 (I don't recall the exact date), I became a prisoner of war with the US army in Germany. I was taken POW near Ingolstadt on the river Danube, close to where nowadays Audi cars are assembled. (Audi is better known to most people than Ingolstadt because it became the export success story of an automobile known worldwide).

I was made a soldier on February 8th, 1945, at sixteen and a half years old. It was no surprise to me because, at the war's end, even younger fellows were made soldiers or had to join the "Volkssturm" along with their grandfathers. In a way, being a regular soldier with a normal "Wehrmacht" uniform was still better than being a Volkssturm man carrying a gun or "Panzerfaust" and wearing civilian cloth or the uniform of the Hitler-youth marked with the swastika. Being captured in this outfit, particularly by the Russians on the Eastern front, was no fun. But at that time, we did not know it.

I was released from the US-POW camp by the end of May 1945, just before my seventeenth birthday. I walked home to Wuerzburg from the camp in Regensburg, about two hundred km away. For part of the way, I got a ride with a friendly truck driver. A nice GI invited me to ride along, for some distance, in his Jeep. My first ride ever in an American Jeep. On reaching Wuerzburg, I found the whole town destroyed, including my parents' apartment. A former neighbor told me my mother had moved to her sister's at Noerdlingen, some 140 km away. She was overjoyed when she saw me two days later.

My mother was certainly not to be envied; her home

(apartment) was destroyed, and her husband, my father, did not come home from the war. He died in France. Of her four boys, only I had professional training. I had completed an apprenticeship and was a mechanic. That was an excellent profession. After the war, I specialized in repairing automobiles. There were no new cars or trucks to be bought in postwar Germany, so fixing old vehicles was much sought after and good business. There were no spare parts either; we had to make those ourselves. The German army confiscated most motor vehicles during the war. Many of them were now abandoned somewhere in a yard or along roadsides.

I got a good job with the Post Office, Transport Department. After some time, however, I realized that I would have to get on with further education. I first learned English, an important language in the US-occupied part of Germany. We still had a military government, and there were so many Gis; it was just useful to be able to communicate with everybody. I did not want to do only "nuts and bolts," so I went back to a technical school called "Meisterschule" and finished with the title "Master of the Automobile Trade." With all this knowledge, I was prepared to realize my dreams.

My dream was to travel to foreign countries, meet people, learn how they live, and learn to speak their languages. I was always a realist and knew that one cannot just take a small savings and travel around the world doing nothing in particular. I wanted to fulfill my dream only on a sound professional basis. So I applied for and was accepted by one of Southern Germany's major truck and bus manufacturers. This company exported more than 50 % of its production to foreign countries. They trained me further for service in their export department and assignments abroad.

After some weeks, I was sent for a trial posting to Switzerland, my first stay abroad. That was not a big deal; abroad was just across the border to the South. Also, the Swiss speak German (kind of) with an accent that we from Southern Germany can understand reasonably well. The Swiss are excellent technicians, and my duties as the manufacturer's technical adviser were quite different from what they would be on my next assignment overseas.

At this time, I met a beautiful girl. In several ways, I was a very lucky guy. Firstly we loved each other; secondly, she was intelligent, spoke languages, and her dreams for the future were similar to mine. Doris worked at the German Embassy in Bern. We married in December 1955. For some time, we had to remain separated. I returned to the factory in Ulm, and she stayed in Bern. All we had were frequent visits to each other's homes across Lake Constanze (Bodensee).

In June 1956, I got the offer of a challenging posting to Damascus to help our Syrian Import Agent. (The company was called Kassioun, named after the big mountain outside the Syrian capital.) My job was to develop servicing and repair facilities. After one month there, Doris joined me. She had given up her job in Bern.

Adapting to the Syrian way of life was not fast and easy. Soon I learned an important lesson. Several trucks came in for servicing with broken rear axles, and I could not understand why. That never happened in Germany. I even telexed the factory for advice. Then I saw one of our customers carrying at least twice the tonnage of cargo on his truck than it was built for. To my way of thinking, this was impossible. I went to the Syrian importer, told him of my observation, and suggested he decline any warranty claims. He listened to me patiently for a while and then said, with an Arab charm, "we could do as you say, but then we would not sell a single truck in this country anymore." He expected me to find a way so that those rear axles would not break. I was furious and thought of leaving at once. Then, I started to think of reinforcing the axle housing. There was no more breakage after that. We reinforced the rear axle locally as soon as trucks arrived from Germany and before they were delivered to customers. Our trucks became the strongest to be had in Syria.

After some time, Doris and I liked living in Syria very

much. In April 1957, our first daughter Renate and in February 1959, our second, Susanne, were born, both in Damascus. We were now a happy family. My work was gratifying; I was young but was given a lot of responsibility. Business was good, and when my second contract ended after four years in the country, the company offered me several posts to choose from.

At this time, I met Louis Gendron, who was French with the UN based in Beirut. I did not know the difference between the various UN agencies present in the Middle East and what they were doing. He was a friend of some very good friends of ours, and a few days later, at a party, I met him again. We had a conversation in which he asked what I was doing. After some time, he told me that they needed a Transport Management Officer in Gaza. He was the Director of Operations with the United Nations Relief and Works Agency for Palestine Refugees "UNRWA," headquartered in Beirut. He suggested I apply for that post and invited me to come to Beirut, meet the Personnel Officer and learn more about the vacant position and conditions. I was not too interested as I intended to return to my company in Germany, where I had prospects for a good new position.

Nevertheless, I discussed it with Doris. She suggested that I should, at least, go to Beirut and see what the position was about. In those years, it was easy to travel from Damascus to Beirut, just about two hours away, over two mountain ranges. The border in between posed no obstacle, and the road was good.

During the visit, I learned that career prospects and conditions in the UN were quite good. I applied for the post, and after some time, I got a message to present myself to the UNRWA representative in Damascus for a job interview. The representative was Dutch. The first thing he said was that he spoke German because he was in a German POW camp for three years during the war. "Oh gosh," I thought, this is it; UN post goodbye. But it worked out differently. I got the position in Gaza.

In January 1960, I landed in an old UNRWA DC 3 plane at the Gaza airfield. (and what a primitive landing place that was). The DC 3 was flown by an Australian Captain Shorter, a good pilot. My family remained in Damascus for a few more weeks and joined me later in Gaza, also known as the "Gaza Strip." This piece of land was occupied by the Egyptian army. UNRWA's mandate was to take care of Palestinian Refugees. About 250,000 people were living in camps where UNRWA provided shelter, food, and schooling for their youth. In UNRWA, there were ten international staff and some eight hundred local employees (Palestinians).

My international colleagues came from the UK, France, the USA, the Netherlands, and Norway. I was the only German. (At that time, West and East Germany were not members of the United Nations. There were very few West German staff in specialized UN Agencies.) I had to develop transport management and delivery systems for the camps. I was happy working in this international environment. UNRWA international people were lucky; we could have our families in Gaza.

Then there was the United Nations Emergency Force "UNEF" with some 5,000 UN peacekeepers in the Gaza Strip. They came from many countries: Canada, the UK, New Zealand, Scandinavia, and others. These young soldiers could not have their families except for a few high-ranking officers. They had clubs; the military called them "A-Mess, B-Mess, and C-Mess." We were invited to be members of B-Mess. Three times a week we could see a good film. (There were no other cinemas in Gaza.) In UNRWA, we had our own "UNIBEC" club (UN-International Beach Club.) We reciprocated by inviting peacekeepers from B-Mess to be members of UNIBEC. They enjoyed being with us very much.

Being all alone for six months without family, or their girlfriends, our ladies were particularly charming to the young soldiers, and we celebrated many parties. I learned to play "darts" from my British colleagues and became quite good at it.

My Scottish colleague John Mitchell was with the Royal Navy during the war. He recounted many times how their fleet sank the German battleship Bismarck in a battle at sea. (Sorry, John, historic research later proved that the crew scuttled the Bismarck after the rudder was gone, and their position was hopeless vis-a-vis the Royal Navy).

We had a sweet, young Palestinian "Nanny" for the children. They also went to an international kindergarten. I must repeat we felt very happy in this international climate, and I was astonished by the excellent cooperation and how well we worked together, considering that colleagues came from so many different countries and backgrounds.

UNRWA was financed through voluntary contributions by governments and private donors. There were several "Goodwill Ambassadors." Celebrities helping to raise money in donor countries. One such fundraiser was Yul Brynner, particularly well-known at the time for the play "The King and I." One day Yul Brynner and his entourage visited Gaza on a PR mission. Our representative invited us all over to his house to meet Yul Brynner. The film star was a kind person. I remember his very deep voice.

By the summer of 1961, I was transferred to a new post in Beirut. We felt sorry to leave Gaza so soon, but life was going on. Soon, we adapted ourselves to the Lebanese capital. In June 1963, our third daughter, Andrea, was born. My Arab colleagues pitied me because we "only" had daughters. The Arabs had a saying: "he has four children (meaning boys) and three daughters!" Doris and I were quite happy with our three girls.

In Beirut, I was in contact with Unicef for the first time. They had several projects in Lebanon and in their regional office in Beirut. They had no vehicle servicing facilities, and as we had a large garage with spare capacity, we offered to service their project and administrative vehicles. The Unicef Transport Officer was an Indian, Ajit Patel, and we became quite friendly. One day his boss Martin Maurer from Unicef,

New York, on a field visit to the Middle East, was told of the UNRWA/ Unicef cooperation in vehicle management. Maurer decided to visit me in my office, and we had a good talk together. The next day Maurer and Adjit Patel told me that a position as "Regional Transport Officer" in Kampala, East Africa, was vacant.

We were not unhappy in Beirut, a pleasant city with schools and all a young family could think of. Nevertheless, the Job with UNRWA was, after some time, not rewarding. The Palestinian situation got nowhere. We only maintained the status quo. The post in Unicef in East Africa seemed to be one where "development" was an objective. UN Agencies have an "Interagency Transfer Agreement," making it easy for staff members to change to another organization. I very much wanted the Unicef job.

Doris and I discussed the prospect of moving again. She was wonderful because she never put an obstacle in the way when she was convinced of a situation that brought us further. I had to apply to Unicef New York, but I got the post. On October 4th, 1964, I landed in Entebbe, Uganda's main Airport, twenty miles away from Kampala. My family arrived a month later. That was already routine.

Now began our long and memorable life with the United Nations Children Fund.

1956

STRANGE PLACES, STRANGE CUSTOMS

Leaving your home country and moving around in foreign places, there is a lot one has to adapt to and get used to. There are different habits, customs, and behaviors, particularly with food. For instance, when we arrived in Damascus in June 1956, we found a lot of fruits and vegetables we had never seen and which were strange to us.

Because of the influx of foreign people into Central Europe, particularly Turks and others from the "Orient," and because of worldwide communication and easy transportation, you find fruits and vegetables nowadays in our countries that were not available in the mid-fifties. Yes, we had bananas and oranges, but we had no zucchini or squash in those days, nor had we avocado or mango, and we had no kiwi. You can now buy all of these in any German supermarket, like in the United States.

Back in Damascus, in those days, there were no supermarkets, just little shops, and there was the bazaar called "souk" (a French word). Souk Hamedie was the largest marketplace in the Syrian capital. Doris and I had only been married for a short while, and Damascus was the first place we lived together. Doris was not the experienced "Hausfrau" that she is now. One of our first shopping expeditions on a hot evening in the vegetable and meat section of Souk Hamedie was crowded, and there were flies all over the place. However, we had to get used to it.

Anyhow, the fruits and vegetables displayed on open kiosks were fresh and tempting. We saw some green vegetables and thought they were cucumbers. We bought some with the idea of preparing cucumber salad, which Doris knew to make very well. She always liked to eat salads of any kind. At home in our kitchen, when she started cutting the alleged cucumbers, it was immediately apparent that these were something different. These were zucchini. Prepared like cucumber salad, it had a funny taste. We learned fast, and nowadays, we like zucchini but not when prepared like a cucumber salad.

* * *

It was a difficult beginning in Damascus. In June, the hot months had just begun. Things didn't go too smoothly with the furnished apartment given to us by my contract.

I worked very long hours daily. We lived outside town on the road to Aleppo; there were no shops around. Doris could not drive the car then because she only got her driver's license later. So late in the evening or on Fridays (In Damascus, being Islamic, Friday was the only day off.), we had to drive together to the souk to shop.

Doris was expecting our first baby and felt very sick during the first three months. The souk was something we were absolutely not used to. "Dirty" is perhaps not the proper word, but different than home. The heat during this time of year was unbearable even after sunset. There were flies everywhere. The butcher recommended to us was adjacent to the vegetable shop, all in the open. The butcher was a friendly Syrian; he prepared the meat nicely for his customers. Whatever he cut away, tendon (sinew) bones, etc., he just threw outside on the street where dogs and birds fought for it.

Believe me, we thought several times about quitting and going home. However, we had no money to buy any kind of ticket. The cheapest means would have been by bus to Aleppo and from there by train, the "Orient Express," by way of the Balkans to Europe. Never mind, we learned to adapt. It did not take long before we liked living in the Middle East.

* * *

One of our expatriate friends knew a nomadic tribe of Bedouins. They roomed around in the desert between

Damascus and Palmyra. Once during the year, they set up camp near Damascus. On one such occasion, our friend took us along to meet them. We were a whole group of foreigners. I think it was a great day for us, but also for the Bedouins. The meal was an interesting ceremony. All was set up for it in the great tent of the chief. There were men but also three European women there with us, including pregnant Doris. The Bedouin women ate in another tent.

There was a big bowl on a pedestal filled with rice. When we were all present, two women brought in a big pot of meat. It was well-cooked goat meat. They poured it over the rice. It smelled incredibly good. So we all stood around the pot and, with our bare fingers, dipped in and got some meat and rice. I should mention there were some bowls with water, so we all cleaned our hands before we dipped in the rice bowl.

By this time, it was apparent that Doris was not a little but very pregnant. So the chief wanted to honor her by fishing around for the eyes of the goat. He then presented them to Doris with a handful of rice. Doris is a brave woman, but she refused to eat this, although it is said in Bedouin traditional customs that the eyes of such an animal are very good for the expectant mother and the baby. Well, the chief then fished again around and found the testicles of the goat, which he presented to me and said that this is good for the man; it produces lots of boys. As Doris was already impolite in refusing the goat's eyes offered by the chief, I could not now refuse the testicles. So I ate them, but they did not help at all. As everyone knows, I have not had any boys but three wonderful girls, Renate, Susanne, and Andrea.

1964

UNICEF NOTES:

- Unicef, as written here, is the present way of writing the organization's abbreviated version. In the old days, it was written entirely in capital letters (UNICEF)
- This book will not in any way be a history book of Unicef. An excellent, well-researched historical book was written by my good friend Maggie Black "The Story of Unicef." There is another book on Unicef written by Judi Silverman.
- The book will not be one of those suggesting better development strategies. Several of my former colleagues have written books with lots of statistics, the number of people saved through their own effort, etc. In this book, I will tell some of the experiences of my family and myself living abroad and working for an international organization. I was not a volunteer working for ideals. I was a well-paid "Professional" doing the best in my power the professional way. I am also of the opinion that effective and continual development work should be done by professionals. Volunteers have their place in this development game, particularly in emergencies or as young people going to foreign countries to gain experience. Long-term projects and development strategies can only be managed by experienced professionals. You cannot live in foreign countries, moving from one duty station to another, from continent to continent with a family, on a volunteer basis. Modern development and emergency projects involve large sums of money, often millions of dollars, and local staff. The responsibility of the

management/administration of large sums of donor money is not negligible. It must be done professionally.

Unicef was first conceived in 1946. At that time, the UN Relief and Rehabilitation Administration (UNRRA), the agency that brought relief and rehabilitation to millions of displaced people in Europe after WW 2, gradually ended its operation. There was a great need to continue the provision of emergency relief to thousands of children, including many orphans, in the postwar period.

The General Assembly of the United Nations approved on 11 October 1946 the creation of the United Nations International Children's Emergency Fund. Unicef was created as a temporary agency. The word "emergency" was still part of the organization's title. For some UN Member States, this was important. It was only much later, in 1953, that Unicef was established on a more permanent basis as the United Nations Children's Fund. The words "International" and "Emergency" were left out then. Still, the abbreviation "Unicef" remained because, over the years, Unicef had established itself in many parts of the world, and everybody knew what the letters stood for.

In Unicef now, "development" has priority over "emergency." Unfortunately, even today, Unicef cannot escape involvement in emergency aid as these occur so often. Some are made by nature (earthquakes, floods, or droughts), and more are made by man (civil war, ethnic cleansing (what a word!), political persecution, etc.)

Major (not an exclusive list) "emergencies" during the last three decades in which Unicef played a key role were in Biafra (Eastern Nigeria), Cambodia, Lebanon (1982), Ethiopia, the drought in Sahelian countries, Bangladesh, Afghanistan, Bosnia, and others. In "emergency" programs, as well as regular "development" programs, logistics is always an essential factor. Except for Bosnia, I was active in all the emergencies mentioned above.

Unicef headquarters is in New York. There are regional offices in critical geographical locations worldwide. There are country offices in most developing countries.

UNICEF BEGINNINGS

In October 1964, I joined Unicef as a "Transport Officer." I was posted in the (then) East Africa Area Office in Kampala, Uganda. (This office later became a Regional Office and was moved to Nairobi, Kenya.) At that time, Unicef did not have offices in all countries; that only happened much later. The Kampala Office was in charge of Unicef-assisted programs in seventeen East African countries, including the islands of Madagascar, Mauritius, and the Seychelles. Transportation has always been a very important factor in the mobility of Unicef-assisted programs.

The island of Mauritius in the Indian Ocean was not a country with the most urgent transport management problems. However, it so happened that the responsible Program Officer for Mauritius had planned a visit to that country. It was an occasion for me to travel with him and get introduced to their activities. Mauritius was my first "Field Trip" for Unicef. There were no flights from Entebbe to Mauritius.

The itinerary was Nairobi, then Dar-es-Salaam, Tanzania, an overnight stay in Dar (commonly used for Dar es Salaam), the following day by Air France via Madagascar, a further stopover on the French (it still is) island of Reunion, and finally Mauritania. The Airport was near the capital Port Louis. For this last stretch, Air France still used the old Super Constellation. That was the plane with three rudders at its tail. So the trip by air was already something extraordinary for me, a newcomer to Africa.

On arrival, the immigration and custom official addressed me in French. I was surprised, as I thought Mauritius was a former British colony and expected people to speak English. (Mauritius had been, at that time, independent for only two years.) Anyhow, the immigration official switched very fast to English when he saw my surprised face. Then he asked: "Do you have sugar cane in your luggage?" Well, I was really flabbergasted. What a question, I thought, he is not taking me seriously. He then explained: "Here in Mauritius, you may come in with anything, such as machine guns, pistols, and other hot items, but under no circumstances may you bring sugar cane to the island." Later I understood. The island grows cane sugar, similar to Cuba, and depends on this product entirely. The risk of bringing in a plant disease is great as such a disease could entirely ruin the country.

Mauritius is a beautiful island with lovely beaches. Tourism is ranked second in their economy. Tourists in the sixties all came from Reunion and Madagascar. That is to say, they were all French-speaking, and the islanders adapted themselves to this fact. Ethnically speaking, most of the population of Mauritius were from the Indian subcontinent. They are, to a large extent, bilingual. Even a taxi driver would first address you in French and then switch fast and easily to English if he feels you are more comfortable in that language. The climate is excellent, it is warm but not hot.

At the time, there was an agricultural expert of the FAO (UN Food and Agriculture Organization). We had a joint project with FAO, and when our business dealing was done, he asked us to his home for a drink. He told us there was a short rain shower every afternoon at 5:30 PM on the Southern part of the island where he lived. So we waited for our watches to turn to 5:30 PM, and sure enough, it started to rain for just five minutes. Now this fellow is to be envied. He can depend on this shower to appear daily; he never has to sprinkle the lawn. He does not even possess a garden hose.

We observed that there was nothing on the island to remind the visitor of the former colonial power. He suggested visiting the town of Curepipe and seeing the big hotel (I forget its name). The people of Mauritius refer to it as the "British

Museum." We went there, it was really British, there were no guests. The hotel completely contrasted with the other ones on the island, which catered to French tourists.

In a previous installment, "The Postwar Years," I wrote about my first job with the United Nations with "UNRWA," the United Nations UN-Works and Relief Agency for Palestine Refugees. I held the position of a Transport Officer based in the Gaza Strip, as it was called at that time. Although I worked with many international colleagues and got positive recognition of my work by supervisors, I was soon dissatisfied with the purpose of my work. I advanced and was transferred to Beirut for a more important job and responsibilities. I felt very sorry for the plight of the Palestinian refugees. Still, I saw that neither my organization nor I could change anything. We just helped to maintain the "status quo."

Let me expand on this: UNRWA, created as a temporary agency by the United Nations, has existed for over fifty years. Ever since its creation, it has been doing the same, providing relief services to refugees. There was and still is Israel and those who support Israel, mainly the United States. Then there were and still are Palestine Refugees supported mainly by Arab countries. In-between was and still is UNRWA, often blamed, cursed, accused of not being impartial enough, and sometimes hailed as philanthropic. It is supported by many donor countries that have voluntarily contributed enormous amounts of money over the last fifty years.

Depending on whom one listens to, the figure is about one million refugees. I do not know what is now classified as a refugee and what is not. More than a generation ago, they left their old homes in Palestine. The situation has not changed much during the last five decades. It is all politics. Anwar Sadat and Yitzhak Rabin were glimmers of hope. The present government of Israel and a converted Palestinian leadership may be a renewed hope for peace in the Middle East, no matter how slow the process may be.

This being the case, I think I was right when I saw no

satisfactory career prospects at UNRWA. I congratulate myself that I looked for and found a position in Unicef. Unicef emphasizes development, a much more satisfactory aim than holding the "status quo." Unicef has existed even longer than UNRWA, but its long existence is nothing negative in this case.

I am a firm believer that underprivileged countries need development rather than relief. Development should be with the principle in mind; provide help to enable people to help themselves. Provide training to trainers so that they can train their own people. Development programs must have dynamics built in to compensate for the population growth (or explosion). The developed world can not permanently look after underdeveloped countries and distribute charity. But we can help, for instance, Africans to help themselves and become real partners.

There have been too many "emergency situations" in recent years, which have taken resources away from relief operations. Example: the Balkans. Emergencies caused by nature, earthquakes, drought, floods, hurricanes, etc., are different. We simply must help and provide aid fast.

But here also, preventative measures can avoid the worst. Earthquake-proof buildings, food storage facilities (droughts occur regularly and are predictable), embankments can avoid floods, etc. National development can be done much more rationally by using local resources.

This will in the end save more lives than dealing with emergencies. Providing charity, like distributing food, creates a dependency. Peasants stop plowing their fields and planting corn if they get it distributed from a relief truck. The better a country is developed and educated, the less likely it will be to ever require emergency aid,

I am more and more critical of food aid in man-made emergencies. I feel angry when local warlords start a struggle for power and plan into their strategy the misuse of the provision of food for the population by the UN and other aid organizations.

A typical example is southern Sudan. (I have written several stories on the situation in Sudan: "OLS," "Predja," and "Khartoum Sudan," and have also referred several times to incidents in Sudan.) Each time there is a man-made emergency situation, UN relief and other aid organizations rush to help civil war victims. In doing this, they play precisely to the strategies of the warlords, who created the situation in the first place. Of course, the armed people, rebels and regular soldiers alike, also get their food rations from such aid.

Hard as this may sound, I think we should be more selective in providing food aid, and if we do, strict conditions should apply. Such aid should be only for a limited time. Further, in such instances, we should not try to bring food to a country's most remote corners using helicopters, airplanes, and what have you. Distribution points: secure, easily accessible locations. The message should go out from there: "Come and get it!" The provision of planting tools, seeds, and fertilizer should accompany food aid. Help them to help themselves.

Again we need to make the distinction between development and emergency aid. I think poverty, famine, disease, illiteracy, population explosion, etc., can only be overcome with development programs, helping people to help themselves. These programs should have absolute priorities over charity. Available resources should be used for this purpose.

DEVELOPMENT

If we are honest, we all practice "learning by doing." An old friend and colleague from Australia, Francis Smithwick, who had a very successful career in Unicef, when asked about his academic credentials, used to reply, he had a "QBE." After this answer, many did not insist on an explanation, probably thinking these people from "down under" have funny titles. To those who inquired deeper into the meaning of this strange-sounding degree (I was one of them), Francis would explain that he had not visited a university. "QEB" simply stands for "qualified by experience."

I also have not attended a university. My education was in technical schools, below university rank. During my whole life, I have not stopped seeking knowledge through self-teaching and attending specialized courses.

When I joined the UN, a university degree was not the most important qualification required. Nowadays, a second-level university degree is necessary for a professional post. Exceptions are some specific field positions, particularly in emergency operations. I made it to the "director's category" without a formal degree, and many of my former colleagues did equally well.

I am not one of those who always brag that in the "old days," we used to do things better. Still, I do feel that my former colleagues and I, with our practical approach to development work, were well understood by the newly freed countries. Some highly qualified UN bureaucrats nowadays speak of very sophisticated development strategies. They are so far up in the clouds that ordinary people can no longer reach them. That applies to UN officials, other donor officials, and government officials on the receiving side who had the opportunity of getting a higher education.

I have frequently spoken with former colleagues my age. When the war was over in 1945, defeated and victors alike were in the same situation in Europe and elsewhere. Those lucky to return from military service without major injuries had more urgent things to do, and few could afford to attend higher schools and universities. Take my own situation (See installment "The Postwar Years"). When I came home in June of 1945, our family's home in Wuerzburg no longer existed, totally bombed to rubble. My mother was alive only because she was not home on 16. March 1945, when Wuerzburg was totally destroyed. She found refuge with her sister in Noerdlingen, 90 miles away. We were four boys, ages 12 to 18 years. I, then, just 17 years old, was the only one with professional training (apprenticeship) as a mechanic.

As mentioned before, my father did not return from the war. One can imagine that I thought only of one thing: finding a job and earning my own livelihood. Furthermore, in Germany, for years, there were no organized universities open for business. And when they finally reopened, they were expensive. Also, they prioritized admittance for those who had begun but not completed their studies. Nevertheless, I always got good jobs, and after some time, I did not feel I had to return to school.

When I landed in Entebbe on October 4th, 1964, on an East African Airliner, I was ready to take up new challenges and was professionally prepared for them. However, I had no clue what "development" was. I had been in a UN position (UNRWA) for four years at my previous job in the Middle East, so I knew about what many observers call UN bureaucracy. But work in UNRWA had nothing to do with developing anything. We strictly provided and maintained the status quo of Palestine Refugees.

Let's face it, in 1964, the whole western world had no experience in development work and didn't expect the colossal task ahead of us all. There was no precedence; independence, for instance, in North America, was quite different.

It was only in the early sixties that African colonies became independent. In the case of Uganda, Uhuru (Swahili for independence) was in 1962. the Western world, bilaterally and internationally (UN), totally underestimated the work and measures involved in making these countries economically independent. While we aid workers in the field started the "learning while doing" process, the Africans were euphoric and completely unrealistic. People's nationalistic feelings grew rapidly. They believed that with freedom from colonial dependence, nothing whatsoever could stop them from reaching undreamed-of heights. They were spurred on by their national leaders, who became extremely arrogant.

If one only recalls Patric Lumumba, the leader of the then Congo (later Zaire, and now again the Democratic Republic of Congo). His fanatic cries against their former masters, the Belgians, and the unrest he created in the country caused, finally, his own downfall and death.

In the Congo, but not only there, whatever little social and economic infrastructure was available at independence, was not maintained and built on, but often because of national pride, was dismantled and not replaced by anything equal or better. It was expected that African leaders demand foreign aid in the form of money, be it loans or donations. Developers in western capitals provided money, often without strings attached. Corruption was the only thing that developed without a problem.

This situation was also helped by the cold-war. The communist East competed with the West for political influence in African countries. Nobody, not even the press, dared to criticize an African leader. Too many African countries are indebted up to their ears. The new demand is that industrialized countries write off debts from the least developed countries. They could not pay back in any case. I am for it, but I am also for conditions to be attached before debts are written off. One condition would be no purchasing of arms, military fighter planes, etc., until health and education services are improved.

In 1964, none of us were really experienced in developing an African nation. We tried and made mistakes, but we also had some successes.

JUST INDEPENDENT

When we came to East Africa in 1964, most countries on the continent had just become independent; one of the last was Kenya in 1963. Spirits were high among the population. The Africans thought that being now free from their colonial masters, nothing could ever disturb their happiness. The leaders knew about the critical question of the economy but still became careless and ignored indebtedness. Huge loans could easily be obtained bilaterally or from international financial institutions, for instance, the World Bank. Nevertheless, most new countries kept a good relationship with their former colonial power. Even countries in which the struggle for independence was bitter and bloody.

One of those was Kenya. Even though the former Mau Mau leader and Britain's most wanted "terrorist," Jomo Kenyatta, became Kenya's democratically elected President, Kenya maintained good relations with the UK. Many former "White Highland" farmers elected to become Kenyan citizens. The Minister of Agriculture was a white man; it all seemed a happy fraternization.

Some new countries, however, broke with their former masters. Congo (later Zaire), Guinea (Conakry), and Mali (Bamako) come to mind. They wanted to do it their own way. Guinea and Mali did not want to be part of the French-speaking commonwealth of nations. The French did not take this very kindly and cut all help. I was told the French, on leaving Guinea, took everything with them that they considered theirs, including wall sockets from buildings that were former colonial or military installations.

These countries also did not share the monetary union,

"CFA," which was backed by France and was a very stable currency from the beginning of independence. As a result, Mali and Guinea had negative development and got impoverished. They needed help from somewhere, so they turned to the former Soviet Union. It was still the time of the cold war confrontation, and the USSR looked for opportunities to get a foothold in Africa. Help from Eastern countries was mostly arms, much more than needed.

East African countries Uganda, Kenya, and Tanzania (including Zanzibar) belonged to the East African Community with common systems. The "East African Shilling" as currency, EA telecommunications, the "East African Airline" (EAA), and other common services. This was a good beginning. Unfortunately, every country in East Africa now has its own currency, airline, and telecommunication systems. In East Africa, the CFA currency is still in use. Even former deserting countries Mali and Guinea rejoined the monitory CFA system that makes commerce and travel between those countries very convenient.

I wrote in an earlier installment about the technical services I was involved with. After independence, they functioned well while expatriate experts were still in charge or present as advisors. "PWD" (Public Works Department-Transport Sections) in former British colonies and "Garage Administratif" in former French colonies were such services. After some years, however, the expatriate staff was gone, and gradually these vital services became ineffective.

It was not that Africans were bad managers or technicians; it was because these professions were, and still are, held in low esteem by governments all over Africa. Their salaries were low. In many countries, government staff must wait months to get their low salary paid. Technical managers of a PWD or a "GA" were not integrated with a ministry's upper management, even though they were responsible for a very large capital investment. For instance, a government ministry might have a vehicle fleet of 120 vehicles (not uncommon), many of which are expensive 4-wheel drive utility vehicles. This would represent a much higher value than anything else that this ministry had, including the total equipment of an African hospital.

Another problem that was and still is predominant, as the saying goes: "The prophet is not listened to in his own country," is very true. For instance, because of the large capital investment for project vehicles, Unicef assigned and paid for a consultant to train a transport organization's technical and management personnel for a limited time, usually two years. As long as this consultant was in place, things worked fine, and well-functioning technical services could be established. Consultants also trained a government counterpart to eventually take over the services. After the expatriate consultant left and the local manager took over, the efficiency of the services got poor, in some instances, collapsing entirely.

It was not that the local person was less capable of managing a government transport organization. Whereas the minister and his upper management listened to the expatriate consultant, they did not listen to and give no support to the local manager in charge after the foreigner had left. This pattern could be observed in East and West African countries alike. Often well-trained and qualified managers, frustrated, leave government services for the private sector, where salaries are better, and they are more respected.

Unicef-assisted programs were conceived for outreach to cover the entirety of a country. That means technical services must also be provided throughout a country. So supervision is necessary. Governments have enormous difficulties paying a supervisor's travel expenses adequately while absent from home on a field trip. The results are that insufficient or no supervision is done.

There is hope, however. After independence, many Africans got jobs in high positions without having qualifications for them. Now 30 years later, African are much better educated and trained and have more experience for management positions.

NIGERIA

My first touchdown on African soil was in Lagos, Nigeria, in early October 1964. At the time, Unicef had only one regional office in Africa south of the Sahara (Nowadays, there are three or four). I had just joined the organization on transfer from UNRWA in Beirut. I presented myself to the Regional Office for briefing. However, my first Unicef duty station was on the other side of that continent in Kampala, Uganda.

The Federal Republic of Nigeria became independent from Britain in 1960. Lagos was their first capital city. Now it is Abuja, situated in the center of the country. While Abuja is now the federal administrative capital, the busiest city is still Lagos, with a population of well over a million.

Nigeria is the most populated country in Africa. Lagos is a very messy place with tremendous traffic problems. You had to make sure to leave in time to get to the airport. From downtown to the airport can take anywhere from one to three hours. Overpopulated as it was, I never liked this town.

The federal government is in Abuja. Some twenty state governments have a certain degree of autonomy, particularly in Unicef-assisted activities. So making contacts and reaching an agreement with the central government was one thing. However, the respective state government was responsible for the implementation of projects. We had to have close contacts with ministries at the state level.

After six years of assignment in East Africa, I was given program logistics responsibilities for Nigeria when I was transferred with my whole family to West Africa.

THE GREAT RIFT VALLEY

My first sight of the Great Rift Valley was in October 1964. I was new in Africa. The valley is very large and actually extends from Russia to East Africa. Still, I want to write mainly about the Rift Valley, where it runs through Kenya. Geologically it is a big scar on the earth's surface, visible even from outer space. The astronauts could identify it while walking on the moon. It has a similarity with the San Andres fault in California.

One crosses the Great Rift Valley when traveling by car from Kampala to Nairobi. A major settlement along the way is Nakuru and, with it, "Lake Nakuru." The area is all agricultural, and the town is a farmer's town where they can get provisions and market their products. During the colonial time, it had been a white farming area, with huge farms, all owned by white people, say British. Kenya only gained independence in 1963, so when I came to Nakuru in 1964, the country had been independent for just one year.

I remember an incident worth mentioning because it was typical for the time. Nakuru, amid this white farming area, had several excellent hotels. These served the farming community who came from up-country to town for recreation and tourists to the rift valley who came for game viewing. In my company, on this first trip, was a visitor from our New York headquarters, Mr. Martin Maurer. Actually, he was my boss. He introduced me to the new work at Unicef.

We stopped over for the night in Nakuru at the Stag's Head hotel, which we had been told was the best. We had a good dinner in a British colonial setting. At this time, there were still plenty of white farmers in Kenya and the rift valley. Cattle raising and farming were the backbone of

Kenya's economy. There was even a white Kenyan Minister of Agriculture in their first independent government. Guests in the Stag's Head were only white.

We were having a British-style breakfast when a big red-faced man, obviously a farmer, shouted "boy" to get a waiter's attention. Gosh, the uproar this caused among the other waiters (there were many in the hall). They shouted and cursed him until the Maître d' came and asked him to leave the breakfast room.

Kenyan waiters were not hostile at all against white people. My boss Maurer from New York, myself, and some tourists who were around at neighboring tables had no problem. Still, being called "boy" a year after independence was too much for the Masais in Nakuru.

Interestingly, in French-speaking countries of West Africa, even today, you can call a waiter "garcon," as you do in France. It means the same thing as "boy" in English. In francophone Africa later, I was always conscious of the incident in Nakuru. I called waiters: "Chef" in the sense of "chief." Naturally, in this post-independence time, one had to be aware of the sentiment of the Africans.

Nakuru has a world attraction on its lake just outside the city. Lake Nakuru is famous for its fantastic flamingos. This National Park had been created to protect the thousands of flamingos. They stand around the shores in shallow water, forming a "pink" ring around the lake. This looks fantastic from an airplane or the rim high up on the escarpment. There are some other small lakes to the North of Nakuru on which one can see flamingos but not in these big numbers. I have seen them take off by the thousands. It is like the sky turns pink.

We came from Kampala/Uganda, and our destination was Nairobi. So, the next town on this road is Naivasha, still in the rift valley. As most towns in the rift valley have, there is a lake: Lake Naivasha, with a magnificent bird and wildlife sanctuary.

From Naivasha, the road leads up some 2,000 feet, the

great escarpment to the high plateau on which Nairobi is also situated. This old road between the rift valley and Nairobi, officially the "B-3," was the only one when I was in East Africa. There is now a new road, much less steep, the A-104. I used it years later, it is good but nothing special, there is nothing to write about. But the old B-3 down the escarpment is an engineering masterwork. This escarpment had been a big obstacle to mobility and the development of the fertile rift valley. Formerly there were small paths down, and the railway made a scary descent on its way to Uganda.

Italian prisoners of war built the first modern road and parallel railway from 1942 to 1944. They had been captured during the campaign in Ethiopia. These men overcame a formidable engineering problem. Several Italians died there during these years. On the bottom of the escarpment stands "The Italian Chapel," a simple structure commemorating those men who accomplished something valuable during a senseless war.

* * *

I do not want to write a tour guide on Kenya and its Great Rift Valley. My journey with my boss from New York through the valley was my first impression of Africa. We were, however, not on a pleasure excursion to see African wildlife. Unicef had activities there, and those were connected with logistics.

* * *

The British had extensive farms all over Kenya. "The White Highlands" was not a geographical concept. It described those farming areas of the British, where Africans (Masai and Kikuyu) were tolerated only as farm workers. The white Kenyans, usually of British descent, never thought of their farms becoming anything else other than what the name says: "White Highlands." After independence, many white highlanders could opt to become Kenyan citizens. At least at the beginning, many did and retained their farms.

But there were also Africans who started farming on

their own. Cattle breeding was natural to the Masai and Kikuyu. What was not a natural thing for them was marketing their products. Unicef assisted the government of Kenya in building up the infrastructure of a dairy industry. They helped with regular milk collection from small farmers, processing in dairy plants, marketing, and helping to bring these plants up to a modern standard. The re-payment by the government was the distribution of dairy products to needy children, thus improving the health of Kenyan children. This project in Kenya became one of the most successful ones in Unicef's history.

Today the dairy industry in Kenya is well established and on a sound economic basis. Unicef has been out of it for a long time, but it helped initially. Naivasha in the Rift Valley has a large dairy plant built with Unicef money and engineering. Milk collection is done by co-ops and functions as it did when we were still in it. Kenyan milk is good. We raised our children on it. (Look how they turned out, having had this good creamy Kenyan milk). We never bought Ugandan but always Kenyan because it was better. Kenyan milk was also marketed in Uganda.

* * *

Here is a story that departs a little from the Rift valley. We had a dairy expert, Harm Brandma, in Kenya working on the project mentioned above. He was Dutch and a good friend to Doris and me. He often came to Kampala and had been a guest in our house many times. That was when Princess Beatrice (now Queen) of the Netherlands dated and married the German Klaus von Amsberg. Doris and I were in Nairobi and visited the Brandsma's. Harm and his wife told us, very frankly, that they did not like their future Queen marrying a German. It had nothing to do with our friendship, but the dutch had not forgotten what the Germans did in Holland twenty years earlier. It made us think, nevertheless.

Now, years later, this marriage turned out to be a good one. Old Klaus produced two sons, whereas the family had only girls for generations. The Dutch royal family is very popular in their country, and that now includes Klaus von Amsberg.

UGANDA

In early October 1964, I arrived at Entebbe Airport. It was the beginning of our many years in Africa. From UNRWA in the Middle East, I transferred to Unicef. The Area Office in Kampala/Uganda was my first posting, and my title was Transport Management Officer.

The East African area office was responsible for programs in 14 countries. Some have changed and/or merged since. Here is a list as they existed at the time; Uganda, Kenya, Tanganyika, Zanzibar, Malawi, Madagascar, Burundi, Rwanda, Lesotho, Mauritius, Seychelles, Swaziland, Zambia, and Rhodesia.

In addition, I was responsible for transport management in Ethiopia, Somalia, and Congo. These three countries were attached to area offices without specialists in this field. From Kampala, I frequently traveled to these countries. I was often away from home, but it was interesting and gratifying work. Unicef had no office in the first fourteen listed countries; they all were covered by the Area Office in Kampala. Later new development approaches required representation all over. Nowadays, there are no more "Area Offices" but "Country Offices" in practically all those countries.

I arrived ahead of my family at the new duty station. We did it this way when the children were young. It allowed me to look for housing and get familiar with the latest job without worrying about the family's well-being. We had another sad reason for Doris to remain longer in Germany. Her mother was very ill. In fact, she died shortly before Doris and our girls left for Africa. On November 4th, 1964, Doris, Renate (7), Susanne (5), and Andrea (2) arrived with SABENA in Entebbe. Doris was in bad shape. Leaving our comfortable home in Beirut, then several months in Germany where her mother was sick, and finally, her mother's death were all very hard on her.

However, we all, including the girls, felt good in Uganda from almost the first day we arrived. I rented a house before the rest of the family came. We moved in, although our lift van with personal belongings had not come from Beirut. Friends furnished us with mattresses and other essential things to be able to live in the house. This, our first residence, was about seven miles outside town on a hill called "Busiga." We had a magnificent view over lake Victoria, and our garden was full of beautiful tropical plants.

Lake Victoria is at 3600 ft altitude. Therefore, the climate was excellent; warm during the daytime but never hot, and cool at night. People didn't have air conditioners; it was not necessary. Kampala is built on different hills, so the various parts of town were: Kololo-Hill, Tank-Hill, Busiga-Hill, Bugolobi-Hill, and so on. Coming on the road from the international airport twenty miles away in Entebbe, Kampala City even had a "skyline." There were several tall buildings. One was the Amber House, where Unicef had its "Area Office."

The Amber House belonged to the Uganda Electricity Board (UEB). Another big tenant in this large building was the Uganda Coffee Board (UCB). Both were very involved in the export business. The UEB owned the power station at Owens Falls in Jinja, fifty miles from Kampala. Where Lake Victoria is the source of the river Nile. It is one of the very big power stations in the world. Electricity is sent all over East Africa from there.

We were in Uganda from 1964 to 1970. It was a good time. The British had left their former protectorate in good order, infrastructure was intact, and the export crops were coffee, tea, copper, and cotton. In Jinja, there was a large textile manufacturing plant. The University of Makerere in Kampala was renowned all over Africa.

* * *

Uganda actually consisted of several old kingdoms. The most important were: Buganda, Toro, Bunyoro, Ankole, Busoga, and Karamotja. Uganda became a republic at independence (1962), and the kingdoms became federal states. The largest, Buganda, was situated around the capital Kampala. The king (Kabaka) of Buganda, Kabaka Mutesa II (called King Freddie), became the first President of independent Uganda. Milton Obote became the Prime Minister.

To us foreigners, it looked like a good arrangement. However, it didn't look good to Milton Obote and his men. They wanted a centrally governed country. With the help of the Ugandan Army and its Chief Idi Amin Dada, they ousted the Kabaka. They created a Uganda with Milton Obote as President of the Republic, greatly supported by Idi Amin. The old kingdoms were renamed regions. Some kings left the country, and some found an arrangement with Milton Obote. Politically they were dead.

One woman of royal blood was the elegant, beautiful Princess Elisabeth of Tooro. She held important government posts and became Uganda's Ambassador to the UN. She even became Foreign Minister under Idi Amin for a short while, but then, when she was abroad, she deserted; perhaps just in time, as Amin killed many of his officials when he was tired of them.

I remember the day when the army deposed Kabaka, Mutesa II. It was a rainy day, with thick black clouds in the sky. From my office window, I could see the palace of the Kabaka some two miles away. The whole morning the city was full of army vehicles, some old tanks, and thousands of soldiers. In the afternoon, they attacked the palace. We saw the shelling and fire. The Kabaka's guards armed with some old rifles were no problem for Amin's army. Soon it was over, but the Kabaka was able (and helped, no doubt) to flee. The Bagandens had never forgotten this, and they did not like Obote at all. Consequently, being in Kampala, surrounded by Buganda, the government could only survive by oppressing its people with force. Obote had, besides the army, a "Special Force," all very tall soldiers from his own northern Ugandan tribe.

* * *

On Saturdays, there was no official work, but usually, we met in the office and looked through some papers and the mail. By 11 am or so, we would go to the "Ugandan Coffee Shop," where one could always meet people and have a cup of coffee. Not infrequently, Idi Amin Dada came to the coffee shop, had some coffee, and talked to patrons. He liked to talk to foreigners.

I have spoken to him. Idi Amin, in those days, was the chief of the army. He was an easygoing guy. He never came with a big escort. Sometimes there were some fellow officers from the army with him. He always came in an open army jeep which he drove himself. You know, he was with the old British army. He was a sergeant, but a very special one because he was a champion boxer and the very best of them. He had all the titles one could have in those days. So he was a popular man, even among the Bagandens.

In 1971, when Milton Obote was away for a conference of non-aligned countries, there was an army mutiny in Uganda, and Idi Amin took over. He ruled Uganda for more than eight years and made the most brutal dictatorship out of it. A shame for Africa.

My family and I had gone by then. In 1970, I was posted to Abidjan, West Africa.

UGANDA II

I enjoy thinking about this next time because we all remember it fondly. The five of us were together (Doris, Renate, Susanne, Andrea, and "Daddy."). Later, when I was transferred to West Africa in 1970, Renate and Susanne had to stay in a boarding school in Germany.

In Africa, we had servants in the house. Actually, in Kampala, we had three. This is neither luxury nor is it always fun. We had to look after them and their families. We had to take them to see a doctor when they were sick. It is practically expected from "expatriates" (and well-to-do Africans, too!) to employ domestic servants. We had to learn a lot.

In the beginning, we had a nanny for our daughters (in Swahili called "ayah."). Our first one was Maria. Shortly after that, we hired a cook. His name was John. Usually, homes have a "servant's quarter," a small house in the corner of the garden. Our servant's quarter was a very good house, with two rooms, a bathroom, and a kitchen. But Maria and John were from different villages and tribes. They could absolutely not live and work together. John stayed only a few days, then quit because he said Maria had bewitched him. She hung a bone or something over the entry to his room.

Maria was a problem herself. One day she was ironing in the pantry when Doris came in and saw a large frog in a corner. She asked Maria to take the frog outside, but Maria said she could not do that because the frog was her grandmother and she needed to feed her. Well, Maria did not stay with us too long either.

Then came Cecilia. Soon her whole family was living in the servant's quarters. They stayed with us for the entire time we were in Uganda, six years. I do not know how many children Cecilia had and whether all who lived in the quarters were hers. Well, she had Rose, who eventually became our second ayah. And she had Celestîne, who was about four years old when we arrived and became a big friend of our youngest daughter Andrea. There were other children, but Cecilia respected our wish to limit the unrestricted growth of her "family."

As I wrote previously, our first place was a house on Busiga Hill overlooking Lake Victoria. Cecilia came from a village on the foot of that hill. Later we moved closer to town, so Cecilia and her family came with us. For her, that was only some seven to eight miles from her village.

Our second servant was Augustino, the gardener. He came from the same village and did not stay in the servant's quarter. He came daily by bicycle and went home every evening. Because Augustino and Cecilia were from the same village and tribe, there was no problem with their working together in and around the house.

The servants got wages. In addition, it was tradition to give them sugar and tea. Cecilia got five pounds of sugar and two pounds of tea per month for herself and her family. Interestingly, groceries and the supermarket where expatriates usually did their shopping had, towards the end of a month, sugar and tea readily packed on the shelf, as a convenience to the customers. This was also a good thing to do because having sufficient of these items, servants would not take anything from the house.

African servants always ask for salary advances, which is standard in East and West Africa. We usually gave them up to a month's wages without arguing too much, thus saving them the trouble of finding reasons why they needed the advance each time.

After John, we never tried to get a cook again. Cecilia, under the guidance of Doris, did the cooking. She cooked simple meals, afternoon tea, coffee, etc., which was always very good. Cecilia would hardly take any leftovers from us, although she had our permission. I think it was just not the Ugandan way. They do not like our food. The Ugandan staple food was manioc, of which cassava was made. Also, sweet potatoes, bananas, and cereals. Cecilia let me sometimes try her cassava. It was delicious.

She cooked outside the servant's quarter, not inside the little kitchen. In the beginning, she built a fireplace out of a few rocks. It scared us, so we bought a portable metal stove at the local market.

Cecilia seldom prepared meat. Sometimes, chicken. It was not that she could not afford meat. By superstition, East African women do not eat fish, though Lake Victoria is full of it. They believe when a woman eats fish, she becomes infertile. Meanwhile, the FAO, Unicef, and others have done a lot of education because fish is an essential source of proteins.

She had an arrangement with Augustino. He always had lunch with her family. Rose, her daughter, became our second house servant when she came of age at 16 or 17 years old. One day her mother told us that she was expecting a baby. There was no man living on our compound. But it didn't surprise anyone. When the baby was born, a girl, she was a real beauty. We all loved her.

We were very lucky with Cecilia. She gave us no trouble. She was also very reliable, and our children loved her. We could easily go out for parties and leave the children with Cecilia. There were many parties in Kampala. We always paid her extra when we were out. For Cecilia or Rose, this was welcome additional pay.

Augustino was a nice guy though he had some faults. He liked "Pompe," locally brewed beer out of bananas, and also locally distilled alcohol. Both were not allowed to be made, but who could prevent this in an African village. Augustino only drank Sundays, and we decided to be tolerant about it, particularly Monday mornings. After the weekend, he appeared with a white handkerchief around his head and said he had a headache. He then looked for a shady place in the garden and slept for hours.

But before we knew his weekly habits, there was one occurrence I surely remember. I was in the office when Doris called me, saying that Augustino was very sick. I should come and drive him home. It was inconvenient for me to get away from the office, but finally, I did. I went home, loaded Augustino into the car, and drove away. With all windows open, I did not notice immediately, but soon I smelled that he was terribly drunk. Anyhow, I got him home, but I felt rather foolish. When I returned to the house, Cecilia had already told Doris that Augustino was only drunk.

Burglary was a big problem in Kampala, but we never had a theft. I attribute this to the fact that we did not change servants often. Some foreigners fired their servants for trivial matters, and it was surely no coincidence that they had the most burglaries.

Of course, one could not tolerate dishonesty and theft. Still, some people were too careless about leaving valuables around the house. We never did this. We made a point of educating the children to be careful with money, etc.

Augustino normally did not enter the house; otherwise, we had only female servants. With males, there was often the problem that they would drink out of bottles. Sometimes they would top it up with water or even with eau-de-cologne. A nasty thought! Sometimes the master of the house would mark the level of contents on the whiskey bottle. It would have been the same effort to lock the bottle away.

Actually, home distilling was a nationwide problem. There were many casualties from mentholated spirits, which could kill a person. The government of Uganda, therefore, decided to open a distillery where "Warragi" was produced and sold to Africans at a low cost. Warragi was actually gin; at least, it tasted like it. We, too, bought it from the distillery. The difference: we got the same spirits in a nicer bottle and paid twice the price.

I realize that I have written quite a bit about our

servants in Uganda. Well, it is a subject one can talk endlessly about. When expatriates get together, servants are the most popular theme to talk about, sometimes the whole evening. (Ladies more than men!)

UGANDA III

I was not a big game hunter. I liked to "shoot" photographs. I sometimes went fishing in the Nile because everyone did, but I was also no great fisherman. Of course, Uganda was the number one country, or at least they rivaled Kenya for that ranking. It is a hunter's paradise.

I had friends who were hunters, and I was popular among them because I could use our office's 4-wheel drive Land Rover for a small fee and gasoline for the trip. So I went on safari with big game hunters. On some of the trips, our families came along. We had all the required equipment, a tent, a stove, cooking utensils, and plenty to drink. One friend even brought his cook along, but this was not a good idea, as it turned out later. The children were excited when we set up camp and when they rode in a Land Rover off-road.

"Safari" (for journey or trip) is a well-known word even for people who have never been to East Africa. It is a Swahili word.

Swahili is a language deriving from Arabic that is understood throughout East Africa. However, it is mainly and best spoken on the Eastern seaboard, Kenya and Tanzania. It is not generally spoken in Uganda but is used as "lingua franca." English serves the same purpose but is used more among the educated.

Uganda has more than eight major languages, and I was told at least fifty dialects. Some tribes understand each other's dialect/language, but many are so different that a lingua franca is necessary. Many expatriates, including us, try to speak at least some Swahili. It is very useful, particularly for an international traveler like I was.

Uganda has two magnificent game parks. I think they

have since changed names, but in our time, they were called Murchison Falls National Park and Queen Elisabeth National Park on the shores of Lake Edward. The most spectacular one is Murchison Falls. There the mighty Nile dashes through a gate some 20 feet wide, down 130 feet. I have seen many great waterfalls, including Victoria Falls in Zimbabwe. Still, none impressed me as much as Murchison Falls. On the bottom is a wide basin, an animal sanctuary. For any big game watcher, this is the true Garden of Eden. I was there several times. When we had visitors, it was a must.

Of course, we were there with the family. There is a comfortable lodge in the park. The trip from Kampala to the park is about 180 miles on a narrow road. The road is only partly tarmac; the rest is graveled. Therefore it was a four or five-hour drive from our house to the lodge.

One could pay for a ride in a passenger motorboat at a boat jetty near the lodge. It held about twenty people in addition to the crew, an African boatman, and a game warden. We went up to the falls on the lower level of the river. It was an unforgettable experience to watch all the exotic animals gathering on the banks of this Nile basin. Elephants, hippos, zebras, many types of deer, buffaloes, you name it. Not to forget the variety of colorful birds of many sizes and features.

But be wary, zebra and deer; there are crocodiles of a size one can not imagine. If you know the Florida alligator, forget it. It is only a small lizard in comparison with those Nile crocodiles. They will catch a zebra, hold it within their jaws and take it underwater until it drowns. Then the crocodile will devour the whole zebra without leaving a thing.

At high noon, crocodiles do not hunt for food; they just lay on a sandy riverbank, tail partly in the water, absolutely motionless, mostly with wide-open jaws and their ghastly teeth in full sight. In this position, birds hop around inside the monster's mouth, picking leftovers from the teeth.

On our excursion up the Nile, the boatman steered the craft very close to one crocodile. The game warden hit it on top of the wide-open jaws with a long pole. This sleeping, motionless monster suddenly snapped its mouth, jumped, and dived into the water. The animal did all this with an unbelievable speed and caused such waves that our motorboat started to rock frightfully.

Our children were still small then. Susanne was about seven, and Andrea was only three years old. I think they were afraid (I was!), although they may not admit it now.

Later I walked alone up a path from the bottom of the falls to the top. Suddenly I was faced with a huge elephant that stood only a few yards off the track in the brush. I wasn't completely shocked because the warden had warned me this might happen. He had advised me to just continue walking.

Elephants in that area are used to people, and they will not do you any harm. Further, the Chief Warden, an Englishman, said with a broad smile: "we never lost a tourist!." With these words in mind, I walked on but was terribly nervous. This mighty animal was just a few yards away, with no fence between us, waving his big trunk while looking me straight in the eyes. It can really cause you stomach cramps.

* * *

I remember we went fishing on the Nile one Sunday, just outside the game park. Our American neighbors, the Wheelers, and their three kids were in the second car. The river formed a pond where fishing was supposed to be good. It was a rainy day, and the fishing was not good. Just outside the reach of my line and hook was a hippo submerged in the pond, only its eyes above the water. Just sufficient to watch my fishing. Susanne and I cast the line again and again. The presence of this hippo made me nervous and even angry. We fished the whole day. Susanne was keen to get a fish, and her patience paid off. Finally, we caught an 18-pound Nile perch. Mike Wheeler did not catch anything.

Lucky fellow, I thought when we got home. Do you know why? We were on that dirt road to and from the Nile for seven hours. And we fished in permanent rain. I was dead tired but still had to clean the fish. While doing this in our kitchen, I saw the light go off in the Wheelers' house and thought how lucky Mike was not to catch a fish. He could sleep right away while I had to do this unpleasant work in the kitchen. (Remember, I wrote at the beginning of this story that I am not a passionate fisherman.)

I spent about seventeen years in both East and West Africa, so I have seen several big game parks, including the famous Ngorongoro crater game reserve in Tanzania. However, I still believe the most beautiful one is Murchison Falls National Park.

Ugandans (Africans in general) do not go to game parks. Their relationship with animals is different from ours. Except for professionals, like game wardens (In the sixties, most were white, but now most are Africans.), scouts, or tour guides, an ordinary African is indifferent to animals or afraid. At the beginning of this chapter, I wrote that one of our friends took his cook along for a hunting trip. This poor fellow was so scared that he climbed a tree and spent the whole time up there while we were gone from the camp.

One day I had to go up country to Gulu and Arua in the North on duty to inspect some of our Unicef activities. I took my logistics counterpart, Mr. Okello from the Ministry of Health, along on this occasion, as I often did because central government officials seldom traveled to the field and saw activities by themselves. Part of this was that the government had no budget to pay travel expenses for their employees, partly also because they were just not used to it. On our trip to Gulu, we passed the Murchison Falls National Park. Mr. Okello told me that he had never been to Murchison's. There is an admission fee to be paid on entry to the park, which is quite high for expatriates but encouragingly low for nationals. Well, we traveled through the park from South to North, and as we were on official duty for the government of Uganda, we did not have to pay anything. My traveling companion saw big game, which he had never seen before in his life, although he was born in the neighborhood about forty miles from the park.

Later, during Idi Amin's time in Uganda, it was reported that soldiers shot elephants with machine guns. What a sad happening.

COMMENTS ON UGANDA

I met Idi Amin and even spoke to him some 34 years ago. My thoughts about him are not scientifically founded, but I have an opinion. In the last 40 years of Africa's history, since most countries became independent, several people became presidents of their respective nations but soon turned out to be brutal dictators.

Most of these politicians, I call them "first-generation," were not prepared to hold public office. Idi Amin was a perfect example. Others were Jean-Bedel Bokassa of the Central African Republic, Mengistu Haile Meriam of Ethiopia, Syad Barre of Somalia, Laurent Kabila of Congo, etc.

All of these were soldiers! They were swept on a post-independence wave up to the top. Once in power, when the euphoria had gone, they and those who helped them discovered they were not equipped to do the job. None of them were educated, had political abilities, or had experience.

In the case of Amin, it's one thing being chief of the army with limited responsibilities for the population, but being president is much more involved. When Amin overthrew Obote, his popularity rose. In particular, with the Bagandans. They did not like Obote because he had ousted their King Mutesa II. Furthermore, he was from a northern tribe, Ankole. He (Obote) was protected by the brutal "Special Force." They were all Ankolies, ruthless; they shot first and asked questions later.

In 1971, Amin, the popular former British sergeant boxer, then chief of the army, ousted their enemy number one. Bagandans had already forgotten that Amin and the military were a tool of Obote when their Kabaka was deposed. When Amin was president, he made himself even more popular by throwing all "Asians" out of Uganda. Indians and Pakistanis had to leave the country within three months.

The Asians were not liked. They held most small businesses, the shops in town, and up-country, too. In colonial times, the Asians stood between the British and the Africans. Africans had no experience with running businesses. After 1971 Africans took over the shops of the Asians. Soon, one could no longer buy anything in Uganda. They mistakenly thought all the money from a sale was theirs to spend; they did not think about replenishment. They had as little idea of managing a large or small business as Amin had of running a country.

Uganda was in a monetary union with Kenya and Tanzania. In those countries, the currency was the East African Shilling. Amin quit or had to quit this monetary union. Economically this was the end of Uganda. Amin stayed in power for eight years and only did this by force and brutal oppression of the population. The life of a person was not worth anything. I really do not know how men can get to this stage of just killing other men, I do not know.

The old kingdoms, Buganda, Toro, Bunyoro, Ankole, Karamodja, etc., and their kings were not just "tribal chieftains." To my understanding, they were extensive and populous kingdoms. Buganda and Bunyoro had an ongoing rivalry as to which was more important. Bunyoro was, in ancient times, a great kingdom. Still, at the time of independence, Buganda was undoubtedly the more important one.

For this reason, Mutesa II (King Freddie) became president of independent Uganda. At the independence negotiations, there was also a dispute regarding the so-called "lost counties." Two counties were given to Buganda during the colonial time, and Bunyoro wanted these counties back.

The matter was not settled at independence, and the two counties were placed "provisionally" under central government administration. Uganda was released by the

British into independence with a federal structure. The kingdoms were the states, similar to the USA, Switzerland, or Germany. But this did not work, and for some time to come, in Africa, it will not work. African leaders cannot tolerate other leaders as rivals around.

For traditional reasons, this may work in India, but not Africa, as the last 40 years have proven. Not even in Ethiopia, which, except for six years of occupation by Mussolini, was never a colony.

I have seen a coup d'etat. In 1966 (I cannot remember the date), the Kabaka Mutesa II was ousted. It was a rainy day. From my office window at Amber House in Kampala, I could see the Palace of the Kabaka. The people of Kampala are Bagandans because Kampala is in Buganda. As Kampala was also the capital of Uganda, there were other people, including Asians and Europeans, in town. During the hours of the attack, there was a thunderstorm, and sometimes it was difficult to distinguish between cannon fire and thunder. People in Kampala went about their daily work. Women went to the local market, pretending that nothing was happening.

But this was only on the surface. I think Africans, on the whole, act like ostriches. They stick their heads in the sand so they don't see what is happening. I had one source from which I could get the people's true feelings. Our maid Cecilia was a Baganda, and she spoke English quite well. She told us how the Bagandans felt about the whole affair.

I even think Obote and Amin intentionally let the Kabaka escape because killing him would have caused an uprising in Buganda. By the way, the Kabaka went to England and had quite a second career as a playboy (King Freddie) afterward.

Tribalism is a major factor in African society. This is perhaps why federal systems do not work. To my observations, except in bigger towns, there were few intermarriages between ethnic groups of Africans, practically never in rural areas. Between Europeans and Africans, yes, but here I think it's more materialism. We seem rich in their eyes. But here again, the offspring of a mixed marriage (half-casts) do not mix with black Africans. They are usually better off than the blacks and are often racists.

These are only my observations as a layman. I am not an anthropologist.

Another thing, we had good American neighbors, the Wheelers. Mike was with US-AID. Shortly after independence, the US State Department also sent African Americans to US embassies in Africa. Among Mike's colleagues were several black Americans. Whether the State Department thought African Americans would have better access to Africans, I do not know. Still, I know they had no better relations. Ugandans were deeply suspicious of African Americans, more than white Americans. We have often talked with the Wheelers and their colleagues about this phenomenon.

* * *

There is a time of year in East Africa, shortly after the big rains, when locusts fly in the evenings. These insects fly around lights. Street lights, for instance. During this time, about two or three weeks a year, women in the neighborhoods go out and catch as many locusts as they can. Fried in a pan, these insects are supposedly delicious. Personally, I have not tried this fried African delicacy.

FOCUS ON LOGISTICS I (RWANDA)

When I joined Unicef in East Africa in 1964, African countries had just gained independence from their former colonial powers. For instance, Rwanda. This densely populated country in Central Africa became independent in 1962.

The majority of the five million people in Rwanda are from the Hutu tribe. Rwanda used to be a German Colony. In 1918 it became a Trust Territory administered by Belgium. The language spoken in government business was French.

With Unicef's help, the Ministry of Health was trying to improve life for mothers and children in the country. There were problems with the availability of transport, not because there were no vehicles, but because most of them were broken down after only a short period of service. Unicef supplied about twenty-five motor vehicles for transportation in assisted programs, mainly in health services. When I arrived in East Africa, Rwanda was one of the first countries I had to visit.

When Rwanda became independent, the Belgians left an infrastructure behind that should have, in theory, maintained government services throughout the country. To support these services, particularly in rural areas, utility vehicles must be in good running order. Unicef vehicles were given to the Ministry of Health in Kigali for their assisted health programs.

Part of the government infrastructure was a "Public Works Department" (PWD) for all public works, such as maintaining roads and buildings. There was also a "Garage Administratif" (French translation: government vehicle workshop). I do not know how efficient the PWD in Kigali was during Trusteeship times when Belgian expatriate experts were in the department. They had now departed the newly independent country.

In October 1964, when I visited Rwanda, tremendous difficulties existed. Roads had deteriorated, and vehicles were out of running order. The whole country had no more than fifty miles of tarred roads. The rest were unimproved dirt roads that had to be regularly graded, especially during the rainy season. About fifty percent of the government vehicles, including those loaned by Unicef, were in operation. Vehicles that entered the "Garage Administratif" never left it; they were "cannibalized." Costly 4-wheel drive vehicles had a short life span.

As soon as a replacement part was needed, or if a tire blew out due to bad roads, the vehicle remained where it was and was soon "cannibalized." This situation was not unique to Rwanda; many African countries were in the same position after independence. Government officials, who were supposed to run the country, often had no qualifications or experience.

The Ministry of Health was headed by a Lady, a former nurse. When I met her on this first visit, I respectfully addressed her: "Your Excellency, Madam la Ministre" She very charmingly replied: "Please, call me Madeleine." She was quite understanding and told me the biggest problem was that government employees were not motivated. Their salaries were low, and their attitude was that government or donor organizations, for that matter, were rich and could replace vehicles whenever necessary.

The missionaries, usually catholic, didn't have the same motivation problem. They kept health services in rural areas going. The missions were run by "White Fathers," named after the white cowl they wore. There were still many Belgians in the missions: fathers and nuns. African priests and sisters were also in responsible positions.

The missions were widespread over the former Belgian colonies (Congo, the Trust Territories of Rwanda, and Burundi). They had the best schools and hospitals. Many government officials, including Ministers and Presidents, were educated in mission schools.

The new governments wanted to reduce the influence of missions by expanding national health and education services to rural areas. The results of these efforts were mixed and depended on the logistical infrastructure of a country. Schools, health, and other public services depended on motivation, supervision, qualified teachers, nurses, doctors, and money. But though the missions had limited funds, the motivation of the missionaries was infinitely better, hence their better results.

Missions also usually had guest rooms where one could stay overnight and have a good meal in the evening. Often no commercial hotels and restaurants were to be found. I frequently stayed in missions during my field trips in Africa, not just in Rwanda and Burundi. I was impressed by their simple hospitality, hard work, and sense of responsibility for development in the country.

Albert Schweitzer was a missionary and a great man. He was famous as a philosopher, musician, and theologian. Later in life, he resigned from all his university assignments. He became a humble medical student. After he qualified as a doctor, he went to the Gabone Province of French Equatorial Africa in 1913 to build a hospital with his own hands in Lambarene on the Ogowe river. There he fought leprosy, sleeping sickness, and other tropical diseases. He was awarded the Nobel peace prize in 1952.

Schweitzer practiced curative medicine and unselfishly helped thousands of people in an exemplary way. Those who made it to his hospital in Lambarene, walking, being carried on a stretcher, or ferried on the river, were lucky and received help. Most people in Africa did not get modern medical treatment. They had to rely on their local "witch doctor."

After African independence in the fifties and sixties, the priority was preventive medicine, and the aim was country-wide coverage. Logistics was the key for any program built on the principles of "outreach" and "preventive medicine."

FOCUS ON LOGISTICS II

In Unicef's definition, logistics meant: "The right project materials, of the right quality, in the right quantity, for the right price, at the right time, in the right place." To accomplish this is no easy matter. The supply line from ordering to delivery is long, and many things can go wrong.

In the early years, Unicef had agreements with various governments stipulating that responsibility ends at the ship's tackle. That meant it was the responsibility of the recipient government to handle donated supplies. They were supposed to clear it through customs, bring it to a central medical store (in case of health supplies and drugs) and finally distribute the supplies throughout the respective county.

That sounds easy, but it is not. Remember, we speak about developing countries. Many of these countries lacked resources and management ability to fill their obligation of receiving and distributing project supplies.

First, supplies would remain in the port for a long time, often for weeks or months, exposed to the sun, humidity, and other adverse weather conditions. There were always excuses for why this happened. No vehicles and no money to pay port fees were popular excuses. Unicef project funds were not supposed to pay customs duties. However, there were usually port fees for handling, small amounts to be paid. For many ministries obtaining the necessary funds was a hassle and a lengthy procedure. Port officials would not trust the ministry's officials; they wanted "cash."

For such reasons, projects were often at a standstill, and health centers had no drugs and other health supplies. These remained unused in a port shed. When supplies were finally cleared and taken to a ministry's warehouse, problems started anew.

I have seen supplies lying in medical stores for years with their validity expired, while health centers complained of shortages of almost everything. Low-ranked and low-paid employees often were responsible for internal logistics. They could be in charge of goods worth many thousands of dollars.

Higher-ranking government officials did not give the necessary attention to get things moving. But they constantly complained of shortages of medical supplies in the country. When I would point out that supplies were lying in the warehouse, rotting away, the standard excuse was: "We have no vehicles, meaning trucks, to distribute supplies in rural areas."

This was a frustrating part of my work. During extensive travels for Unicef to countries, the first thing I always paid a visit to were ports, airports, and warehouses. Often I saw appalling conditions, and it took time and convincing to get things moving. The government naturally always wanted more. More supplies when an earlier consignment was still in the warehouse. Larger warehouses and, if possible, Unicef's help to build extensions. Now there, I was very critical in supporting such assistance. I was known for repeating religiously: "A good warehouse is an empty warehouse!"

Project supplies should be out at the projects, not in a central warehouse. One thing governments were insatiable in asking for was more vehicles, meaning Land Rovers and trucks. Unicef provided such transport means. However, it had to be within the whole concept of the respective project. There was also the question of the expenses to run vehicles: fuel, spare parts, and repair costs. That, too, was a government responsibility.

In the sixties, after independence, governments often easily accepted conditions under which project supplies, including the operation costs of vehicles, became their responsibility as soon as these were in their country. Over the years, it has become increasingly difficult for governments to do so. Partly this was because of growing bureaucracies in those countries. It was also the unavailability of funds to meet such commitments. Countries got more and more indebted. The budgets of participating ministries were so meager they couldn't meet costs such as port clearance, vehicle repair, and fuel.

As a result, Unicef (but also other aid organizations) took on operating costs that were initially government responsibilities. I was an advocate of this. It did not make sense to provide a $20,000 vehicle and see it later not being used because our partners, governments, could not afford to run it. If a small, inexpensive part was needed, a ministry probably could manage to buy it. However, if, for instance, four tires were worn out, replacing them was a significant cost factor. Vehicles were often "temporarily" parked, waiting for someone to provide money for four tires. Left in this condition, "cannibalism" commenced, meaning that parts required elsewhere were taken off the "temporarily" parked vehicle. Deterioration set in, and soon, a relatively new vehicle, which only needed replacement tires, was gone. What a terrific waste of resources.

In taking over internal costs, somebody had to manage logistics in those countries on the spot. In later years and even now, Unicef had to station a logistics person in such countries.

1965

RWANDA

A few remarks on Rwanda. The country had only fifty miles of tarred roads when it became independent. These consisted of three short stretches, one in Kigali, the capital. One in Butare, the university town. And one in Kisenyi, a lovely town on the shores of Lake Kivu. Each of these places had about fifteen miles of improved roads. Overland there were only dirt roads which were quite difficult to travel on.

There were spots where local youths would dig a hole or a ditch across the road and wait until a vehicle came along. Then, they would offer to repair the road for a small fee. You had no choice but to pay. Another thing was the airfield at the capital. It was a grass field outside Kigali on which only small two or four-seater planes could land. There were no international flights to the country.

So on my first visit to Rwanda, I traveled by road with a colleague. The distance from Kampala to Kigali is about 380 miles, two-thirds of which was not tarred. For this journey, one needed a whole day. I remember the return journey. Halfway from Kigali to Kampala, we met a car. There were not many cars traveling, and when you met one, usually both would stop and tell each other news of the day as well as the condition of the roads.

The car we met was occupied by a UN colleague from the World Health Organization (WHO). The news he had was not good. He told us that Maurice Pate, the first Executive Director of Unicef (That is to say, my boss), had died the day before on 19. January 1965 in New York. I had only been in Unicef a short while and had never met Maurice Pate, but it was still a shock to be told this on the road in Central Africa.

Maurice Pate was replaced some months later by Unicef's second Executive Director. He was Henry Labuisse, an American from the South. Labuisse had been the director of UNRWA (my first UN-Organization). Then he became the US Ambassador to Greece. Finally, he returned to the UN, becoming chief of Unicef.

As I said earlier, Kiseny was a lovely little place. Lake Kivu was special because one could swim in it. Many African Lakes and Rivers were invested with bilharzia (schistosomiasis). Their waters were infested with parasites: water snails that entered the body through cuts or abrasions and caused bilharzia, intestinal and worse infections.

However, because of its sulfide water contents from the volcanic mountains nearby, Lake Kivu was not infested by these water snails. For this reason, Lake Kivu was an old resort area frequented by Belgian planters from the Eastern Congo, Rwanda, and Burundi during colonial times. There were splendid hotels, but in these post-colonial times, no tourists; they were all empty. So we planned and eventually did spend a vacation over the Christmas holidays in Kisenyi with friends from Kampala, about 400 miles away. We all had children and a wonderful time. I wonder whether the children remember.

The world has heard terrible things about Rwanda and the refugees crossing the border to Goma in what is now called the Democratic Congo (formerly Zaire). In Rwanda, Burundi, and to some extent, in the Congo, there are basically two ethnic tribes: Hutus, the majority, and Tutsi, a minority.

The taller Tutsis usually hold power because they are military. At regular intervals, they kill each other. That happened in Rwanda. So, many people fled to Goma, where the infamous refugee camp was. Goma is actually one big town with Kisenyi and is only separated by a border. Well, during our season holidays in 1965/66, we could not imagine that Western Rwanda and Goma would one day be where this terrible genocide would happen in the 90s.

* * *

As mentioned earlier, Unicef's policy was outreach health services covering an entire country. Project supplies often remained sitting in stores in capital cities. Some of the best vehicles were used by Ministry Officials in the capital and, worse yet, sometimes by their families. Vehicle replacement parts and drugs often lay unused in central government stores. They did not get to rural areas where they were needed. You may ask, did I have a miraculous recipe to remedy this situation? No, I could not do miracles. It required much follow-up work, convincing, persuasion, field trip supervision, and negotiations.

CONGO

My first mission in logistics to the Congo was back in 1965. I flew to Leopoldville, as it was then called. Later the country's capital was renamed Kinshasa. Congo became independent from Belgian in 1960.

When I visited for the first time five years after independence, it had not really become a quiet place. I traveled from Entebbe first to Goma, then over endless tropical forests, enormously big rivers, mountains, and savannas, but no roads except sandy tracks in the bush. I thought to myself: who could rule a country like this from the other (Western) end of it. Today, some 35 years later, I wonder about the same question. This country is not really free yet. There have been years of warfare, corruption, and misery.

It began shortly after independence. The players were President Joseph Kasavubu, Prime Minister Patrice Lumumba, the chief minister of Katanga Province, Moise Tschombe, and already then Josef Mobuto.

Trouble started in the Western Congo in a military camp near Matadi when African soldiers of the "Force Publique" started a mutiny against their (still) Belgian officers. The ensuing disturbances swept through the whole country. Not too severe in big towns like Leopoldville and Elisabethville but horrible in some rural areas, where white plantation owners and women came to harm. Also, there was a power struggle among the first-generation Congolese politicians from the beginning.

These events made the UN Security Council decide to send UN peacekeepers to the country. The Secretary-General of the UN at the time, Dag Hammarskjölt, gave the marching order. Shortly after that, when the UN blue helmets were already in Leopoldville, Moise Tshome of mineral-rich Katanga Province wanted to break away from the rest of the Congo and declared the Katanga Province independent. Of course, there were vital economic issues at stake. The Belgian-owned "Union Minière" of Katanga and Kasai had vast mineral wealth, not just copper. They were rich enough to buy a man like Moise Tshombe and finance a whole army.

But now the big powers in the world got into the chaos. It was in the midst of the "Cold War." The UN Security Council met again in New York. It came up with a resolution, ordering the UN peacekeepers to go into Katanga and end this unilateral declaration of independence. That took some time to achieve.

In the meantime, the power struggle in Leopoldville continued. President Kasavubu fired the prime minister, Patrice Lumumba. Marauding army factions took him into custody and killed him. To make a long story short, only one of the "old guard" survived: Mobuto. He changed his Christian first name from Joseph to Sese Seko. In one way or another, Mobuto Sese Seko got rid of all the independent politicians and ruled the country for 35 years. Later he was ousted by the next president, Kabila.

Shortly after that, Mobuto died of cancer in exile in Marocco. In September 1961, UN Secretary-General Dag Hammarskjölt was killed in a plane crash on a mission to the Congo. In the first years of engagement in the Congo, the UN had a difficult time. They could not control the various political and power groups, were not liked by the Belgians who stayed behind, and were not respected by the first-generation African politicians.

Things had settled down a bit when I visited the Congo in 1965. Mobuto had calmed the various tribes and got the country back to work. He protected the big mining corporations in Kasai and Katanga. They could now work efficiently exploring the Congo's enormous wealth. Mobuto became one of the wealthiest people in the world. Surely, no coincidence. The mining companies could buy whatever they needed.

At about that time, a lot of names were changed. Congo became Zaire, Leopoldville became Kinshasa, the Congo river changed to River Zaire, Elisabethville to Lumbumbashi, Katanga to Shaba Province, and many more, all "African names." The people were satisfied.

Unicef and other branches of the United Nations were involved in one of the largest development programs in their history. Logistics was of prime importance. Our mandate, of course, was women and children. An infrastructure of health centers, and hospitals, particularly on the government side and in rural areas, did not exist. The only institutions that kept health services and schools alive were missions, mainly catholic ones. The government of Zaire wanted to, but could not, change this situation. All the missionaries were badly needed.

The eastern part of Zaire, Goma, Bukavu, Albertville, etc., had no land connection with Kinshasa. Our supplies came in through the Kenyan port of Mombasa. My mission was to find supply routes and see what became of the approximately 750 vehicles, mainly Jeeps, and 4-wheel drive vehicles, that had been sent after independence to the Congo, now Zaire. Could they still be used in health services? Well, some could! The UN peacekeepers established countrywide vehicle servicing stations and agreed to maintain the Unicef vehicles.

Unicef had no office in Kinshasa. The office on the other side of the river in Brazzaville looked after Unicef's programs in Zaire. The country opposite Kinshasa is Congo/Brazzaville, a former French colony that also became independent in 1960. A bit of a situation like New York, NY, and New Jersey, NJ, except that most of the time, the two countries quarreled with each other, and the only means of communication, a ferry, did not operate.

Brazzaville had not only the Unicef Area office but also the regional headquarters of WHO (World Health Organization). Both organizations had personnel stationed in

Brazza responsible for projects in Zaire. So when, as often happened, the ferry did not work, these staff had to travel via Paris to visit Kinshasa. No other connection was available. One of the problems in Africa that still exists today is there are no, or very few, air routes East/West but plenty of North/South ones. This remnant of colonial times, when the colonies were oriented toward their colonial powers in Europe, created this situation. To a large extent, this has not changed.

* * *

On this first trip to Zaire, I flew from Entebbe to Kinshasa (That was one of the very few routes East/West). The airline was called Air-Congo (later Air-Zaire). The aircraft was a DC 4, a really scary old plane. Because of technical problems, it was three days late departing from Entebbe. The pilot was an East African adventure type, and so was his co-pilot.

We were only three passengers to Goma. A few more people boarded the plane there. The flying time was some five hours, partly very near to the ground. I think they needed to fly low and navigate along rivers and roads. I did not use that airline for subsequent visits (Then I traveled with the British airline south to Johannesburg and from there north again with the Belgian Sabena to Kinshasa.)

At the stopover in Goma on that DC-4 flight, I talked to the pilot. He calmed me a bit and told me the plane was quite safe. This pilot, a freelancer who flew all over Africa, also told me an interesting theory on how the plane accident in which Dag Hammarskjölt died happened.

This accident has never been entirely explained, and the cause has never been established. There was wild speculation as to whether it was an accident or sabotage. Was the KGB or the CIA involved? Was the pilot sick or drunk? Nothing of the sort, our East African flier told me.

The UN Secretary-General's plane, a DC-6, crashed on its approach to Ndola in Zambia. The plane came in too low, collided with treetops, and crashed shortly before the runway. One person, a UN security man of Swedish nationality, survived, but I think he died later.

The town of Ndola is in the rich copper belt of Zambia, at an altitude of 1268 meters. It is on the border to the former Congo, now Zaire. OK, so far, so good.

In the Congo, on the fringe of Leopoldville, now Kinshasa, is the old airport of the former Belgian-Congo capital. It is practically just behind the splendid Boulevard Albert. Almost mid-town, this part of town is called "Ndola." This old airport is still used for private and small military planes and helicopters. This airport's altitude is 307 meters.

When they examined the plane wreck where Dag Hammarskjölt died, they found a map of Ndola near Kinshasa, Congo, in the cockpit but no map of Ndola, Zambia. The weather at the time of the accident was foggy with minimal visibility. The Swedish pilot of the DC-6 had no African flying experience. Could it be that this DC-6 crashed because of a mistaken approach map?

CONGO II

Over the years, Zaire became "my baby." That is to say, I traveled there many times. In the sixties, I traveled from Kampala, Uganda, where I was stationed for six years. From there, I also frequently visited the Eastern part of Zaire, meaning Bukavu, Goma, and Lubumbashi. It is like being in another country.

One can drive by car from Kampala to this part of Zaire. Which I usually did, taking advantage and also visiting Rwanda on the way. The Lake Kivu area is particularly beautiful with volcanoes all around (These are not active and are all green.) Previously when it was the Belgian-Congo, it served Belgian plantation owners of the region as a holiday resort.

There are beautiful, luxurious hotels, particularly in Bukavu and Kisenyi on Lake Kivu. Kisenyi and Goma are actually one big city divided by a border. Kisenyi is Rwanda, Goma is Zaire. In Belgian times, this did not matter.

The hotels had no guests even though the lake is one of few where one can swim. There is no bilharzia (schistosomiasis). I have written about Lake Kivu in the installment entitled "Rwanda."

One thing I did not mention before: this mountainous area in Eastern Congo is an ideal climate for medicinal plants (herbs), the basis for many medicines. There are now plantations owned and operated by big European pharmaceutical companies. I do not think Kinshasa has any control over this activity; they export via the East African port of Mombasa.

* * *

"Chaos" ruled the Congo in the early sixties when

Katanga declared independence. Later when the UN did some arm-twisting, they agreed to rejoin the "motherland."

When Lumumba died, the President of Congo, Joseph Kasavubu, appointed Moise Tshombe as Prime Minister. He recruited mercenaries. They came from all over, mainly from South Africa, Belgium, the UK, and Rhodesia. Usually, the mercenaries were ex-soldiers and adventurers. There were an estimated four to five hundred in the Congo. Some made headlines in the Western press. For example, Mike Hoare, who lived in South Africa. Others were the Belgian Jean-Pierre Schramme and the African-American pilot "Colonel Julian." These guys were tough. The Congolese Army or Rebels were no problem for them.

They could take over a whole town with a handful of fellow mercenaries, which they proved in Stanleyville (now Kisangani). Tshombe had plenty of money. The USA was much more friendly to him than they were to Lumumba. Anyhow, finally, Tshombe was ousted by Josef Mobuto and went into exile. That also was the end of the mercenaries. They gradually faded away when the money dried up. Mobuto had no money; by definition, a mercenary only works for money.

* * *

I want to bring up two short stories of the mercenaries' time in Congo: These people had no hesitation in taking a Unicef vehicle if they needed one. The white UN color and/or the Unicef decal were no hindrance for mercenaries. Near Stanleyville, they took one of our jeeps. Apparently, it helped them conquer that city from Lumumba's loyal forces.

Whether it was during warfare or the ensuing victory celebration can no longer be established with certainty. But, later, some 30 miles outside Stanleyville, a most likely drunk mercenary smashed the jeep against a tree. It is not known whether or not he came to harm. The tree was knocked down, and the jeep was no longer operational, so it stayed there on the leftover remains of the tree.

Years later, a Unicef colleague of mine came by and

found a tree with a jeep on top of it, its Unicef decal still readable. What happened was, at the time of the accident, the tree was knocked down, but its roots were still OK. In the tropics, almost anything re-grows. So that tree, after some time, grew with the jeep on top of it.

The mercenaries had plenty of money, and they were simple-minded. So "off duty" drinking was their main occupation. One could always see and meet mercenaries at the Hotel Memling in Leopoldville (Kinshasa). One could not mistake them; they were always armed and in a good mood. They would invite anyone who wanted to sit with them and listen to their stories. Often they were in female company. The girls benefited from their generosity. Not only free drinks. I usually stayed in the Memling, it was a good hotel.

One evening, I saw a very attractive blond lady sitting with the mercenaries, which was a little unusual. The following day I took a SABENA Flight to Johannesburg (SA). And, as very seldom ever happened, in the seat next to me was an attractive blond lady. I soon recognized her as being the lady who sat with the mercenaries the day before. Over lunch, we started to talk; she was very pleasant. She then told me that she was Mrs. Mike Hoare. According to her, she had succeeded in talking Mike into giving up this mercenary existence and coming back to South Africa for a more decent job.

TONI NUTTI

Susanne asked me to write about our visit to Toni Nutti, a respectable Italian lady who lived in the wild Kagera river. We were there in 1965 with the whole family. Susanne was about six years old, but she vividly remembers our stay in her guest house.

Some people may tell you that the source of the White Nile is at Jinja, Uganda, where its waters dash out from Lake Victoria over the mighty Owen Falls. Do not believe that, even if you find it in a reference book. Lake Victoria has one contributor, the Kagera river. Its source is in mountainous Burundi. It joins the lake in the West, near the town of Bukoba.

We were on a safari trip and wanted to spend a few days of local vacation with friends on a lake in Rwanda. We were told by a hunter that it was possible to spend a night at Toni Nutti's guest house on the way. It's a bit risky because she does not accept everybody. Travelers have to be to her liking. Besides, the house has no telephone to make a booking in advance.

"Well, where is the place?"

"Toni Nutti's guesthouse is in the river Kagera, on the border between Uganda and Rwanda."

"In the river?"

"Yes," was the answer, "it's a small island in the river which forms the border at this point. As you arrive on the river bank," the hunter continued, "there is a cord which you have to pull, it rings a bell in her house. On the sound of the bell, she will come to have a look at you. After that, she will pronounce if she accepts you. Do not be too late. If she rejects you, the next possible place to stay is a lodge (Lodge Kizinga) fifty miles away in the Kagera National Park, a Rwandan game park. It's not as nice as Toni Nutti's, but you can find a room in the lodge."

We left Kampala for Bukoba, just about 190 miles. The road was not too bad. As we arrived at the river, we made sure to look civilized, then rang the bell. Toni Nutti came from her house and approached the river bank. She was a gray-haired lady in her senior years. She shouted over, asking us who we were and what we wanted. We said our names and, as a reference, the name of the hunter who sent us. Her face lit up, and she said we could stay.

It was a small island in the river. One could not even walk on most of it. It was partly swampy. The river was full of fish and crocodiles, a bit scary for us all, not just the kids.

Now getting over the river was something I had not seen before. A hand-operated cable car (funicular) extended from one strong tree on the mainland to another strong tree on the island side. The river was only about thirty to forty yards wide. A cage for two to three people was suspended from the cable on a wheel. An African on the island cranked the cage forth and back.

As we were nine people, including children and our luggage, five trips had to be performed. The fellow was perspiring quite a bit. "Too many guests," he remarked. The scary thing was that the wire mesh cage cleared the water by just a few inches. The water was full of crocodiles, patiently hoping the steel cable might snap one day.

We made it, and we all had the most delightful evening. Toni Nutti had lots of stories. She had spent most of her life in Africa near the Kagera river. She had been on the island she and her husband had built for the last thirty years.

We stayed up late in the night. Her husband had been a professional hunter. Some years back, while guiding a group of tourist hunters, he was killed by a buffalo.

Her brother, too, was killed by a buffalo. African buffalo can not be compared with the American buffalo. They (African) are the most dangerous animals you can hunt. They are unpredictable. Even if they are already down, you must be careful how you approach them. (I write this from hearsay, I am not a hunter myself, as I have written in a previous story.) Toni showed us photographs, proving that she had shot several buffalo herself. She was an assistant to her husband in guiding tourist hunters. We had such a good meal that evening in her guesthouse. She was a delightful hostess.

The night was perfect. It cooled off after dark, and we slept to the rushing sound of the wild water.

At breakfast in the morning, Toni Nutti asked whether we had met Lord Nelson and Lady Hamilton. We thought she was joking. However, it turned out that there were two older hippos in the river. At night they usually came out from the water, as hippos do. The pair trot around the house, examine the trash cans, and feel at home in Toni's garden. The two had been near the island for years. At one point, she and her husband named them Lord Nelson and Lady Hamilton.

1967

ZANZIBAR

Zanzibar and Pemba, two islands to the East of the African continent, were formerly colonized by Arabs. Both islands were significant places for the slave trade. The unhappy people were brought over from mainland Africa, auctioned, and shipped from the islands. In 1964 Zanzibar and Pemba merged with Tankanika. This marked the birth of the Republic of Tanzania.

Unicef assisted with various basic health projects in Tanzania, including on Zanzibar and Pemba. I visited Zanzibar several times and also Pemba once. Besides standard basic health programs, the islands also had a malaria eradication project. The technique used then was spraying each house twice a year to destroy the mosquitoes and interrupt the chain of infection. Thousands of huts and structures in rural areas also had to be sprayed. Such campaigns were very logistically demanding, hence my involvement.

In the sixties, Germany was still divided into West and East Germany. President Julius Nyerere decided to structure Tanzania along socialistic lines. They called it African Socialism. Tanzania was one of the first countries to recognize East Germany, the GDR (German Democratic Republic). The GDR sent aid to Africa at that time.

In addition to other aid, their bilateral aid also assisted public health projects. In eastern Africa, the GDR concentrated its support on Zanzibar and Pemba. The GDR had an incredibly large number of "specialists" on the islands. Going out in large groups, they always had a political supervisor.

So here I came, not just as a Unicef official but also as a West German, and they knew it. My contact was with government officials, but they, in turn, often consulted with their advisers from the GDR. On the surface, I had no particularly big problems as far as organizational questions were concerned.

Some of the GDR people stayed in the hotel on Zanzibar, where I had booked a room. Sitting together and having a drink on the hotel terrace was unavoidable in the evening. As long as the political supervisor was around, the conversation was very much checked and boring. However, this one in Zanzibar had the habit of drinking a bit too much and finally went to bed. Then the conversation became much more lively, and we felt that we were very much one people, Germans.

* * *

In East Africa, at that time, there was an airline owned by the three countries Tanzania, Kenya, and Uganda. It was called East African Airways (EAA) and was quite good. EAA had a modern fleet of aircraft (Remember, this was in the 60s.): Vickers VC 10s, several Fokker Friendships F-27s, and a few de Havilland Comet jets. They also had one de Havilland Rabbit, a two-engine biplane with about eight passenger seats. The outside was still fabric, and its captain was as old as the plane. This Rabbit EAA was used on the run between Zanzibar and Pemba and from Pemba to Tanga on the Tanzanian mainland.

It was quite an experience to fly on this plane. The journey to the airport at Chaka Chacka lasted about one hour. Here too, were many GDR experts in health services. The island had no hotel but a government guesthouse. The room looked alright to me until I looked in the guest book and read the last entry by a fellow boarder: "too many rats!" That was an encouraging thought for the night.

The medical chief of the GDR team was Dr. Schlesinger. His wife was also a medical doctor and Dr. Schlesinger. They both worked in the island's hospital. They invited me for dinner, which I found very nice. When I arrived, there were two other doctors present. We had a very good meal and a lively, relatively free conversation. Physicians seemed to have a little more freedom to invite "foreigners" without having a political supervisor around. So here we were, all Germans but still from different countries, speaking about a future Germany in the same language.

* * *

The big event on Pemba in these January 1967 days was a little sensation. A nurse, about 28 years of age, was on the GDR team. On the other hand, the WHO (World Health Organization) had a Belgian entomologist in the malaria eradication project. The two fell in love, which would have been a natural matter under normal circumstances. But here was a citizen of a socialist country, the GDR, and, on the other hand, a young man from the capitalist world. That caused quite a problem.

Anyhow, I heard later that the young lady from East Germany stood her ground, and one day they were married by a priest who visited Pemba once a year. The nurse got permission from a high-ranking government official in East Berlin to leave the GDR team and take residency in Brussels.

* * *

The following day I took the de Havilland Rabbit with the old captain from Chaka Chaka for Tanga and, from there, an EAA Fokker Friendship to Kampala. By the way, this is one of the most beautiful flights in Eastern Africa. It travels low over several game parks. The majestic Kilimanjaro, with a snow-covered peak, is to the plane's left side.

EMERGENCY LANDING

My family and I lived in Kampala for six years. These were good times in the Ugandan capital. The country became independent in 1962. In the beginning, it was a fairly well-functioning democracy. The democratic system, however, deteriorated, and by 1971, the then-president Milton Obote was ousted by Idi Amin Dada.

Idi Amin was well-known all over the world. This is a strange phenomenon. Very few people know the names of good leaders in the developing world. Yet, everybody knows bad dictators like Idi Amin. So that means one has to be nuts to be known. We left for West Africa before Idi Amin took over in Uganda.

Unicef had its Regional Office in Kampala, even though neighboring Nairobi in Kenya was more of a center with well-functioning communication, air connections, and other facilities. The reason was that when Unicef opened an office in East Africa, Kenya was a British Colony. Uganda, however, was "only" a British protectorate. (I never exactly understood the difference between the two statuses.)

I was a Regional Transport Adviser and traveled throughout the region to eighteen countries where Unicef-assisted programs benefited mothers and children. There was rarely a direct flight out of Entebbe Airport (Uganda's International Airport, 20 miles away from Kampala!) to other East African countries. I always had to travel first to Nairobi and stay overnight. It was the only place with air connections to many of the region's countries. For the return travel, it was the same thing. Arriving in the afternoon in Nairobi, one had to stay overnight. Only the following morning was there a flight back to Entebbe.

This one Saturday morning, I think it was in 1967, I had stayed overnight in the famous New Stanley Hotel in Nairobi. I went early to the Airport for the EAA flight to Entebbe. All went smoothly; we started on time. The plane was only half full. It was a Fogger Friendship F-27, the airplane most frequently used for this run. It is an absolutely beautiful flight out of Nairobi. Heading west, one can see Kilimanjaro's snow-covered summit to the south, over Lake Naivasha. The lake appears to have a pinkish shore from twelve to fourteen thousand feet because thousands of flamingo birds use it as their "home base." Then, you fly over the Rift Valley, the great Mau Escarpment clearly visible. And finally, Lake Victoria, the biggest lake in Africa. Entebbe Airport is right on the shores of Lake Victoria.

The pilot did not approach as usual this morning, flying over some small islands. I had landed many times and knew the approach well (from the passenger's perspective!). No, the Friendship flew over the tower, not once but twice, until the captain came on the intercom to announce that we had a problem. The nose wheel of the plane would not deploy. He had flown over the tower for the people on the ground to confirm that the wheel was actually stuck inside. The captain had hoped the control panel light was faulty. He said we would fly back to Nairobi as they were better equipped for emergencies.

This was not a pleasant feeling at all. I knew Doris was waiting with the children to meet me and take me back to Kampala. It later turned out that airline officials were not forthcoming in explaining why the plane circled but did not land to her and others.

It so happened that there was a second aircrew traveling on board our aircraft as passengers. They were scheduled to be the crew on another flight in Entebbe. They gave us ignorant passengers useful information, saying the plane could land perfectly well without the nose wheel.

We all sat in the rear as the plane was only half occupied. We even moved the luggage to the back. The crew offered something to drink, which was nice.

As we arrived in Nairobi, the plane circled once over the runway. During the one-and-one-half-hour flight back from Entebbe to Nairobi, the press had been notified, so hundreds of journalists and photographers were near the runway. Also, there were ambulances, fire trucks, and what have you. The runway was foamed: prepared with liquid to prevent the plane from catching fire.

When I saw all the preparations being done, I remarked to my equally frightened lady neighbor: "They don't seem to think much of our chances here."

Anyhow, the landing was superb. The pilot kept the nose of the plane up until the very last meters before the aircraft came to a halt. The spare aircrew we had among us were really helpful. They gave us lots of confidence. At the moment of touchdown, they opened the emergency windows and doors, which we did not need in the end.

I must say that I was very much relieved when I was down on the ground again. Then came the reporters. I was immediately surrounded and interviewed. They asked how I felt, whether I was scared, and other things to which I would not have answered truthfully in any case. (A young Unicef staff member is never scared.) So not entirely seriously, I replied: "This was the first time on an East African Airliner that I got a beer free of charge.

In the afternoon, EAA took us back to Entebbe in another aircraft. The following Monday, "Uganda Argus" (A local paper in Uganda!) had a front-page headline: "BEER SERVED WHILE PLANE PREPARES FOR EMERGENCY LANDING." In the story on the landing, my name and the fact that I was a Unicef staff member were specified.

In a way, Kampala was a small place, and everyone knew everybody. All my acquaintances asked me about the emergency landing. When I met the Czechoslovakian Ambassador to Uganda, he said he did not know I liked beer so much. He invited me to his house, where he had a stock of good

Czech beer. (Pilsner Urquell).

1968

SAFARI

Expatriates, as we were, live a "perfectly normal life." That, of course, is a little exaggerated; it was not so normal. For instance, we could take our children on a "safari," a trip to the beautiful East African countryside.

We had good German friends named Lueck. Arno was a diplomat with the German embassy. He was a hunter. Hunting big game was special for him. Irmgard was a perfect hostess. She taught us to play bridge. As a perfect hostess, she was also a very good cook.

Now, we all had servants. It was expected that expatriates have servants (I have written about this before). The Luecks had a cook named John. But the hostess always did the last touch of a meal (particularly when guests were invited).

The Luecks live only about twenty miles from our place in Heidelberg nowadays. We meet regularly, play bridge, and reminisce about the good old days in East Africa.

We also had a Bavarian friend, Peter Riedmann, a bachelor, who represented BMW and some other German companies in Uganda. Riedmann decided he wanted to be a hunter too. He bought a gun and obtained the necessary license to hunt game. On such a license, animals and how many of them the licensee is allowed to shoot are listed. As soon as one game is shot, particulars had to be entered by the hunter immediately in the license.

In our time in Uganda, wildlife, hunting, fishing, and this sort of thing were very well organized. The respective Ministry (I think it was under Agriculture) had plenty of expatriate staff, usually British, who had lived in East Africa all their lives.

Easter came, and there were some holiday days off. We got together and decided to go on a hunting safari, taking our families along. We were five adults and five children. With four vehicles, we set off from Kampala to a hunting area about 80 miles away. There we put up our tents and established a comfortable camp.

The Luecks had taken two of their servants, John and Isaac, along to help prepare meals and what have you. (The Luecks had male servants. It was no problem to take them along. We had only female servants. It was not possible to take them.)

In the evening, we sat together around the campfire. Hunters always tell fantastic tales. It is well known that they usually exaggerate. I will never forget sitting there in the African night with all the sounds. These sounds continued later when we were in our tents.

In addition to the sounds of the night, there was the chatting of the Africans. John and Isaac had met some fellows from the nearby village. Africans always chat and laugh long into the night. I think this is because they are frightened of wild animals and also perhaps of ghosts. The campfire burned the entire night to keep lions and other naughty animals away.

The following morning we went out game viewing; the hunters to shoot. They had a 4-wheel drive vehicle; we only had our VW station wagon. It was dry, and there were plenty of trails. It was OK in a regular car for our viewing.

The Lueck's youngster, Reiner, and Susanne (our tomboy) went in the jeep with the hunters. We met again for lunch at the camp. They had nothing for the frying pan. It was good we brought plenty of provisions along from the Kampala supermarket.

After a light meal and a siesta, we went out on foot. Of course, we kept close to the hunters to be protected in case of an attack by something big. It was not actually lion country; this was known. But sometimes, there were some. One never knew exactly. However, it is an experience to "still hunt." (Is this the expression if you quietly creep close to an animal?) To creep up against the wind, trying to come as close as possible to a zebra, for instance.

Peter Riedmann, on his first hunting safari, wanted to shoot a zebra. They (the hunters) talked about it all day long. Now, supposedly, in the evening, around five PM, was the best time to shoot a zebra.

I felt sorry for the zebras because this is also the time when lions hunt zebras. A zebra's destiny seems to be to die around five or six in the evening, whether by lions or hunters.

We secretly believed Peter Riedmann did not actually want to or was mentally unprepared to shoot that zebra as a new hunter. When we approached the zebras, he moved around, whispered too loudly, and did everything that a huntsman does not do. As a result, the herd ran off. Peter had no chance to come within shooting range.

In one of my stories, I wrote that daylight, so close to the equator, is from 6:30 AM to 6:30 PM year-round. So we had to return to the camp. On the way back, Peter shot a pheasant, so at least we had something to fry that evening.

As we returned to camp, we looked for John and Isaac. At first, we did not see them. Then it turned out they were both sitting up in a tree. It is not really a laughing matter. They were simply frightened when dusk set in. We must understand they were both "urbanites" (city dwellers). They rarely, if ever, had gone on a hunting safari, hence their fear. Rural Africans, too, are scared of wild animals. But they know better where the safe places are.

That hunting safari in Uganda, I think it was in 1968, stayed in our memories. Often we talk about it. Peter Riedmann never became a real, passionate big game hunter. Another thing, when the real hunters go out to shoot game for trophies or fresh meat, they do not take their families along.

1970

DORIS STORY

Doris recalls: "For many incidents, you must be young to possess just that little bit of flexibility to not pack your children to run off.....where to? Home is where your husband is posted at that moment.

"Abidjan, the capital of the Ivory Coast, was our marching order in the fall of 1970. When we finally got our lift-van and unpacked, we had lived without our belongings for weeks.

"They were sent to us in West Africa from Kampala on the other side of the continent. Our stuff had been in a port shed for a long time without anyone telling us. In the end, Horst went to the customs office. A few days later, the big case was offloaded in front of our house.

"When we opened the case, we found our belongings in more or less good condition. A few items were missing, and some were inside that weren't ours. Strangely enough, most of the missing items were kitchen utensils. But the African masks and a small table we found inside did not belong to us.

"As we were putting all the wrappings and packing materials back into the wooden crates, our newly engaged night-watchman (His name was "Zango") came to help. The next thing I knew, my husband was running through the living room to the bathroom, blood dripping from his right hand.

"Why he ran to the bathroom, I did not know. Nothing useful was unpacked yet, and nothing was there to help in this situation. I followed Horst and looked at his hand. I saw that two of his fingers were badly injured.

"Zango had lifted a heavy piece of something and dropped it just where Horst's hand was. What to do next? No telephone, no car, and no idea where Horst could find medical help. Obviously, his fingers had to be stitched.

"We had neighbors, British, French, and a family from the Netherlands. The latter we had met already. We had heard the family's daughter Daniella was about the same age as our daughter Andrea.

"By this time, it was seven PM and already dark. We had already learned that, by about seven AM on the equator, it became daylight, and at seven PM, it became dark.

"Anyhow, our new neighbor took his car out and drove Horst to a nearby medical clinic. He brought him back with seven stitches in his hand. Three months later, we heard the clinic was closed and locked up by the health department. Too unsanitary, below acceptable standards.

"We were able to return the favor later when the neighbor needed to borrow a tuxedo for an event, and we were able to lend him Horst's.

"The next day, after our unpacking and the drama, I was trying to organize the kitchen when Horst came with a telegram and the sad news that his mother in Germany had passed away. That was the moment when I cracked up and started to cry."

ABIDJAN

In April 1970, our good time in East Africa was over. We had to move on. West Africa was our destination. I sometimes wondered why we had to transfer every now and then to another location. Each change of duty station involved uprooting the family, packing furniture and personal belongings, giving up the home that was yours for years, and taking your children away from the school they were in for years.

The family must get used to a new place and language. Then comes finding an apartment or house, a school for the children, making new friends, getting used to a new environment, and new servants in the house. Parting with their friends is often hard for children.

Why could one not just stay in one place? It would be cheaper for the organization and easier for the staff members.

When hired as an International Civil servant, one signs a contract agreeing to accept at any time any station one may be sent to by the UN Secretary-General. Further, you agree to be on call twenty-four hours a day, seven days a week, anytime this is required. You are paid a proper salary for this readiness and flexibility, distinguishing you from locally employed colleagues.

It is good to move. There is less risk that you will adopt a "laissez-faire" attitude and start seeing things as locals do. One must remember that you are sent to a place because you have special knowledge unavailable locally. Secondly, you are more likely to stay alert when a new challenge arises in a new location.

On a practical note, there are "nice" and easy duty stations, and there are so-called "hardship stations" (For instance, Somalia or the Congo and earlier Cambodia). Colleagues who are there want to move out after a reasonable time. Colleagues in a "nice" station wish to stay as long as possible. These are often tough decisions for management.

The organization does take your personal situation into account, if possible. For instance, the availability of schools for your children is considered when you are transferred. When your situation in this respect changes, you are expected to move to a less agreeable place.

Of course, language is important. You are much more functional if you speak the language of a country. That means the "lingua franca." French in most West African countries. My school French was, mildly speaking, rusty.

Unicef sent me to France for two months to brush up on the language at Alliance Francaise, a top French language institute. So I spent two interesting months in Paris. Doris and the kids stayed in Germany with our family during this time.

The classes at the institute were in the mornings. In the afternoons, I roamed around on foot in Paris to practice what I had learned that morning. I loved to go to those little Parisian Bistros where I met French people over a glass of beer or a "pastis" (A mixture of anise alcohol with water) in the evenings.

It was easy to start a conversation with the older generation, single men of some 60 years. These men were in WWII or at home in the "Resistance." When, after some introduction, they found out that I was German, the conversation inevitably came to the subject of the war. The French, by then 25 years after the armistice, had a fair attitude towards Germans. Discussing the war was not unpleasant at all. Usually, they told me of their heroic deeds.

Generally, they respected ordinary German soldiers and the "Wehrmacht." They knew our military leaders by name, even those I could not remember. Of course, war crimes and criminals were not included in their admiration. The French did not bring up the latter unpleasant events over a conversation in a bistro. Everyone I met was pleased by our new friendship, for which we are all grateful to General Charles de Gaulle and Konrad Adenauer.

* * *

In October 1970, Doris, Andrea, and I arrived in Abidjan after French language training and spending our leave in Germany. We had to leave our two older daughters, Renate and Susanne, in a German "Internat" (boarding school). The first thing we noticed after leaving the airplane was that the climate in West Africa is much hotter and more humid than in Uganda.

Abidjan, the capital of the Ivory Coast, is a very modern cosmopolitan city. A beautiful town, very French. They call it the "Paris of Africa." I must explain that although we are German, the British or American way of life comes more naturally to our children and us. One thing is the language. We speak and can express ourselves better in English than in French. We always had more British and American friends than French ones. I am unsure exactly why this is, with us being European and Germany being France's direct neighbor.

The traveler arrives by air at the elegant International Airport at Port Bouet. It is to the south near the Atlantic (Gulf of Guinea). The city is about ten miles inland on an extensive lagoon. Lagoons extend to the west (one hundred miles) and to the East (fifty miles) from Abidjan, parallel to the Atlantic coast, and form an important inland waterway. They are also quite beautiful. However, the quality and cleanliness of the water, particularly near the big city of Abidjan, is anything but good. Actually, it sometimes stinks.

Housing for expatriates was readily available but expensive. We found a good, new villa at Marcory, across the lagoon from the city center, which is called Plateau. In this part of town, rents were a little more affordable. Our landlord was Lebanese. There are many Lebanese in the Ivory Coast and other West African countries. They play the role of small business people, like the "Asians" in East Africa.

Living in Marcory was pleasant, except we had to cross the bridge over the lagoon to the Plateau. That was as much a bottleneck as any bridge in New York during rush hour.

We found a school for Andrea, our youngest, then seven, in Marcory. In the beginning, it was tough for her. The school was French-speaking, and she started without knowing a word of this language. Three months later, she spoke it better than Doris and me.

Doris also found work as a secretary with the regional office of the World Bank. Her office was on the Plateau in the same building where Unicef had their offices, the "Shell Building." She had the same work hours as I had, so we only needed one car and therefore did not greatly add to the congestion on the bridge over the lagoon, called "Pont General de Gaulle."

The Unicef Office in Abidjan was the West African Regional Office. I became responsible for program logistics management in over twenty West African countries, four of which (Nigeria, Ghana, Sierra Leone, Liberia, and part of Cameroon) were English-speaking. Sixteen countries spoke French, and two (Angola and Guinea Bissau) spoke Portuguese. This language I have never learned.

I traveled a lot with this responsibility, leaving Doris and Andrea at home. They were not lonely. Soon after our arrival, we had many friends, some even in our immediate neighborhood.

I was lucky in one respect, I was assigned an excellent secretary. She was British and had been the secretary of the British Ambassador. Her name was Jean. She had met and married a nice Italian man, so she had to quit the British foreign service. Their (British) loss was my gain.

Jean spoke French well, but it is a difficult language, and one easily makes mistakes when writing it. The other secretaries in Unicef were French or French-educated Africans. French is an official UN language, and so is English, but the latter is spoken more commonly in Unicef. Some

French-speaking colleagues insisted on writing to the NY headquarters in French. They could do that. However, the reply took some time if the letter had first to be translated. Letters to African governments all had to be in French.

We had a perfect arrangement. Our secretaries consulted and helped each other. Only well-written letters, whether in English or French, left the office. Most of my international colleagues in the office were French. When I arrived, our director was Senegalese. When he left after about two years, he was replaced by a Frenchman.

We lived in Abidjan for seven years, and after some adjustment, we loved the Ivory Coast. In the beginning, it was difficult for all of us to have our two older daughters away in a German school. They visited with us twice a year during their vacations, glorious weeks.

In my next chapter, I shall write about the severe drought that started in the Sahelian countries of West Africa shortly after we arrived there.

ABIDJAN II

The semiarid countries on the Southern rim of the Sahara, referred to as "Sahelian countries," were affected by severe drought in the early seventies. As a result, famine struck the poorer population again. Rains had failed to come or were too short in certain areas. Other factors were a growing population and too many cattle, hence overgrazing of the scarce fertile land.

There is also the phenomenon that the desert (Sahara) is steadily advancing to the south. So land for agricultural planting is being lost. In countries of the Sahelian belt, from Mauritania in the West to Ethiopia and Somalia in the East, the wealth of a family, or better say, a man, is measured by the number of cattle he possesses. Veterinarian services are often prioritized over human medicine, resulting in too many cattle. These don't have to be either good milk or beef cows. The only thing that counts is the number of cattle heads to assess a man's wealth. Therefore overgrazing is a big problem in those countries.

Unfortunately, these countries hardly had any food or grain storage and management. If a drought hits the region, food prices increase immediately, affecting the poorer population first. So during the drought emergency of the 1970s, the international community was again asked to help.

In West Africa, the countries affected were: Mauritania, Senegal, Mali, Niger, Burkina Faso (formerly Upper Volta), and Chad. Except for Senegal and Mauritania, all of these are landlocked countries. Even in Senegal and Mauritania, the affected areas were in the interior, hundreds of miles away from ports. The bulk of food came by ships to ports on the West Coast.

There were also flights by military transport planes of donor countries from port cities to most places hit by the drought. Western countries donated money and food generously, including agricultural products like grain. The World Food Program (WFP) and Unicef were the lead agencies of the United Nations involved with the relief operation.

Distances were immense, roads were poor, and logistics were crucial. Take, for instance, Chad. Food had to be imported through the port of Douala, Cameroon, a distance of more than 1700 miles over inferior roads. Relief supplies were carried over these distances by commercial transport companies.

African truckers are tough, highly professional people. In case of breakdowns, there are no automobile associations to call, and garages are in major cities. But truckers just fix problems themselves. They always arrive, sometimes a bit late, but they arrive. Except in some war situations, we never lost cargo carried by African trucking companies.

Another affected country, Mali, had a railway connection from Dakar/Senegal to Bamako/Mali. This inter-state run railway system was very inefficient and unreliable. To add insult to injury, sending relief cargo was expensive. And Bamako was not a drought-affected area at the end of the railway line. The drought was hundreds of miles away in Mopti, Timbuktu, and Gau.

To avoid the inefficient railway and double handling in Bamako, we shipped relief cargo to Abidjan and, from there, on commercial trucks up through the Ivory Coast to the drought-stricken part of Mali. Relief supplies to Niger and Burkina Faso arrived in the ports of Cotonou/Benin and Lome/Togo, respectively. They were trucked up North, in each case more than 1000 miles, to the drought-affected areas.

These logistics activities required me to travel extensively all over West Africa. The main cities were connected by the service of Air Afrique. They flew the French two-jet engine "Caravelle," not a bad airplane but already a bit old in those years. In Mali, the national airline flew a two-turboprop Antonov 24. I had to fly in it often, and that was scary. Because of their affiliation with the USSR after independence, Air Mali used Russian airplanes.

When I left, most were out of service, and several crashed. The last one, an Antonov, crashed in the eighties, killing all on board, including a Unicef colleague. She was stationed in Bamako. (During the pilgrimage, Air Mali flew Muslim pilgrims from West Africa to Mecca in Saudi Arabia with a Tupolev. That one crashed, too, killing some 180 pilgrims.)

Air service existed only in major cities. From there, my colleagues and I traveled a lot on bad roads to follow up on food distribution and implement the drought emergency programs.

* * *

On my travels, I remember one Friday in Ouagadougou / Burkina Faso when I wanted to be home for the weekend. The only plane was an Air Afrique flight, which stopped in Ouaga (as Ouagadougou was called for short). But this one was hopelessly overbooked, and I could not get on it. I did not feel like staying in Burkina Faso over the weekend.

Then I remembered a train to Abidjan, supposedly an overnight night service, leaving Ouaga Fridays at five PM and arriving the following day at eleven AM. The fare was very reasonable. There was no sleeper class, but I was told there was lots of space in the first class, and I was advised to travel in that class, which has air-conditioned wagons.

We left only one hour late, which in Africa may almost be called "on time." It turned out that the first-class wagons were crowded, and the air conditioning was not working. After a while, it got very hot in the wagon. The windows could not be opened, and there was no way of stretching out. So I decided to go to the rear of the train. This was the class for not too-well-off Africans. It was crowded too, but there was no glass in the windows, and a nice evening breeze made traveling more agreeable.

In the early night, the train stopped somewhere along

the track. There was no station. The train stood in bright moonlight in the middle of the African bush for over two hours. We were not told why the train had stopped. Fellow travelers told me that this is often the case. Engines are old and frequently break down.

When Africans travel, they usually combine it with trading. So the wagon was full of trading passengers and their merchandise, such as fried fish, fruits, live chickens, some goats, and what have you. Burkina Faso and the Northern part of the Ivory Coast are famous for their delicious mangoes. So my fellow passengers had large baskets of big mangoes and were still buying mangoes whenever the train stopped at a station.

One amusing thing was that when the train entered a station, the conductor yelled, "ill n'y a pas commerce sur le perron" (no trading on the platform). Of course, people did not take what the conductor shouted seriously. Trading of all sorts went on. I think, perhaps, local traders had an arrangement with the engineer that he would stop at a station as long as required to complete all commercial deals.

The whole trip was very folkloric. I would have been sad to have missed it. I sat the entire night and the following day with genuinely nice people. Everyone was very friendly. At the border to the Ivory Coast, passengers were required to fill in immigration cards. Many on board could not read or write, at least not in French. So they came to me with their passports and asked me to fill in the cards for them. They paid me for my writing service by giving me a mango or an avocado. I bought a basket at one station to carry this delicious produce.

Instead of eleven AM, we arrived in Abidjan at eight PM. I called my surprised Doris to pick me and my baggage, including a big basket of fruit, up from the station.

COLONEL ODUMEGWA OJUKWU

We watched the secession of the Eastern Region and the creation of a "Republic of Biafra" by Colonel Odumegwa Ojukwu from a distance in West Africa. We heard over the BBC of the hazardous night landings of supply planes on the legendary "Uli-airstrip." That was a stretch of ordinary highway within Biafra. For most of its three years, from 1967 until October 1970, Biafra was surrounded by federal troops.

The civilian population in Biafra was brought urgently needed supplies only through intense diplomatic efforts by Unicef and the ICRC (International Red Cross). Hunger has been a factor in war strategies for thousands of years. This was no different with the Nigerians.

During the civil war, ICRC's and Unicef's help via the "illegal" air bridge was again and again construed as an infringement on Nigeria's sovereignty. After the civil war was over in early 1970, Unicef and other aid organizations were involved in saving the Ibo population of Eastern Nigeria from starvation.

When I arrived in Abidjan in 1970, my first field trip was to Enugu in "liberated" Eastern Nigeria. Life had just returned to some degree of normality after that war. Nevertheless, the requirements of food and building an infrastructure for basic health services were crucial. As it often is in such a situation, logistics was important.

I traveled from Lagos by Land Rover to Enugu. As we got close to our destination, I saw in a local street market what I thought were giant rats, hanging dead, head down, in a market stall for sale. Then I remembered press reports suggesting that the people of former Biafra had to eat rats to survive. The actual truth, however, was a bit different.

I was told by an Ibo that these were field rats, nothing to do with our common sewage rats. Actually, these field rats are a delicacy, he said. I never tried to confirm this myself.

* * *

Two more things on Biafra. First: Colonel Odumegwa Ojukwu and his fellow officers fled to Ghana just before the federal forces recaptured the territory. Second: the blood bath on the Ibo population that many people predicted and feared did not occur. The federal soldiers were quite civilized in victory.

THE CANNIBALS

When we had been in Abidjan for some time, a German family arrived from Monrovia/Liberia. They had three children, two white girls, some eight to ten years old, and a younger African girl, perhaps four years old. She was a full African. There was no question of a possible affair that an unfaithful spouse might have had. You know how people sometimes speculate.

In Monrovia, the couple, let us call them Hilde and Hans, had a female servant. As sometimes happens, their maid became pregnant, and a baby, Jessica, was born in due course. A beautiful little girl. Hans and Hilde kept the maid and her baby. In an expatriate household in Africa, that was not an unusual thing to do and was no problem.

When Jessica was about a year old, her mother fell very sick and died. We do not know what of. The maid had no known family or relatives, no one who would claim the baby. So Jessica, a beauty, was kept in the house. No one was responsible, and the local authority's social services could do nothing. They looked for a family who would take Jessica but found none. Jessica grew up with her white sisters. She started to talk and, of course, learned primarily German, the language spoken in the house.

When Hans was transferred by his organization to Abidjan, they asked themselves: "What will happen to Jessica?" There was only one option, to adopt the little girl. The family stuck together. The two natural daughters loved their new sister very much. The fact that Jessica had dark brown skin did not bother the family.

Under the circumstances, being adopted by Hilde and Hans was the best thing that could have happened to Jessica. In

Abidjan, we often met them and quickly became good friends.

We rented a beach hut (French: "paillote") on the South Atlantic. Hundreds of "paillots" covered the beach between Abidjan and Grand Bassam. The highway was parallel to the lagoon, separated from the sea by a narrow stretch of sandy land with palm trees. It was quite beautiful. From the main road, we had to turn off towards the ocean, over a small bridge onto a sandy track zigzagging like a ski-slalom through those palm trees, constantly worried that a coconut might fall on the car. After a one-and-one-half-mile drive on this track, we were at our paillote.

Next to us were friends and colleagues. They all had their own beach huts. The whole year round, every Sunday, our friends and we were at the paillote. My colleagues and I were all traveling a lot. If I was not in Abidjan on the weekend, it would be no problem for the family. There were always friends on the beach.

In the afternoon, we would play volleyball. Teams were mixed, men and women, youngsters, boys, and girls, a jolly nice social event every Sunday. I always knew that Doris and the family were well cared for if I could not be with them on the weekend.

Hilde and Hans got, by chance, a paillote close to ours, and we were together at the beach every Sunday. (Funny, nobody ever went to the beach on a Saturday for unknown reasons.) Their two daughters were close in age to Andrea. They went to the same school. Then there was, of course, little black Jessica. She was now about four years old and spoke very clear German.

The highway to the beach was the main link between Grand Bassam and Abidjan. On this roadway was an illegal shantytown known as "Bidonville." ("Bidon," meaning canister or can, was the material the shacks were built of.) Bidonville was situated just after the turnoff to the International Airport. The way to the airport was a splendid boulevard. A much simpler road went on to Grand Bassam.

By design or not, travelers to and from the airport never saw that shantytown. Sometimes the authorities decided to tear down the structures. A bulldozer would come and level part of it. A few days later, the shacks would be erected again. Rumors had it that there were cannibals living in Bidonville. Further, (supposedly) on an occasion when some of the shanties were torn down, human bones had been found on the grounds.

Our beach huts were about two and a half miles from Bidonville. The people did not bother us, and we did not believe in the cannibal story.

* * *

One Sunday afternoon, there were a lot of people eating and drinking at the beach. We had just decided to play volleyball when, suddenly, Hilde said: "where is Jessica?" It seemed like she had just been seen, but now she was nowhere to be found.

A search in the immediate surrounding was not successful. We all got alarmed, and a frantic search for Jessica set in. Although it was not mentioned loud, we all thought of the alleged cannibals at Bidonville. Apparently, Jessica had been gone longer than Hilde thought. We ran to the dangerous ocean beach. Normally, children were not allowed to go there without adults. Then we split up to run up and down the long line of paillots. We could not find Jessica. It was scary.

An Austrian friend, Annemarie Kogler, went further south than any of us thought the child might have gone. Sure enough, Annemarie found Jessica in the paillote of a French family. These people just wanted to find out who Jessica was and to whom she belonged. Remember, Jessica did not speak any other language but German.

The French family first thought she belonged to some African people. Then they realized that her language was not a local dialect but was instead German. What happened was Jessica had been exploring the neighboring paillots by herself. One looks just like another. She could not find her way back from where she was and went further and further in the wrong direction. It must have been very confusing for the little girl because of the similarity of the paillots. Then with her language, she could not ask or was reluctant to ask for help. Anyhow, a sigh of relief went through our camp.

We never found out if there were cannibals in Bidonville or not. It may indeed have just been a rumor. Society is suspicious of people living in shantytowns and believes they can do the most horrible things.

Hilde and Han's three daughters have all done well. Jessica finished university with honors and is now in a well-paid position in the computer industry.

SUAT

I had a colleague from Turkey, Suat Cobanoglu. Most of the time, he was alone in Abidjan, his family, because of schooling, resided in Turkey. During holidays and vacations, our Turkish friends were together in Abidjan. We had a good relationship with the family: Suat, Bilge (his wife), and the two boys. Susanne and Renate were only with us during their school holidays, as were the boys of Suat and Bilge.

Suat had a paillote just next to ours, but he was practically always sitting with us. Often we asked him why not give up his paillote and move in with us. (By the way, rent for beach huts was not cheap. And there was a shortage. Interested people were waiting to get one.)

* * *

One time when Suat returned from home leave, he had a brand new car, a Ford. On the Sunday following his return, he drove with a mutual friend to the beach.

She told us the story later: He went fast to demonstrate the new car's advantages. He turned right over the bridge from the highway onto the sandy track, zigzagging between palm trees, all at high speed.

A moment of inattentiveness was enough. Suat collided slightly with one of the palm trees, causing a dent in the body of his new car. Angrily he got out to inspect the damage.

"Merde," (shit!) he shouted, kicking the left front tire. At this moment, a coconut fell, hitting and cracking the windshield of Suat's brand-new car. Poor Suat, our sympathy was limited, and even when we meet now, years later, we will not fail to recount the mishap he had with that coconut.

DOMESTIQUE

Servants are a vital subject, measured by the time and frequency they are discussed during evening invitations, bridge circles, coffee parties, at the swimming pool, and other occasions when expatriates meet in Africa. It seems that ladies discuss domestic help more than men, which is natural because ladies usually have more to do with household management.

I have written about the servants we had while we lived in Uganda, East Africa. So this story will be reserved for those we had in West Africa. Domestique is the French word for household help. We had one in the house in Abidjan, and Zango, our combined nightwatchman/gardener.

Initially, we had two in the house: Vincent, the cook and senior person, and young Bienvenu, the junior helper. Vincent came from Dahomey, which is now called "Benin." Most good cooks came from Dahomey. That was tradition. Bienvenu came from Upper Volta, now called Burkina Faso. Voltaiques are not usually cooks; their specialty is more in the field of watchmen/gardeners.

All our domestic help came from outside the Ivory Coast. Ivorians were more often found in hotels, restaurants, and with higher government officials. The usual expatriate household had "aliens" from neighboring countries. Admittedly they were often less trouble.

The names of the "domestiques" were interesting. We had "Bienvenu," meaning welcome. Some friends had one called "Onvient," meaning "on vient" for: "he is coming." We knew one called "Innocent," meaning the same in English or French: "naive." The best we heard was "Fetnat." It took us some time to find out what this name meant.

Africans often have an African name, which is not usually used, particularly not by people who work for expatriates. So parents give their children also a Western name, just in case! There are calendars listing the name days of saints. When a child is born, African parents look at the calendar. If a son is born on the name day of the holy Vincent, they call the boy "Vincent." If it is the name day of Mary, they call the girl "Mary." It is a simple system.

Now, the French and their former colonies (some are more French than the French, particularly the Ivory Coast) celebrate their national holiday. In France, it is called "Fete Nationale." (Like the fourth of July in the USA and the third of October in Germany.)

In the calendar mentioned above, "Fete Nationale" was abbreviated as FET NAT. That poor boy, the domestic help in our friend's home, was born on the national holiday and was named "Fetnat."

* * *

Vincent was a good cook. We could definitely not complain about him. He was clean, honest, a good cook, quiet, and reliable (meaning he came on time and daily). However, he never smiled, ever! West Africans are usually cheerful people; they laugh a lot. But our Vincent always had a stone face. It got on my nerves.

Vincent made the best, really the very best cheese soufflé you can imagine. He needed the whole morning for this and prepared it with great ceremony. We had it twice a week, just soufflé with lettuce. I have eaten in great places, including French restaurants famous for their soufflés. Doris is the best cook you could think of. But I have never had a soufflé as good as Vincent's.

One day Vincent came and told us that his brother had found a job for him in the big hotel in Paris where he (the brother) worked. The brother had sent him an air ticket and asked him to move to Paris. So we lost Vincent. Andrea and the two of us were sorry we would no longer get Vincent's good soufflé. On the other hand, in one way, we were pleased that he was gone. His stone face, with never a smile on it, was not nice to have around in the house.

At this point, Doris thought we did not need a fully trained cook. She worked full-time at the Regional Office of the World Bank in Abidjan. Still, she wanted to give Bienvenu a chance to become an assistant cook. So Doris trained him to do simple things himself. Bienvenu was an amiable chap and very willing to learn.

We had him for more than five years until we left Abidjan. Ultimately, he learned remarkably and could rightly be called a "cook."

Of course, he learned to do some German specialties in our house. Most of his fellow cooks in Abidjan learned French cuisine, why should Bienvenu not learn about German cuisine. One thing he learned how to make well was South-German style noodles called "Spaetzle."

One can make spaetzle entirely by hand. My grandmother used to do it. However, nowadays, there are simple machines, a strainer that you pass the spaetzle dough through. When we left Abidjan, Doris gave Bienvenu our spaetzle machine as a gift. He was proud of it and took it to his next employer.

Our neighbor was a Hungarian, Monsieur DeGorgy, a bachelor. He had a small printing business in town and came to our house often when it got too lonely for him at home. He was anxious to get Bienvenu as a cook when we left.

They apparently had a good employer/servant relationship. They even sent seasons greetings to New York, signed by both.

Some ten years later, I returned to Abidjan on an official Unicef mission. One afternoon when I had time, I visited Monsieur DeGeorgy's business in town. He was pleased to see me and quickly invited me for lunch the following day. I accepted. The next day I was in his shop in time to drive with him to the house in our former neighborhood. Bienvenu greeted me with a broad smile and was quite excited. Guess what I got for lunch? Yes, you are right, I got spaetzle. It was the best I had eaten in a long time.

Having domestic help was not always paradise on earth. They came to you with all of their small troubles. We didn't have too many problems with our servants. Perhaps it was because of how we treated them. We returned them the same respect they showed us. One thing we never did: "hiring and firing." That was not good. The only reason for us would have been "stealing" in the house. That we would not have tolerated. But in this respect, we were lucky.

We also paid social security, including health insurance, for our domestic help. Not everyone did, but we felt it was important to do so, as we enjoy the same privilege in our country. The Commonwealth of West African French-speaking countries agrees to recognize each other's social security systems. So no matter where aliens came from, they were insured as long as they came from the Commonwealth of West African French-speaking countries.

When we were settled in New York, at Waterside, after we got used to the American way of life, we said to ourselves: "Thank heaven we no longer have servants in the house!"

1971

ABIDJAN EASTBOUND

In August 1971, I set off on a duty trip, in the company of my family, from Abidjan, Ivory Coast, to Ghana, Togo, and Dahomey. In this part of Africa, the coast runs from Sierra Leone in the West to Cameroon in the East. There are several West African English-speaking countries: Sierra Leone, Liberia, Ghana, Nigeria, and part of Cameroon. This anglophone line of nations is interrupted by the "Cote D'Ivoire," Togo, Dahomey (Dahomey was renamed "Benin" in 1975), and the larger part of Cameroon.

I wrote "Cote D'Ivoire" purposefully because, under their able but very French-oriented President of many years, Felix Houphouet Boigney, the government had decided by law that there was only one name, the French. No translation for the Cote D'Ivoire was allowed. Therefore even in official English UN documents, the Ivory Coast is called Cote D'Ivoire. However, our book is not an official document. We may call it the "Ivory Coast" (the German Word is Elfenbeinküste).

Looking at an older Atlas of the World is interesting. You find the old names: Ivory Coast, Gold Coast (Ghana), and Slave Coast (Togo, Dahomey, and Nigeria). From the Slave Coast, also called the "Gulf of Benin," no doubt many ancestors of present African-Americans left the black continent in the hull of a slave ship.

That was one of those rare trips where I could take the family along. Renate and Susanne were with us in Abidjan for the summer vacation. Our first destination was Accra, which does not look too far on the map. An airplane flies there in only 30 minutes. By car, it was a long drive.

One has to travel up North to Abengourou, cross the border by Niable, then head down South again to Accra. The distance on the road is five hundred miles. After thirteen hours of driving on poor roads, we arrived late and totally worn out.

Due to lagoons, rivers, and mountains, no direct coastal road connects Abidjan and Accra. The lagoons and rivers are no insurmountable obstacle, technically speaking. But Ghana has remained British-oriented since independence, while the Ivory Coast looks towards France.

Although ethnically, they are the same people on both sides of the border, there is only minor trade between these neighboring countries. Also, the road connection from Abengourou, where the main road leads, to the border at Niable (20 miles) and from the border on the Ghana side to the main Accra road is shockingly bad. It almost seems they intentionally discourage trade and the exchange of people. So much for African unity.

* * *

As I said, we arrived at the Ambassador Hotel in Accra very tired and took it easy the following day. While in Accra, I had to make a few business phone calls, so we stayed until lunch. After lunch, we set off for Lome, the capital of Togo. The distance is only about one hundred and thirty miles, and the road is good. Here again, are two countries, one Ghana, oriented towards Britain. The other Togo, towards France. Most of the 130 miles mentioned above are on Ghanaian territory. The border is just outside the town of Lome.

Interestingly there is much more trading of goods and border crossings of people going on between Ghana (anglophone) and Togo (francophone) than on the border between Ghana and the Ivory Coast. What is it, the good road? Is this a chicken/egg situation? Do you first have to build a good road and then expect traffic? Or does heavy traffic justify building a good road?

After a pleasant trip along the coast to Lome, we moved into a very nice place, the Benin Hotel, situated on the seaside with a large pool. I was busy negotiating logistics questions with project and government personnel for two days. Warehousing of project supplies, etc. It was important for me to know that Doris and the girls were in a good hotel and could enjoy themselves in the pool.

Togo used to be, up to WWI, a German colony. Its people and government are very friendly towards Germany even today. As a result, there are a lot of German investments, including a beer brewery and a butchery where one can buy good sausage German style. But also other, more critical industries. Togo has a large branch of the "Goethe Institute," a worldwide German cultural institute. No wonder many Africans in Togo speak German.

When WWI started in 1914, the Kaiser's Governor in Togo, estimating their chances, surrendered to the joint British/French forces without firing a shot. The German colony was then divided between France and England. Present-day Togo was taken by France. It is a narrow country, only 75 miles wide at the coast, extending about 380 miles to the North. The other part of colonial Togo, taken by Britain, is now part of Ghana. We spent two full days in Togo and had a good time with friendly people.

This West African safari story will continue.

ABIDJAN EASTBOUND II

So, we were in Togo when I ended the last chapter, and I must now make a slight correction. I wrote that Togo was a German colony. When it was a German colony, it was called "Togoland." It only became "Togo" when the Eastern part became a French colony after WW1. A small detail.

I also wrote that the Benin Hotel in Lome is on the seashore. The coast from Liberia to Cameroon is absolutely beautiful. However, it is too dangerous for swimming. There was a lovely beach with cozy paillotes (beach huts).

We had a Paillote in Abidjan. However, we couldn't swim in the ocean. The undercurrent is too strong, and someone, often a tourist, drowns at least once a week. People who boast that they are strong swimmers still do not come back.

The Togo coast is no different. There were some swimming possibilities where a river ran into the ocean, forming a small bay, or a lagoon, providing swimmers protection from the waves. Hotels often had a pool filled with ocean water because of this.

We continued our journey eighty miles along the coast to another country, "Dahomey" (now Benin). Its capital is Cotonou. Again we were in a good hotel: "De La Plage," with a large pool.

In Dahomey, Unicef was assisting with a vehicle maintenance project. They assigned a Swiss transport/logistics consultant, Heinz Rieben, to start it. Heinz was there with his wife, Rita. She cared for my family and showed them around while Heinz and I attended to official business.

After a discussion with the Minister of Health at Cotonou, it turned out that I had to fly 260 miles north of

Dahomey to a place called Parakou. Unicef was assisting a large project where logistics problems needed to be solved. Heinz Rieben came along on this trip.

The Minister arranged for us to take a military flight on special service for the government. The plane left the military part of the Cotonou airport early in the morning. It was supposed to be back that evening. That was about the worst flight I have ever been on. The plane was an old DC-3, a military version, meaning there was no sound insulation inside, and it had longitudinal bench seats.

The passengers were mainly family, dependents of military personnel. Beside me was a woman with a live goat. There were also chickens and a dog on board. Actually, the goat behaved well. It seemed to me it had flown before. On takeoff, one engine misfired, and long flames came out of its manifold. After one and a half hours, approaching the Parakou airfield, this wretched right engine stopped in midair, and the plane landed with just one engine.

On board, only the goat was not alarmed. After we disembarked, the pilot approached us and apologetically said he had a slight problem with the engine. He was not sure whether he could return to Cotonou that evening. Actually, his announcement was quite immaterial to me. I had already determined that I would not fly back on his plane.

We did our official business and then checked into the hotel, which was not too bad. Heinz visited his country's people in a Swiss bilateral project. He discovered that one of their men was driving to Cotonou the following day. This friendly Swiss offered us a ride. We called Rita Rieben on the telephone to inform her of the next morning's delayed arrival. Rita passed the news on to my family.

The hotel had an excellent French cook. We had a pleasant evening sitting outside on the veranda under a magnificent, starlit African sky. The following day we drove back South. Only the last sixty miles of the two hundred and sixty were asphalted, but the other section was not too bad.

One more day in Cotonou, then we drove back to Accra via Lome. On this coastal road, there are always merchants selling their products, for instance, pineapples. The merchants would peel a pineapple for you with a big knife, leaving the stalk on it. This provided a convenient handle while eating it without getting too messy.

Another thing our daughters had not eaten before was cut-up sugarcane. You sucked the sugar out of it. It was delicious. There was plenty of dried fish on sale. It is a bit smelly, so we did not buy dried fish.

In Accra, we stayed at the Ambassador Hotel again for two nights. I had a full day of business with the Ministry of Health at the main ocean port at Tema, twelve miles from Accra. I also had to arrange for some visits to major health centers up North with the Ministry. I intended to make these visits on our way home to Abidjan.

ABIDJAN EASTBOUND III

We left Accra in the morning. Our destination was Kintambo, a trip of two hundred and eighty miles. Portions of the road were very poor. In Kintambo, there was no hotel, but we were told that we could stay in a government guest house, supposedly a nice one. We did not know that there was also an old guest house.

We arrived at twilight and, by chance, came to the old house. It was old, shockingly old. Actually abandoned. Susanne said at once she would not set foot in this ghost house and would remain in the car. But we all did not feel like staying there. That shack could not be described as being "quite nice." I asked people who gathered. They laughed and finally directed us to the new guest house. That was very comfortable accommodation indeed.

Kintambo is not a big town but rather an African village. But there is an extensive provincial government administration. My contact was chiefly with the Provincial Medical Officer (PMO), an important official in the governmental hierarchy.

Unicef assisted the whole range of rural development programs in this province in central Ghana, mainly under "health." Here again, logistics was crucial. Health services were provided for the village of Kintambo and the rest of the province. Distances were far, and roads poor. Unicef had furnished many vehicles for the mobility of outreach health programs and for support of the rural health centers it served.

The PMO suggested I accompany him to Tamale, a town bigger than Kintambo, with a large Medical Training Center for many types of health personnel. He intended to travel in a VW Minibus (provided by Unicef). He suggested that my family should come along.

Of course, they were pleased to do so. The prospect of spending a day in Kintambo was not exciting. The distance from Kintambo to Tamale was about one hundred and twenty miles on a rural, not tarred, road.

In this part of Ghana, there are two rivers, the Black Volta and the White Volta. They flow into a man-made reservoir called Lake Volta. This vast man-made lake extends some two hundred and twenty miles from North to South. It ends about seventy miles North of Accra in the gigantic Akosombo, or Volta, dam.

The dam's huge hydro-power station serves many West African countries with electricity. On the Northern end of the reservoir where we were, we could not see the blue waters of the lake. It was a rather swampy area. The roads were frequently flooded, which naturally did not improve their surfaces.

In Tamale, we visited the Medical Training Center and the old hospital, where "outreach" health facilities were also based. Then the PMO showed me an interesting sight that would make the blood of a taxpayer freeze in their veins.

A large building on the fringe of the town turned out to be a hospital. Big gates, a modern entrance, marble flooring, most modern hospital equipment, an x-ray station, an operating room, you name it, it was there. Finding such a modern hospital in New York might even be hard.

The bizarre thing was this new hospital was utterly empty. It had been finished for years but had never been put to use. The PMO told me they didn't have sufficiently trained personnel or funds to run it. The area had insufficient patients to justify such a "monster installation." People would be horrified to even enter the building. If brought there on a stretcher, they would probably think they had already died and gone to heaven. The old "open-air" hospital in town is what rural Ghanaians liked and needed.

Who was responsible for this scandalously bad

planning? I can only guess, but I think this guess is very much what happened. Some local politicians sold the idea to the Minister or the Ministry of Health in Accra. They, in turn, suggested it for financing to donors. I could not find out who the donors were. The PMO could not tell me. It is actually straightforward to raise money for this kind of thing.

Which donor organization or country does not want to sponsor a hospital in the bush of a developing country, thinking the "poor people" need it? The Albert Schweitzer syndrome. Unicef was not involved. Our organization does not finance hospitals but instead concentrates on preventive medicine. This was an interesting "field trip" for Doris, our daughters, and me.

Back in Kintambo the following morning, I had some free time and decided to walk a little. Susanne and Renate came along. We strolled through the village.

It was unusual for a white man and two girls to be seen on foot on this African village road. But the people were friendly. They are always almost friendly and open-minded to foreigners in Ghana. (the Secretary-General of the UN, Kofi Anan, comes from this region in Ghana.) Another thing, Ghanean are well educated. In Kintambo, where many provincial government employees live, practically everyone speaks English.

On our stroll, we passed an African house. Several men were standing outside. They greeted us and invited me inside to try their local distillate.

What followed, Susanne can tell you almost better than I. I went inside and drank only a small tumbler of this stuff. It ran down my throat like fire. I first thought I was being poisoned. I excused myself, went outside, ran to the guesthouse, and drank a liter of water. The girls giggled and laughed, finding it funny. I did not think it was. Ever since this experience, I have refused to drink a local distillate, no matter where I am. The following morning we left Kintambo for home.

On the way back to Abidjan, our daughter Renate learned a lesson that I think she will not forget. At the Ivoirian side of the border, we went inside to present our passports to the immigration officer. Crossing borders anywhere in Africa is a bit tedious. The uniformed staff sometimes feel too important and powerful and are not always friendly.

In this instance, the immigration officer was a young, arrogant fellow with a smart uniform. He looked for a long time at our travel documents. I, traveling on official business, had a UN Laissez-Passer. We all had international certificates of vaccination, which were required.

After some time, Renate said something in German. I can not remember what she said, but it was undoubtedly not respectful as far as the immigration man was concerned. I am sure he did not understand German, but he felt this was not a nice remark that Renate had made. So he started to make a lot of trouble. He said Renate's vaccination certificate was fake because her yellow fever vaccination had occurred on the same day as another vaccination. He said this could not be done as it would result in death. Ridiculous!

Anyhow, he was very unpleasant. I had to wave my UN Laissez-Passer and threaten to officially complain. Finally, he let us go.

Later we discussed the incident in the car. Renate, then about 15 years old, knew it was wrong of her to make this remark in German. People everywhere can instinctively feel if a comment is nasty or friendly. You do not have to study a language for this.

We were home in Abidjan by four PM, and all went well. I think this was an unforgettable trip for us all, one which you would never experience in the same way as a tourist.

CITROEN 2CV

As a logistics officer, I had to advise my organization on suitable transport equipment, meaning vehicles, to do the required job at an economical cost. At that time, Unicef had a budget of thirty-five million US dollars for transport equipment. Proper vehicle selection was no small matter for a project.

For even longer than Germany manufactured the VW-Beetle, Citroen of France manufactured the ugly but inexpensive 2CV, a simple, 2-cylinder, two-horsepower car, its body built of corrugated iron sheets. It was so simple an American might not understand it.

The French and the francophone Africans loved this car. In the Ivory Coast, it worked for many years. There were thousands of Citroen 2CVs. It was the "normal" people's car. When one was finally worn out, it could still be sold. It fetched a high scrap price.

The Citroen 2CV was the cheapest vehicle Unicef could get on the world market under a fleet sales agreement. Logically you would think that if we needed small cars in Ghana, the Citroen 2CV, a success story in the neighboring Ivory Coast, would be our first choice.

The 2CV absolutely did not work in Ghana. Unbelievable! Africa, same region, same climate, same poor roads, partly the same ethnic people, but a 2CV would not last for a month in Ghana. This cannot be explained on technical grounds.

The Ghanaians wanted the "Morris Minor" as a small vehicle. It was a much better-looking, nice, cheap British car. Technically not as robust as the Citroen 2CV. The life expectancy of the Morris was much less than the French car.

As this cannot be explained on technical grounds, I believe it is a matter of philosophy. You must be French or a French-educated African to accept, like, and drive a Citroen 2CV. Likewise, you must be British or educated in England to accept, like, and drive a Morris Minor. If a neutral outsider tries to impose something else for sound technical reasons, it will not work. No matter how thoroughly you have studied it, they will prove you wrong.

* * *

A follow-up story: We had to follow UN financial rules as a UN organization. That meant: for procurement, competitive bidding was required for items of more than $5000. There are exceptions for proprietary items, standardization, serviceability, etc. We had "internal auditors" from Unicef. They had field experience and were reasonable.

But there were also "external auditors" in the UN. The UN Board of Audit appointed a member state to provide auditors every two years. These "external auditors" were often people who had studied and knew the rules. However, explaining to them when to apply the exceptions was difficult.

Try to explain to a Pakistani external auditor that you provided the slightly more expensive Morris Minor car to a project in Ghana because you thought the basic Ghanaian philosophy would not accept the cheaper Citroen 2CV.

HANS VON SPONECK

How independent are UN officials anyhow? When I read in the newspaper that the UN Coordinator in Iraq, Hans von Sponeck, requested Secretary-General Kofi Annan relieve him from his post in Baghdad, effective 31 March 2000, I had to ask myself this question. His request to leave his post was under protest.

Von Sponeck denounced sanctions imposed nine years ago by the United Nations against Iraq several times. He said that these sanctions hit the poor, particularly the children of Iraq. Saddam Hussein and his cronies, the real culprits, do not suffer. Their regime can certainly not be toppled by these measures. For his frank and open statements on this issue, Von Sponeck was heavily criticized by UN member states, particularly the USA.

Now he is quitting. I think the UN Coordinator has to report his observations in all frankness, even if it is not to the liking of some member states. Iraq, too, is a member state of the United Nations, and its population must not be held hostage for the misdeeds of Saddam Hussein.

Member states of the UN signed the convention on staff privileges and immunities in February 1946. This convention stipulates, among others: "In the performance of their duties, members of the Secretariat shall neither seek nor accept instructions from any government or any other authority external to the organization."

* * *

Reading that article reminded me that I have known Hans von Sponeck for a long time. I met him during my travels in Africa. Von Sponeck (a countryman of mine from a noble family, as indicated by the "von" in front of the name) is a career UN diplomat. His organization is the UNDP, the "United Nations Development Program."

Like Unicef, UNDP is a "field organization." Approximately ten percent of its staff are at headquarters in New York. The rest are in field offices worldwide. The chief of a field office is called the "Resident Representative." Habitually the UNDP "Res-Rep," as they are usually called, represents the United Nations at large, vis-à-vis the country in which he or she is posted. There are exceptions to this rule where a higher UN office is located, for instance, in Ethiopia with its headquarters of UN-ECA.

I met von Sponeck for the first time in the early 70s in Accra, Ghana, where he was UNDP Res-Rep. I wrote above that the UNDP Res-Rep also represented Unicef in countries where Unicef had no office. This is no longer the case today because nowadays, Unicef has offices in almost all developing countries. The relationship and cooperation between Unicef and UNDP have traditionally been good, barring some incidents in countries where personalities (of the Res-Rep and the Unicef Rep.) clashed.

On one of my earlier visits to Accra, when Unicef had no office there, we informed UNDP by cable of my arrival by air. We requested that they make appointments for me to meet with the Ministry of Health, collect me at the airport, and make a hotel reservation.

I arrived in Accra late one evening on a stopover after a long journey to Central Africa. I intended to stay only two days before returning to Abidjan, where I was posted. There was no UNDP driver at the airport to meet me. OK, a little unusual and inconvenient.

It was not snobbism that we UN travelers expected a car and driver when we came to an airport. There was a practical reason behind it. These countries, Ghana in particular, had very strict currency regulations. You could not get Ghanaian currency, called "Cedi," outside the country. One was not even allowed to bring Cedis into the country.

You had to declare your foreign money at the entry point and exchange only what you needed at official banks or exchange offices. None was open at the airport for business on that evening. So, how to get and pay for a taxi?

Well, of course, the old African traveler I was, there was a way, and I was not totally stuck. Another thing was that I did not know which hotel I was supposed to be booked in. There were two hotels where UN people mostly stayed in Accra: the Ambassador or the Continental (Not to be mistaken with the "InterContinental" chain). As it turned out, I was not booked in either of them, as the UNDP office did not get our cable, but of course, I didn't know this then.

I managed to get local Cedis and a taxi. We first drove to the Continental and found no room there. Then to the Ambassador with the same result, no room available. The taxi driver suggested other decent places, but I had no luck there either. There were just no rooms.

An international meeting was in town, and all the hotel rooms were taken. I ran out of taxi money, but the driver was friendly and took me to places that were not so "decent." Places where girls were sitting in the lobby, and the guy at the reception desk asked me how "many hours" I wanted the room.

Well, that was too much for me. I returned to the airport, where I could make a phone call. I called Herrn von Sponeck and told him my situation. I asked whether he could put me up for the night.

Of course, I could stay at his house. He apologized that I had not been picked up and no room was booked. Unfortunately, he could not come to the airport, as he had an official dinner party going on right now at his house, to which he also invited me.

He explained to the driver over the phone how he could get to his place and further told him that he would get the money for the taxi fare on arrival at his house. Now it was my turn to be embarrassed, crashing a dinner party, and having no money to pay for the taxi.

This was not a problem for Hans von Sponeck and his charming wife; she was British and warmly received me. It was a very large and official dinner that had just begun. Tables were set up in the garden. Accra on the coast had a lovely climate in the evening. The guests were from the UN, other diplomatic circles, and the government. I was shown to one of the smaller tables where a plate had been set for me.

I will not forget the tall, good-looking African gentleman and his elegant wife, who were with me at that table. It was Dr. Nkrumah, son of the first Ghana President Kwame Nkrumah. Pres. Nkrumah was overthrown and left the country in 1966. His son was a pediatrician, and he worked in an Accra hospital. As is customary in Africa with low-paid government hospital doctors, he also had a private doctor's office in town.

He was very entertaining. He recounted stories of Ghana and his father's first post-independent government. No, he had no problem with the military government in power at the time, even though his father had been the president of the overthrown former government. I was later told by the Sponecks that Dr. Nkrumah was a very good and sought-after pediatrician by the expatriate families living in Ghana.

In any case, he and his wife were very pleasant people. I vividly remember that evening under a clear African sky after all that hassle I had on arrival in Accra.

I met Herrn von Sponeck several times after that in different locations in Africa, where he was posted as UNDP Res-Rep after Ghana. His last assignment in Baghdad was probably the most difficult one.

IRAQ

This is a follow-up to the last story, "Hans von Sponeck." I just heard that a second high UN official in Baghdad, Jutta Burghardt, incidentally also a German, quit her job as Chief of Mission of the World Food Program (WFP) under protest.

She told reporters that she can no longer be part of a system that causes mass starvation of children through sanctions imposed by the United Nations on Iraq. The "Oil for Food" program, under which a small amount of oil can be exported by Iraq in exchange for food and medicine, is insufficient to avert famine conditions for the population.

On the same subject, I heard on CNN that earlier this week, some eighty members of the UN Congress appealed to President Clinton to work on giving up these sanctions. (Unfortunately, I have no record of this news, I must have missed it in German newspapers.)

Why am I concerned about it? I am certainly not a sympathizer of Saddam Hussein, but I find it unbearable that the world sees no other way to fight him except by making his population suffer and countless children die. On the other hand, most people do not care or know about the children in Iraq.

Another story most people in Western countries know about and are concerned about is whether or not a five-year-old boy should be sent back to his natural grandmothers and father in Cuba (Elian Gonzalez). Such a cruel thing to do!

Are we civilized if politics is made on the backs of children?

1972

VACCINES IN MALI

The Republic of Mali is a landlocked country in West Africa. Their outlets to the sea are Dakar, Senegal, to the West, and Abidjan, Ivory Coast, to the South. The country was a French colony until it became independent in 1960. The capital city is Bamako.

However, the town better known to many people is Timbuktu (Tombouctou in French). This old town just south of the Saharan Desert is known for many stories about Trans Saharan Caravans doing their trading there.

I visited Mali several times in the early seventies. The roads were terrible, particularly those north of Bamako. The one from Mopti to Timbuktu was a nightmare. There was an air link from Bamako via Mopti, Gundam, and Gao, Timbuktu. This route was serviced by Air Mali with an old Antonov 24, a Russian two-turboprop aircraft. I was scared when I used it. Years later, the same plane crashed. All on board were killed, including a Unicef colleague. She was on an official field trip to Gao.

Often the country is hit by severe Sahelian droughts. Although these are challenging times, there are always tourists, usually Americans, in Mali, particularly in Timbuktu. Hotels were poor throughout Mali. They were horrible in Timbuktu. At that time, I observed that never had a place done so little for so many tourists. Besides, there was not much to see in this old African trading town. It was folkloric, nevertheless.

Unicef supported a vaccination project for children in the whole of Mali, therefore, also in Timbuktu. One of the difficulties with immunization programs, not known to many, is that vaccines must be kept refrigerated at all times.

Therefore the cold chain must be maintained from when the vaccines leave the factory until they are applied to—in our case, children. Vaccines lose their potency if the cold chain is interrupted at any time. One of Unicef's priorities for many years has been child immunization programs. The cold chain question is a colossal logistics challenge. (More on this will follow!)

On one of my visits to Timbuktu, I was in the company of a director for preventive medicine from the Ministry of Health (MoH) in Bamako. We went to see the local health department and found that the refrigerator at the immunization office was not working. A second backup refrigerator was not plugged in. There were sufficient stocks of required vaccines, but they were all gone, kaput. The provincial health officer tried all sorts of excuses about why this had happened. The MoH director accompanying me was not pleased by what we saw.

For some reason, we also visited the provincial veterinarian department (Usually, I had nothing to do with agriculture/veterinarian officials). We found perfectly functioning cold chain equipment and properly stocked vaccines for livestock vaccination at their installation. I thought: This could not be true, the same town, same adverse climate, here it works, there it does not?

An agriculture person explained it to me as follows: We here in the outback of Mali regard cattle higher than humans. If there were an outbreak of disease among cattle, this would affect the livelihood of the whole region and must be prevented by all means.

He did not continue to explain what, by implication, that meant for humans, considering the mess I had earlier seen in the health department.

MALI

Mali is one of those African countries that one can easily get attached to. It is fascinating, an old culture, and people are proud of it. As in so many African countries, there are several ethnic groups living in Mali. The majority are Muslim. There are the Mandingo, the Dogon, and nomadic tribes in the North; Tuareg and Fulbe.

After independence from France in 1960, Mali turned socialistic under its head of State and government, Modibo Keita. Guinea did the same under Sékou Touré; they were friends in the region. Both countries turned around later. Mali in 1969, when M. Traoré took over in a military coup d'etat.

Keita, who was very popular, was kept as a prisoner by the military. Where he was interred was one of these secrets, where everybody knew the answer. He was rumored to be in Kidal in the Saharan desert near the border with Algeria.

* * *

I visited Kidal in February of 1972. The region was affected by severe drought. The starting point for a visit to Kidal is Gao, on the Trans-Saharan Highway. I landed in Gao on a wretched Antonov 24 with Air Mali. As described in "Vaccines in Mali," the plane crashed later.

I was surprised by the enormous runway in this relatively small Sahelian town and later learned that Gao had been used by the Allied forces in WWII as a staging point to support the West African campaign.

We were three colleagues (a Swiss, a French, and myself) from Unicef. We asked the Malian Regional Medical Officer to accompany us to Kidal. He arranged for the military escort required to visit Kidal.

The Trans-Saharan Highway, on which we traveled

north for the first one hundred and sixty miles, would not require the escort. But from Anefis onward, for another one hundred and twenty miles, it was a military zone and off-limits for regular people, particularly foreigners.

On this desert track, called the "Trans-Saharan Highway," we saw the terrible consequences of the drought. Especially around "water points," places where animals gathered to water (drink). Numerous skeletons of cattle and goats lay around, and the soil had deep cracks. There had been no rain for years in this area.

We made a few stops on the way up. On each one, the escort's soldiers and our Regional Medical Officer, Dr. Fumba, drank whiskey instead of water, and quite a lot of it. It was unbelievable the quantity that the doctor could take in. I saw him take a handful of pills. They were mainly vitamins (I think) but also painkillers. He shoved them into his mouth and washed them down with whiskey.

They, the doctor as well, were good Muslims. I later heard that Dr. Fumba died of an unknown disease. His disease was known to me; he drank himself to death. A pity; he was a nice fellow.

We drove in a Land Rover on this desert track. I had hallucinations of a mirage or Fata Morgana. I constantly saw high green mountains on the horizon in a haze. The distance always remained the same. We never came closer. In fact, I knew that the landscape was flat in this part of the desert. When we arrived in Kidal, we were given a local hut with a thatched roof. It was quite clean.

It so happened that the governor of the region (the Gao Region) was on an official visit to Gao at the same time as we were there. So we were invited to the festivities in his honor.

On the evening of our arrival was a bizarre barbecue. I have never seen anything like it before. There was a huge fire on which a whole cow was roasted. The beef was pinned on a simple rotisserie mechanism of poles and a wooden skewer. Two Tuareg in their desert turbans, covering even their faces, turned the rotisserie for hours. When the outer part was done, one of the elder Tuaregs cut it with his bent dagger and handed it to us. We were honored guests. It was all done by hand. There were no plates, forks, or knives. It was delicious meat.

Eating continued until late at night, and there were dances for entertainment. Only men danced. The women were around; they kept to themselves and did not dance. They were served the delicious meat last. Moonshine made the evening even more romantic. As this was an official celebration in honor of the governor, no alcoholic beverages were served with the meal.

The next day, still in honor of the governor's visit, there was a camel race. That was quite a sight. On a large field outside the village, some fifteen camels and their Tuareg riders raced around the place three or four times with a cheering, ecstatic crowd. I think their favorite won because they carried him away on their shoulders after the governor gave him a dagger as a prize.

Anyhow, we also managed to do some business. We visited the new health center and spoke to the local health assistant and the nurse. We inspected the cold chain, saw vaccination records, established drug requirements, and other things for carrying out primary health service.

We knew, and our man from the Ministry of Health in Bamako, with us on this trip, told us that former President Modibo Keita was kept here in Kidal. This was not a subject to be spoken of by local people. A very memorable visit for me and my colleagues.

On the way back to Gao, the Land Rover lost a ventilator belt, and the vehicle dangerously heated up. The driver, an experienced desert driver, knew what to do. He fitted a rope in place of the belt. He had the rope stowed away in the vehicle's toolbox.

1973

ELEPHANTS HAVE THE RIGHT OF WAY (MALI II)

As described in "Abidjan II," there was a West African drought in the seventies and the corresponding long haulage of emergency supplies to the affected areas in the continent's interior.

I have always felt that sound decisions on transportation can only be made if one knows conditions, distances, roads, border and customs arrangements, and what types of trucks are required. Therefore I did not make decisions from my desk in the air-conditioned Unicef Regional Office in Abidjan; instead, I traveled and saw the conditions for myself.

I was known for constantly being out on "field trips," as they were called. Sure, I used to fly in airplanes to where large airports were situated, but trips to rural areas could only be made with a 4-wheel drive vehicle.

In those years, the port of Abidjan was the most efficient port on the West Coast (I think it still is today!) The second best was Dakar, Senegal, but here we had the problem of an inefficient railway to Bamako for cargo to Mali. So we decided to use Abidjan as much as possible as a port of entry for Mali.

I also believe a staff member's family should know what the husband and "daddy" was doing on a field trip. So I thought taking them along occasionally was good practice if it did not hinder duties. Such an opportunity arose in July 1973.

I had to survey the supply route from the Ivory Coast to the Sahelian part of Mali. I wanted to know more about distances, road conditions, and the border crossing point to Mali at Pogo. Our two older girls, Renate and Susanne, were staying with us in Abidjan during their German boarding school's vacation time.

I decided to travel in my own car. (We had an arrangement whereby if one used his/her personal vehicle on a duty trip, the organization reimbursed a mileage allowance.) So I made arrangements and invited the whole family to come along. There were five of us: Doris, myself, Renate (seventeen), Susanne (fifteen), and Andrea (eleven).

We set off on July 25th from Abidjan towards the North. The road to Bouake and some miles beyond was easy, a broad dual-lane highway. The President of the Republic, Felix Houphoet Boigny, was a native of Bouake, so the president's hometown and its roads were rather over-developed.

As we drove on, the road got unpaved and narrow. Soon, our car was covered in red dust. Despite the narrow road, there was heavy traffic. Particularly scary were the big trucks carrying undressed timber, up to eight massive logs, piled up. They were at least twenty meters long and must have weighed twenty tons or more. And the speed they drove made you go off the road voluntarily to let them pass and pray they would not turn over.

The Ivory Coast is a large exporter of tropical timber. More and more sawmills and factories were established to process this timber, for plywood and other ready products, instead of exporting raw trunks. Environmentalists were also insisting on reforestation. It took some time after independence before this was accepted by the government.

Our first stop was intended to be at Korhogo in the North of IC. Before we reached Korhogo, we had an unfortunate mishap. There was a small herd of cattle led by a herdsman along the road. I passed the cows at what I thought was a respectable distance. Nevertheless, as I was next to a young cow, the herdsman hit it with a stick. The frightened animal jumped sideways onto the fender and hood of my Mercedes, causing considerable damage, including a broken left headlight.

I could not continue driving without first bending the

fender back so the wheel could freely turn. In no time, a crowd of people started arguing with me, saying I killed the cow. That was not true. The cow ran away. We all saw it.

After some palaver, I got into the car and drove away. Even to the local folks, it was obvious that the cow was not dead. Otherwise, they would not have let me go without paying for it.

Interestingly, in my long experience on African roads, I found that cows and chickens are much more likely to run into your car. Goats and camels never cause such accidents. So you can quite safely travel in Mauritania or elsewhere in the desert.

My experience with elephants in this respect is not entirely clear. When an elephant is in your way, you automatically slow down. (On entering the game park at Murchison Falls in Uganda, there is a big sign reading: "Elephants have the right of way!")

The following morning we continued from Korhogo in our damaged Mercedes. Bamako was our destination for the day, about four hundred and ten miles, not all on bad roads. I had a business meeting for about an hour at the halfway point in Sikasso.

This town in Mali is an important logistics point. Relief supplies to the drought area would continue from Sikasso to the North, avoiding the capital Bamako.

We arrived late in the evening in Bamako. I was pleasantly surprised to learn that the Ministry of Health (MoH) had reserved an apartment in their guest house for my family and me. Hotels in Mali were bad; the capital was not an exception.

There are two major hills in Bamako. On one, called "Point G," are most government offices, including the President's Palace, and several ministries, including the MoH and their guest house. It overlooks a wide area of the beautiful landscape and the mighty Niger River. On the other hill is the University of Mali, an institution with a good reputation in West Africa. People jokingly refer to them as Montagne de Pouvoir (mountain of power, meaning "Point G") and Montagne de Savoir (mountain of knowledge, meaning the university hill).

Because of Unicef's significant investment in vehicles in the country, we had a transport consultant in Bamako. He looked after these vehicles, including their maintenance, spare parts requirements, and how they were used. He was a Frenchmen with an Italian name: Bruno Gabrielli. Bruno was a nice guy. He had been to Abidjan many times and usually stayed in our house. So the children know him well.

It was he who had arranged our accommodation in the guest house. He made our stay in Bamako a very pleasant one. He patiently answered all the many questions that our daughters asked about Mali. Together we discussed my mission to the drought-affected places with various ministries in the government. Bruno then traveled with us up-country and was a big help to me in my duties.

Two days later, we traveled to Mopti, an important old city on the river Niger. The same hotel situation existed. But there was quite a comfortable riverboat in Mopti. This ship was used, during regular times, to transport tourists from Mopti (up to this point, roads were good) to Timbuktu and, further, to Gao (where roads were practically nonexistent at the time). One could use riverboats (two were in service) from Koulikoro, just outside Bamako, for a leisurely journey to Gao via Timbuktu, some nine hundred miles.

However, due to the drought, the water level was too low during our visit. The Niger hadn't been navigable for two years. So we could stay on one of the two boats in Mopti. Our children are patriots and immediately noticed that the boat was of German design. Assembled in Mali, but its power plant and other equipment came from Germany.

When we woke up in the morning, it was interesting to see many people come to the river, fishing, washing clothes, taking a bath fully naked, and drinking from the river in the belief that the water had purified just a few meters downstream. Again a folkloric sight and quite an experience for our young daughters.

We continued our journey to many places in the area, including Kutiala, San, Bandiagara, and the interesting old town of Djenné. Bruno and I were busy following up on the implementation of drought emergency measures, requirements, the situation of transport, means of distribution, the condition of vehicles, and so forth. That gave my family plenty of time to look around for interesting things to do.

Speaking about the drought, in Bandiagara, we hit the biggest tropical storm you can imagine. We were stuck for a whole day because the streets were flooded. One rain does not end a drought, but any drought eventually ends.

That was a very eventful trip to Mali. We like to think it was memorable for our daughters. Often when we get together, we recount little stories about this journey.

MALI III

I wanted to bring up one more rather funny story about Mali. Once, I traveled to Bamako in the company of a Unicef colleague responsible for managing projects in Mali. He was from Cameroon, Maurice Diwouta. Maurice was a well-French-educated African.

The "elite" in the former French colonies had one particular education path. They were all, even before independence, educated in this very well-known institute in France. (I do not know the correct name for this institute, and for now, I will just call it the "French Institute.")

Anyone in a higher management position in African French-speaking countries was educated in this "French Institute." The top staff of governments, banks, and organizations like Unicef were all the same. Consequently, they knew each other intimately. Going with Maurice on a field mission opened doors that I, as a European UN Official, would not have been able to open without prior formal arrangements.

He also could name bad situations very bluntly as he saw them. He could call a mess a mess, which I could not do without risking a diplomatic conflict.

So, I was with Maurice in an official meeting with the Director General, MoH, in the latter's office on the "Montagne de Pouvoir." Well, Maurice and the director had both been in the before mentioned "French Institute" at the same time. They greeted each other very cordially and exchanged names and news about the whereabouts of their fellows. I was sitting around patiently and could not participate in this part of the old boy's conversation.

When they were in the midst of it, a door opened behind

the Secretary-General's desk. In came a woman in an African dress with a basket of eggs. Without a word, she threw one egg after the other toward the Secretary-General. Some went on his desk, and some hit him directly. One even in his face. When all the eggs were thrown, she left again without saying a word.

What a mess! The whole event took only about half a minute in silence. We, the visitors, were stunned. I do not know whether our host was. Saving face, he only said: "Je m' excuse." We continued the meeting without cleaning up the mess as if nothing had happened. I do not know whether she was his wife or a disgusted employee with a bone to pick with the SG. Maurice and I had a good laugh after we left.

1974

NIGERIA

In November 1974, I went on a memorable mission to Nigeria. The office in Lagos requested I visit some of the federal states on transport and logistics issues. They suggested that the Program Officer responsible for these states accompany me on this trip. That was Alexander Kukolevski.

Alex was from Moscow. Rumor had it that he was a nephew of Leonid Brezhnev, then Prime Minister of the USSR, though he never confirmed this to me himself. (I have written about him in the chapter entitled "Inside Kampuchea." The Kampuchea happenings were later, in 1980).

Russians in these years who were "assigned or commandeered" to UN positions were privileged. We had several in Unicef. They were usually with us for two to three years. After that, they had to return to the USSR. Some came back for a second term after several years. Most of them served in headquarters. They were all housed in a high-rise apartment up in the Bronx. Where we were sure they were closely guarded.

Except in the office, where the USSR colleagues were friendly but generally uninformed, they did not mix with others. Socially you never saw one outside regular duty hours. They were brought and taken to their housing in the Bronx together in several buses.

Alex had been with Unicef for longer. He had been in the Lagos field office, lived with his wife in a rented house as other Unicef staff did, and could go on field trips into the interior of Nigeria. All of this was unusual for a USSR UN staff member. Perhaps he was "controlled" by the USSR Embassy in Lagos, but we could not tell if so.

We were supposed to go on a field trip to Benin, Bendel

State's capital, and Ibadan, Ojo State's capital. Before we left, he directed the driver to his house in the morning, saying that his wife had received permission to travel with us. Permission, in this case, meant from the USSR embassy. Unicef usually had no objection if a family member joined in a field trip, provided that no additional expenses were involved.

So the three of us and the Nigerian driver traveled for several days in that interesting country. But equally interesting for me were Alex and his wife. I think her name was Elena. I learned that she was an embassy official herself. She was a teacher and taught Russian kids at the embassy school.

We had a very frank discussion about world affairs as they presented themselves in 1974. Both of them were aware of it all. They read Western papers. When Elena bought a Time Magazine at the hotel, I asked whether she could take this to the embassy. "No problem," she replied. They told me about the life of "the privileged" in Moscow. I had no doubt that Alex and his wife were among the most privileged in the USSR.

In Ibadan, we stayed at the "Ibadan State University" guest house and ate in their refectory. Ibadan is one of the biggest and most important universities in Africa. The university was involved with implementing the Unicef-assisted project in Oyo state.

Then we got stuck for two days simply because we couldn't get gas for the Land Rover. Nigeria, one of the most significant petrol-producing lands on earth, had a refinery in Ibadan. And still, their pumps ran out of gas. Ultimately, the driver spent a whole night in line at the gas station and got sufficient gas to take us back a hundred miles to Lagos.

I met Alex Kukolevski again in New York and then in Cambodia. The last time I visited headquarters in New York, I heard that Alexander had died of cancer in Moscow the summer before. He was a good colleague and interesting too.

I realize there are no notable highlights in this Nigeria story; all routine. However, on many of my missions, nothing extraordinary happened, or at least, that's the way I felt.

1975

JOHN BRADFORD

John Bradford, an American citizen, was a Unicef colleague in the Information Division at headquarters (NY). He came to Abidjan when I was posted there, accompanying a TV crew filming a movie for fundraising purposes.

So I knew John. However, professionally we did not have much to do with each other. He was a friendly person, I think an "old" bachelor. At least I never heard him talk about a family.

Later, I was sorry when I read in one of our staff bulletins that John had retired from Unicef. He didn't seem that old to me. I was proved wrong. At least he remained very young in his heart. (Note: Retirement age in the UN system is sixty. Early retirement is possible at fifty-five with a reduced pension.)

I was on a logistics mission to Liberia, I think it was in 1975. I inspected a warehouse where international aid items, including Unicef supplies, were stored. I saw a man in the office of that warehouse and thought, I know this guy. As surprised as I was, he got up and said: "Hello, Horst. How are you doing?" It was John Bradford!

It turned out that he joined the US Peace Corps after retirement from Unicef. They sent him to Liberia to work as a volunteer in a US-assisted health and nutrition program.

I had only ever met young fellows from the Peace Corps. But I learned that they also provide motivated elderly, healthy persons the opportunity to join this noble institution. We met that evening in his apartment and talked about the "good old times."

The US Peace Corps and Unicef assisted the same government program in Liberia. We worked together to solve common problems. Before parting from Robertsfield (Liberia's International Airport), I told John he should visit us in Abidjan, only one hour by plane from Liberia.

* * *

Some weeks later, John turned up in my office in Abidjan on a stop-over, bound the following day for Bamako, Mali. I invited him to stay at our house. I also arranged that he could get to the airport the next day to catch the Air Mali flight to Bamako.

Doris was pleased when I brought a guest home; she always was. Having a foreign guest always meant interesting discussions and news from the outside world. And interesting it was this evening on our porch under an African sky.

John told us a fascinating story. As a young man in the late twenties, he participated in an expedition led and financed by a well-known American philanthropist and adventurer. (I can not recall his name, but I believe he may have been a son of the Vanderbilt dynasty.) They traveled in a convoy of motor trucks from East Africa via Kenya (British), Ethiopia (independent), Southern Sudan (British), Congo (Belgian), Central Africa (French), Chad (French), Niger (French), Mali (French) to Timbuktu and from there to Dakar/Senegal (French) where they embarked on a ship and sailed back to the US.

At that time, trucks (no Jeeps or Land Rovers were available) were not as reliable as they are nowadays. Fuel was not available everywhere, and roads were miserable or nonexistent. They had to travel with barrels of fuel, spare parts, tents, and several mechanics to keep the vehicles rolling.

John was full of stories about the details of this expedition. One of the highlights for the adventurers was Timbuktu, the legendary old town on the fringe of the Sahara and the river Niger. Doris and I had long since noted that Americans have an absolute weakness for Timbuktu. John Bradford was fascinated with Timbuktu. Later in life, he had never been able to return to the place. Going there again was a lifelong dream of his.

Now on Peace Corps assignment in Liberia, he saw an opportunity to fulfill his old Timbuktu dream. On this evening in Abidjan, he was on the way and showed his excitement.

For some time, we did not hear from John. On his return trip from Mali, he traveled by another route back to Liberia. At the end of the year, we got a letter from America. It turned out to be season greetings from John Bradford. He had completed his year as a volunteer in Liberia and wrote from his retirement home in the US.

This communication made it clear that his trip to Mali had been disappointing. He wrote that going from Bamako to Timbuktu was a nightmare (I have written about the Air Mali experience with their USSR-made airplane, the Antonov). John wrote what I also wrote in a previous story about Timbuktu. He said he had never seen so little done for so many tourists.

Most of the tourists were American (Apparently, going to Timbuktu for an American is the same thing as going to Mecca is for a Muslim). Then he wrote: "I was a young fellow when I saw Timbuktu some fifty years ago, and during my whole life, I remembered it the way I had seen it then. Timbuktu remained the same, but I had changed and gotten fifty years older."

That made me think at the time and even more today as I write my memoirs; there are so many places I like to remember. But deep in my heart, I know that I should not return. Some places have a reverse development. Many remained as they were. Anyhow, one remembers only the good things. The unpleasant events are often forgotten.

1977

BRIDGE IN NOUAKCHOTT

Mauritania in the western Sahara was a French colony until its independence in 1960. Many of the former French colonies became independent that year. The capital of Mauritania is Nouakchott on the southern Atlantic. It is a new city built for the country's independence. The population of this vast desert country is only 1.6 million people.

Mauritania has a Moorish nomadic majority and a black farming minority. The latter live in the South along the Senegal River, which also constitutes the border with the Republic of Senegal. There is an airport in Nouakchott. However, as many travelers do, I arrived by car from Dakar.

In the late seventies, Unicef didn't have an office in Mauritania. A Program Officer responsible for the country was based in the Unicef area office in Dakar. He visited Mauritania frequently for programming work. When the Program Officer was not in the country, the Office of UNDP (United Nations Development Program) represented Unicef to the government. Unicef personnel in Mauritania on business usually visited the UNDP representative to explain their mission.

There was a good road from Dakar/Senegal to Nouakchott. I traveled there in a Land Rover from our Dakar area office with a Unicef driver for better mobility in Mauritania. My Itinerary was: Dakar, Saint-Lois, then Richard Toll. Two hundred and twenty km so far. There was a ferry over the Senegal River at Richard Toll. On the other side of the river is a place called Roso. About twenty km out of Roso, the desert starts, until one reaches Nouakchott after two hundred more km. The Mauritanian capital is not a green city. On the contrary, it is very desert-like.

Water is expensive. Actually, I found out that whiskey is not much more expensive. France helped the new country construct a plant for converting seawater to drinking water at independence. However, this plant was too complicated and costly to run; more recently, good water has been piped from a source in the desert, some 180 km from the capital.

The morning after I arrived in Nouakchott, I went to the UNDP office for the customary visit and to inform the representative of my mission. He was a Scott with an, at least for me, unusual name. Aprees, I think it was, though I am unsure of the spelling.

He listened to me very patiently and did not interrupt me at all. After some time, he asked: "Do you play bridge?" I was flabbergasted because this was a question that I had not expected. He smiled and explained that they had invited people to their residence for dinner and bridge that evening.

Their intention was to play at three tables rotating after every four games. One invited guest had to cancel. They were now short one player. I could play bridge and told him I would be happy to oblige. Actually, I was pleased because a hotel evening in Nouakchott was not an exciting prospect.

So I went there in the evening and was received by a very charming Ms. Aprees. Dinner was delicious. The game started, and my first hand was excellent. I often experience this, only to find that my cards get worse from there. Not in Nouakchott! My cards got better with each game.

I never started a game without at least twenty points, no matter which table I played on or who my partner was. Being there as a guest and having such outrageously good cards, I was almost embarrassed. I knew that I could not come to Nouakchott again. At least I could not accept an invitation to play bridge.

Years later, I met Aprees again. He was then the UNDP Representative in another African country. He remembered the bridge evening in his residence in Mauritania. We both had to laugh remembering it. However, Mr. Aprees did not invite me to play bridge on this occasion.

* * *

Another brief story on Mauritania: As I wrote above, most of the population, those living in Nouakchott among them, are Moorish nomadic. I had a lady colleague who was French and a Unicef Program Officer. Her duty station was Bamako/Mali. So she lived in Bamako but occasionally visited Nouakchott to see her husband, a Mauritania Moor. Her children were grown up and no longer at home. (By the way, Unicef has a large quota of women in leading positions among the staff. Because moving around from one duty station to another is necessary, separation from the family is often the price.)

Marie and I were good friends, and it so happened that she was in Nouakchott when I was there as well. So she invited me for dinner to meet her husband. He was a high-ranking government official, and I was not surprised to see a lovely villa on arrival.

I was led into the house, it was sparsely furnished, and I was curious. But then I was shown to the yard; believe it or not, a big tent was pitched there. The tent was warmly lit with a very comfortable interior. There were lots of thick carpets.

We had a fabulous dinner, barbecued meat with rice and whole leaves of green salad. As is the custom, we ate with our bare hands. I had been in desert tents before, but this one in Nouakchott was the tent of a chief and splendid.

In our line of work, one got a broader view of colleagues from other countries. I found that working with people from different countries in the team goes surprisingly well. I think everyone does his or her best. Perhaps sometimes subconsciously.

I have worked with many nationalities. For some time, I had an African director from Senegal. You have to give allowances to people from other cultures as you expect them to give allowances to you for your own culture.

NEW YORK

I was posted to headquarters in New York by Unicef in the autumn of 1977. We subsequently lived there for twelve years. New York was part of my own and my family's lives. Doris and I lived longer in New York and Waterside than anywhere else. As one can imagine, it brought a significant change to our lives.

I had only been to New York once and only for a few days. That was in May of 1975 when I was invited to attend the Unicef Executive Board Session. At that time, I was posted in Abidjan.

After returning to the Ivory Coast, I told Doris enthusiastically about all I had seen and done in the Big Apple. We decided to work and aim for a transfer to headquarters.

Of course, that was a little ambitious. There was only one post in the organization in my field. Robert Walker was in this position in headquarters and did an excellent job. It also meant getting a promotion. So, how could I possibly reckon on having a chance of getting this post?

I got that position two years later, and we moved to New York. By the way, I did not push Robert Walker, our dear friend, out of his post. He became the chief of Unicef's Emergency Section, an even more important and rewarding position.

As we were preparing to leave Abidjan, our suitcases already packed, we read an article about New York. It was written negatively about muggings, stealing, burglary, murder, noise, dirt, and rubbish in the streets. Gosh, we thought, we are going to this place.

Coincidentally a colleague from headquarters, who had lived for many years in New York, was on a field mission in Abidjan. We showed him the magazine and asked whether it was as bad as described. He read the article and said wisely, "Yes, it is bad. But, there is one thing wrong with the write-up; it is only half the story. This big metropolitan city has as many good things as bad things. The article is only talking about the bad things." Well, that was encouraging again.

Coming from Abidjan, after two months of "home leave" in Germany, I landed at JFK on Monday, August 15th, 1977. I was alone. Doris stayed in Germany with our daughters for two more weeks. I took a cab to Manhattan. A room was booked for me at the Doral Inn Hotel at Lexington Ave.

I walked down East 49th Street to the Unicef offices the following morning. At the time, the offices were in the Alcoa building, First Ave. 48the Street, north of the UN gardens. That was my start in the USA.

Two days later, I moved into a small furnished apartment at Beekman's Tower, the next building north of The Alcoa. I settled here for the time being, very close to the office, where I could start the new assignment and look around for a more permanent place to live.

I was not a stranger at my new workplace. Having already been with the organization for some fifteen years in field locations, I knew many people personally. Be it from their visits to the field or assignments to Africa at one point or other.

Many had been guests in our house on such occasions and knew Doris and the girls too. Take, for instance, Louis Gendron. I had known him since the fifties from Damascus. Later we were both in UNRWA and neighbors in Beirut. Louis was now Chief of Personnel at Unicef.

I had known some of my colleagues for years from correspondence. I thought it was high time to put faces with the names I had read on memos and cables for so long. They all were very helpful to me as a newcomer to New York. I got invitations to their homes and was invited almost daily for lunch around the UN mid-town vicinity.

It was nice to see and meet all those people, but there

was a practical reason apart from the social aspect. I wanted to see my colleagues' homes to help Doris and me decide where to settle in New York. We had spoken of this together and thought we should try and find a house up country in NY State. Having lived in a house with a garden since our marriage, we could not imagine living in a high-rise Manhattan building.

A Swedish colleague from Information Division had been a guest in our house in Abidjan only a few weeks earlier. He asked me to come for dinner at his place near the UN one evening. He said we could walk there together after work. I accepted he called his wife, and it was OK with her too. So after work, we left the office together and walked south on First Avenue. It turned out that of all places in New York, my Swedish friend lived at Waterside, building 30, the "A" apartment on the 29th floor.

What can I tell you? I liked Waterside at first sight. My friends told me all the advantages of living in Manhattan: walking to the office, not spending hours on a train, and what have you. I was persuaded at once and called Doris in Germany the following morning. It did not take me long to convince her that we should give up our dream of a house and garden upstate NY.

We decided to live at Waterside and gave ourselves one year, after which we could move. The rest of the story is that we lived at Waterside for thirteen years. Because of Susanne, we still visited and stayed at Waterside whenever we went to New York for many years after that. At that time, in 1977, it was easy to get an apartment at Waterside. Actually, we had two options. We took the one in building 30; 30-A.

Doris and Andrea arrived in New York on September 9th. We stayed in the apartment of Katia Fisch, a colleague of mine, for several weeks. Katia went on an extended field trip to Africa and was quite pleased to have someone stay in her home while she was away from New York. Our new apartment at Waterside only became available on October 1st. This location was also good for Andrea. She went to the UN School (UNIS) from the beginning. Living at Waterside was ideal for her.

NEW YORK II

Old New Yorkers will only shake their heads in disbelief when I tell some of our experiences during our first weeks in the Big Apple. You must understand that we were basically ignorant African bush people who had just arrived in that big town, actually in one of the biggest towns in the world.

Can you imagine? We had no credit cards, and I had just opened a bank account when I arrived some days earlier. My credit rating was absolutely zero.

You have probably never experienced a thing like what happened to us when we bought furnishings for our dining room at Macy's. We hadn't brought any furnishings along from Abidjan. We had sold whatever we had there. So we needed new furnishings in NY. We found a lovely set of dining room furniture at Macy's.

When we spoke to the salesman, he noticed that we were foreigners and was suspicious. He asked whether we were from Israel. "No," we said, "we are from Germany." So he was even more suspicious. The dining room furnishings were about $15,000. The delivery time was about five weeks.

The salesman asked how we would pay, and I told him by check. He said I needed two kinds of photo IDs. A driver's license would do. Having just arrived, I had none of these IDs.

He asked me where I worked, and I told him at the UN. Then, he inquired, "What company is that?" He asked for my phone number. I gave him the number of Katia Fisch's apartment where we were staying. He took the information and went to see his supervisor.

I think he checked the phone number against my name and found it did not match. Finally, he returned and told us that the check was unacceptable.

I asked what his problem was. Delivery is in five weeks. If you take my check now, and it bounces, you will know it after three or four days, then you just do not deliver. That was too simple for the Macy's salesman. It was final. No check was acceptable, only cash, cool cash.

So I went to the Chemical Bank, UN branch, where I had my account and withdrew $15,000 in cash. I had just come from Africa, where I had read that article in that wretched magazine about all the mugging in the streets of New York. I distributed the money in all the pockets of my suit. Then I ran like mad from the UN to Macy's, always looking behind me for possible muggers. Hooray, I arrived safely and paid cash for the dining room set, which was finally delivered five weeks later to our apartment in Waterside.

UNKNOWN FLOUR

After we moved into apartment 30-A in building 30 Waterside, we met a young couple in the "B" apartment on the same floor. We became friendly and invited each other for drinks. It turned out that the young woman and the young man were both lawyers. I think they even worked in the same office.

Their office represented the soccer club called the NY Cosmos. Actually, the Cosmos was only "sort of" a New York club because they played soccer in Giant's Stadium in New Jersey. (I think their successor club is called the NY/NJ MetroStars. They also play in the Giant's Stadium. At the time of this writing, they were just joined by a famous German soccer star: Lothar Mataeus)

Anyhow, soccer only started becoming popular in the US in the mid-seventies. At first, they engaged well-known soccer players from Europe and Latin America. The Cosmos then had the famous Brazilian star Pelé and the not-less-famous German Franz Beckenbauer.

One day our friendly attorney neighbor came over and said the following Saturday was "Beckenbauer-Day" at Giant's Stadium. He could easily get tickets on account of his office representing the Cosmos. He asked us to come and watch the football match and honor this occasion for Franz Beckenbauer. So we went along. It was an interesting match. Both Beckenbauer and Pelé played, and the Cosmos won.

* * *

Having been treated so generously by our neighbors, Doris wanted to reciprocate and invited them for dinner. They accepted and said they would very much like a typical German meal. "Oh, that is easy," Doris replied, "I will make 'spaetzle,' a typical southern German meal." (I wrote about how Doris taught our local cook in Abidjan to prepare spaetzle: see "Domestique.")

The big evening came. Doris had already started to prepare the spaetzle dough in the afternoon. By November 1977, Doris was a much more experienced housewife (German: "Hausfrau") than when we started in Damascus.

What she had no experience with was the American self-rising flour. Coming from the African bush, Doris had never cooked with this sophisticated processed flour. This may be unbelievable for an American housewife. So Doris took the quantity of flour she was accustomed to using and added baking powder.

She did not expect what would happen. The bowl overflowed quickly, the dough grew more and more, and she could not stop it. To make a long story short, she could not use the dough anymore for spaetzle. Our guests just had spaghetti and a meat sauce, and they enjoyed it.

1978

AFGHANISTAN

I have been in Afghanistan three times on logistics missions. Afghanistan is landlocked and challenging to reach. The country, and Kabul, with the Hindu Kush mountains in sight, always fascinated me for their wild beauty.

I landed in Pakistan in 1978. This was my first time in the country. I had a routine visit about logistics there before traveling on to Afghanistan. I planned to drive from Pakistan to Afghanistan via the Khyber Pass to Kabul.

After some days in Islamabad, where Unicef's country office is, I continued to Peshawar on the North Western Frontier. We had some Unicef activities there, basic health, including a water and sanitation project.

There was a Polish Drilling Master, Ted. He was training Pakistani technicians on a huge rig for drilling boreholes. He collected me at the airport and showed me some project activities.

When we traveled in the nearby mountains, I remember his Pakistani counterpart was with us. They told me about the influence and power the tribes up here in the Northern Frontier District had. For instance, there was an official government road where everybody could travel safely. However, off the road was tribal land. Without the permission of the tribal chiefs, nobody, not even the police, could go there.

We visited a village just off the main highway in the tribal land in the foothills of the Khyber Pass. Craftsmen there manufactured, I should say copied, from the originals, guns, pistols, just about any kind of weapons, with the most primitive means. It was unbelievable. They had no modern machines at all to make these weapons.

They worked with a hammer and chisel, a file and emery paper, and a hand-powered drill. These were about the only tools they had. The end product was astonishing, to say the least. From the looks, one could not distinguish between the original and the copy. However, from the material quality point of view, there must be a difference.

Peshawar is the most oriental place I have seen so far. Their market is something. I could not resist purchasing a beautiful oriental carpet, a Bukhara rug typical for this part of the world. The carpet was too big to fit in a suitcase, so getting it to New York was another story.

As I said, my planned itinerary was to drive through the Khyber Pass to Kabul. After all, I was a logistics specialist. Part of my mission was to find access routes for our project supplies. So, I could combine duty with my keen interest in traveling the Khyber Pass, a dream I have had since I was a boy, and read adventure books about this region.

Days before, I had sent a cable to Kabul, advising the date and time of my arrival at the Pakistan/Afghan border. My colleague, and new friend, Ted, drove me up the Khyber Pass. It is only about fifty miles from Peshawar to the border.

Now, that was a big disappointment for me. It was not the rugged trail of my imagination. Thanks to generous US-AID, the Khyber Pass is now a broad highway similar to any American freeway, like I-80 through the Donner Pass in California.

It was a good road but not romantic at all. We did stop several times, and one could see what used to be the old pass where local tribesmen led caravans of donkeys up to the summit.

I would do an injustice to nature if I did not mention the magnificent scenery, the mountains, and the beauty of this land. We came to the border too quickly; there was nothing spectacular to report there.

The Pakistan border post is about half a mile from the Afghan post. We were not allowed to cross this no man's land by car, so I had to say goodbye to Ted, take my luggage, and walk the half mile to Afghanistan. Thank god there were some young fellows who, for a few rupees, took my baggage across. That included the carpet that I had bought in Peshawar. One young man carried it on his head. It was quite a sight.

The Afghan border guards were easy. My visa in the UN Laissez-Passer was enough. One customs official asked about the carpet. He thought there were better ones to be had in Afghanistan. When I told him I wanted to buy a second one in Kabul, he let me go and did not charge any customs fee.

Unicef had sent a Toyota Land cruiser, a delegation of three staff from the Kabul office, and a driver to receive me. My Danish colleague and logistics counterpart, Mogens Munck, had already lived in Afghanistan for some years. He was very knowledgeable about the country.

While I was disappointed by the "modernized" Khyber Pass, I was one hundred percent rewarded by the wilderness of the road that led down about thirty-five miles from the border to Jalalabad on the way to Kabul. This was the country I had dreamt of in my youth; the narrow winding road with scary bends, where one would not want to fall off the edge; it would be fatal. Our Afghan driver was excellent, and I never felt insecure. The wild Kabul River accompanied us the whole distance (about 150 miles) to the Afghan capital.

In Kabul, the UN had a "Staff House." Actually, it was the UN Club with some rooms for accommodation to rent. I was lucky to get a room there because it was much better than the local hotels.

Mogens turned out to be a big help. Everything I needed to know he had right at his fingertips. As mentioned above, he had been in Afghanistan a long time, though not long with Unicef, so it worked both ways. I learned from him about the country and, on the other hand, could give him a lot of Unicef inside tips.

He was just married, and his charming wife was Spanish. They had met in Kabul. We made some "field trips";

that is to say, we drove in a jeep to rural areas to see Unicef program activities. Mogens, in addition to being a logistics expert, was also a refrigeration engineer. That combination came in handy.

As I wrote earlier, Unicef was heavily engaged in immunization programs. It is essential to keep the "cold chain" intact to preserve the potency of vaccines. Mogens was the right person to organize this very efficiently.

Politically speaking, Afghanistan was between revolutions in the autumn of 1978. The president of the "Democratic Republic of Afghanistan" was Nur Mohammed Taraki, and the prime minister was Hafizullah Amin, a pro-USSR communist who later became the president.

Both were, of course, communists; their party was "Khalq." Taraki was much more moderate. He and his second in command had earlier ousted President Daud, a cousin of the previous king Mohammed Zaher. Well, the Afghans were not sorry to see Daud go.

At the time of my visit, one could not have foreseen that events would gradually bring Hafizullah Amin to brutal power and eventually the Russian invasion of Afghanistan. Both Taraki and Amin were Pashtuns, the ruling majority. Afghanistan is a melting pot with varied ethnic groups of Uzbeks, Turkomans, Tajiks, and Baluchs, a mixture predestined for conflicts.

Besides official business and politics, Kabul was, at this time, not destroyed by rockets and mortar shells. It was an interesting oriental town for Westerners to visit. Its market streets were fascinating. Besides carpets, there were many other things to be seen and bought. Precious stones were plentifully available.

That was not my only visit to Kabul. Two more followed. They were not, particularly the last one, as pleasant as the first one.

1979

KAMPUCHEA

Shortly before the conclusion of the Vietnam War in April 1975, the "Khmer Rouge" entered the capital of Cambodia, Phnom Penh, and renamed the country "The Democratic Republic of Kampuchea." (NOTE: during my involvement with this country for Unicef, it was called this. Although it is now again Cambodia, I shall use the name "Kampuchea" in my writing, neglecting the "Democratic Republic" part because the country under its leader Pol Pot was anything but democratic.)

The Khmer Rouge were enthusiastically greeted by the people on entering Phnom Penh. Soon, however, they showed their true faces. Within days they moved the entire population into the countryside. Then they started a genocide without parallels in modern history.

Pol Pot introduced "stone age communism" in Kampuchea, a curtain went down on this country, and it was cut off from the outside world for more than four years. Only in mid-1979, after Vietnam "liberated" Kampuchea from the Pol Pot regime, did the ICRC (International Committee of the Red Cross) and Unicef jointly revisit the country. Then the tragedy the people of Kampuchea had suffered during these four years was revealed.

Later the motion picture "The Killing Fields" became a synonym for this horrible time in Kampuchea. I shall describe only my involvement in the aftermath of it.

In September 1979, the Secretary-General designated Unicef the "lead agency" of the United Nations relief operations in Kampuchea. Unicef teamed up with ICRC for what was known then as the "Joint Mission." That began Unicef's biggest and most challenging logistics operation ever.

At that time, apart from advising on field logistics, I was in charge of vehicle procurement at headquarters in New York. The huge relief operation in Kampuchea got underway with minimum preparation time to save a whole population from starvation. The equipment most required, apart from food, of course, were means of transportation to bring food to Phnom Penh and for the distribution thereof in the entire country.

My concern was inland transportation and distribution of relief supplies. Foremost for this, heavy trucks were needed. But we also required river transportation: barges, and tug boats, given the many navigable rivers in Kampuchea. We estimated that at least six to eight hundred trucks, each suitable to carry ten to twelve MT (metric tons), were initially required. Later these numbers had to be almost doubled.

From the standardization point of view, the ideal would be to provide only one make and model truck. That would solve many servicing problems, including spare parts, know-how, etc. However, no manufacturer of heavy trucks worldwide has that many trucks fitting our specifications, just waiting in a yard for someone to buy them.

So our procurement section in Geneva explored Europe. We in New York searched in the US and Japan for suitable trucks that were available immediately. During the first few months of the Kampuchean operation, I was mainly at my desk in New York, coordinating the procurement of as many trucks and other logistics supplies as possible, calling manufacturers, and sending cables of inquiry.

In those days, telephones and cables were the fastest means of communication. The Internet and e-mail option was not available to us then. The vital communication link with Phnom Penh was frustratingly difficult and slow.

Actually, telephones to the Kampuchean capital did not work at all. Cable communications were unreliable; under the best circumstances, they needed several days to connect. Therefore messages were written and sent by daily relief planes flying to the Unicef Office in Bangkok, from where they were dispatched to New York. Return cables went the same way. SITREPS, as we called them (Situation Reports), that reached us made it clear there was a severe famine throughout the country. On the other hand, means of transportation in the country were so scarce that no distribution of any importance could be undertaken.

Fundraising in New York and Geneva was done at the same time. Contribution of money was one thing, but in addition, food, air transportation means (planes), and suitable ships to transport relief supplies to Phnom Penh were requested from donors. It was exemplary how East and West stood together and helped the Khmer people by pledging money, food, and vehicles to the United Nations.

Apart from some airlifting of food, the bulk came by ship from Singapore and Thailand via the Mekong and the Tonlé Sap rivers (which connected the Mekong with Phnom Penh) to Kampuchea. The Seaport of Kompong Som on the Gulf of Thailand was another option. However, inland transportation from there was a problem due to impassable bridges for large trucks. Simultaneously with the first food arriving in Kampuchea, Hercules and big Transall transport planes airlifted several trucks from Bangkok. The Transalls were Belgian military planes, and the Hercules was a commercial company charter.

An unexpected problem occurred in Phnom Penh. As spring (1980) went on, the level of the river (Tonlé Sap) became very low. That meant food had to be hauled from river barges up a very steep rise to the warehouses at street level. An Offloading bridge at Phnom Penh harbor could not be used. Firstly, because there was no operational crane available, and secondly, the bridge was in bad shape to the point of collapse. Due to the famine in the country, Kampuchean stevedores had enormous difficulties carrying fifty kg bags up the steep river banks.

My good colleague Philippe Heffinck, a Belgian, was with Unicef's first relief team as a Supply and Logistics Officer in Phnom Penh. Philippe sent a message to New York, calling for eight auto cranes with five-ton lifting capacity and eight conveyor belts to arrive, if possible, yesterday. We bought this equipment in Japan. The US Airforce agreed to lift the auto cranes from Yokohama to Phnom Penh with two gigantic Star-Lifter aircraft, four in each plane. Phnom Penh Airport was suitable to accommodate the Star-Lifter.

Now came the snag we hadn't reckoned with. The new Kampuchean government under Heng Samrin, entirely backed by Vietnam, did not want US military aircraft to land in Kampuchea; that was politics again. Therefore the US Airforce lifted the cranes to Singapore, and we shipped them to Kompong Som. Then they were driven to Phnom Penh with difficulty. With much smaller planes (Hercules and Transall), the conveyor belts were airlifted direct to Phnom Penh.

At this point, it was time for me to see the operation more closely. Our headquarters Kampuchean support group, where I was a member, decided that I should go out to consult with Heffinck and with our Bangkok Office. A visit to Phnom Penh would have been ideal. However, this required a visa/permit issued by the Kampuchean Authorities. That took time which I did not have. We decided I should fly to Bangkok and meet Philippe Heffinck there. On November 4th, I departed New York for a long flight to Bangkok via Alaska, Tokyo, and Hong Kong.

KAMPUCHEA II

Being an "old African," the "East" and the whole of Asia was new to me. Busy Bangkok was impressive, although I lived in NY and should have been used to big cities. A driver from the Unicef office collected me at the airport and took me to the Amarin Hotel, where accommodation was booked.

I ran into Knud Christensen in the hotel foyer. A Danish national, an old friend, and a colleague. He was formerly Unicef Representative in Brazzaville and Dakar and had often called me to his areas on logistics problems. Only recently called back from retirement on active duty, he was appointed "Unicef Special Representative" to Kampuchea.

"I thought you were in Phnom Penh?" I greeted him.

"Yes, I was," he said. It turned out that he had only been in PNP (Phnom Penh) for a few days when, on the road to Kampong Som, the Landcruiser in which he was traveling turned over, and he was injured. He had two broken ribs and bruises. He was evacuated to Bangkok.

Anyone else but Knud would have been in bed in a hospital or flying home to Denmark with the injury he had suffered. Not Knud; he did not want to leave. He stayed in the hotel, killing pains with aspirin, met people, and was ready to help wherever possible. In those days, so few had actually been to PNP that first-hand knowledge of Kampuchea was sought after. Sick as he was, he gave endless information to concerned UN and NGO (Non-Governmental Organizations) officials.

Shortly after I arrived at the Amarin Hotel, I met John Saunders (British). He was going to PNP to become the new Unicef Special Representative, replacing Knud. With the Supply Officer of the Bangkok Unicef Office, Lorenz Ostlund, a

Swedish national, we had our first meeting in the hotel. It was very informative for me.

We must remember that in November 1979, Vietnam had "liberated" Kampuchea from the Pol Pot regime. It was still a communist country with difficulties and deep suspicion against Westerners. However, for the Khmer people, it was indeed a "liberation" from the "stone age communism" of the Khmer Rouge and the killings. Kampuchea was now under the Vietnamese. They controlled everything, including the number of aid people and aid organizations allowed to come to PNP.

The following morning Phillipe Heffinck arrived with a relief flight. Once you had a permit to stay in Kampuchea, using one of the flights out and in again was no problem. After two days of discussion, I understood the magnitude of the logistics problem and knew the necessary details.

In the four years that the Khmer Rouge were in charge of Kampuchea, they ran the country down to zero. There were no vehicles and no equipment whatsoever still available. Nails, bolts, nuts, and, of course, food all had to be imported. Heffinck stressed the need for river craft. Due to many bridges being down, various areas of the country could not be reached by road.

A VIP visitor from NY arrived, Mr. Labouisse, the Executive Director of Unicef, accompanied by Mrs. Labouisse née Curie. They came to Bangkok on a fact-finding mission. (Mrs. Eva Curie, still alive when I write this, at 95 years old, is the second daughter of the legendary Madam Marie Curie, two times French Nobel Price winner.)

Those meetings in Bangkok in early November 1979 were critical and helped enormously in planning and coordinating Unicef's strategy for the "Kampuchean operation," which, I say with pride, was very successful.

Anyhow, a cable was sent to HQ-NY. Ed Kenny, our top Shipping Officer, had to come to Bangkok immediately. He was with us two days later. He and I went together to Singapore.

Our order was to buy two powerful tug boats, four motorized cargo barges, eight tow barges, and a passenger barge for the port of PNP. We had not procured such items before in our lives.

As we made inquiries in Singapore, we were a minor sensation. The shipbuilding industry in this City/State seemed to laugh at us. So we hired a consultant for this ship-purchasing business. He came up with good suggestions and an efficient approach to quickly get our fleet of river crafts from Singapore and Thailand.

In addition, Ed negotiated warehousing space at the Freeport in Singapore, which became our base for all ocean-shipped supplies. Here everything was consolidated for onward shipment to Kampuchea. Airfreight was received in Bangkok and, from there, lifted to PNP.

From Singapore, I went to Japan. Unicef has a liaison Office in Tokyo. My colleague Honda-San was notified of my arrival and met me at the international airport in Narita. We contacted all possible truck manufacturers, Hino, Mitsubishi, Toyota, Fuso, and others, to see where we could get trucks that fit the required specification.

One thing was that local Japanese trucks had the steering wheel on the right side, as the Japanese drive on the left side of the road, like the British do. Kampuchea drives on the right side and therefore needs to have the steering wheel on the left side.

Generally, in Western industrialized countries, truck manufacturers, as mentioned above (but also US, British, French, and German factories), manufacture chassis and cabs but not the cargo platform and canopy required for transporting food. We were successful in finding trucks. Now we had to look for platform builders to furnish the cargo platform. Everything went well. Some days later, I took a plane back to New York.

Fundraising for the starving people of Kampuchea was very successful. Naturally, the logistics equipment had to be procured based on available funds. However, the world's people donated money in a commendable way. It was unbelievable. There was no real shortage of funds.

Nevertheless, it was public money and procedures exist throughout the UN system. Certain shortcuts were possible in emergencies, such as the famine in Kampuchea. However, a minimum of procedures had to be followed. Neither I nor anyone else could spend millions of dollars without approval.

So when I arrived back at my desk in NY, I had to prepare and present these purchases to the Unicef CRC (Contract Review Committee) for approval. In some urgent cases, this had to be done retroactively. Without being careless with public money, Unicef can respond flexibly to emergencies and is only reasonably bureaucratic. This is why the (UN) Secretary-General appointed Unicef as the lead agency in the Kampuchean operation.

While I was in the East, my colleagues in NY and Geneva could also buy trucks and other equipment in the US and Europe. Furthermore, through diplomatic contacts, East Germany donated 150 five-ton 4-WD trucks, spare parts, and engineers to service these vehicles.

* * *

Over the X-mas holidays, Doris and I went on leave to Germany for a few days. We had just landed in Frankfurt and gone home when I received a cable from NY. The US army had offered to donate some mobile maintenance units for servicing the transport fleets in Kampuchea. I traveled by train to the US Base at Kaiserslautern and inspected the mobile units. Regrettably, we had to reject the donation. The vans were specialized for military purposes and unsuited for civilian operations. The Authorities in PNP would never have let these military vehicles come to Kampuchea. Realities five years after the Vietnam War.

1980

INSIDE KAMPUCHEA

At the beginning of April 1980, I was sent to PNP (Phnom Penh) for a three-month assignment in Kampuchea. I was to replace Philippe Heffinck as a Logistics Officer. My visa had already been requested weeks before my arrival. However, I had to personally collect it at the Bangkok Vietnamese Embassy.

On Friday, April 4th, 1980, I flew on an Italian military Transall transport aircraft from Bangkok to PNP. The flight was two and a half hours long, although the distance seems closer on the map.

The plane had to fly south across the Gulf of Thailand, first entering Vietnam at Ho Chi Minh City (Saigon) and then flying north again to PNP. The reason: Thailand did not recognize the Heng Samrin regime in PNP. Therefore planes could not use the direct route that would have taken less than one hour. The money wasted by such prestige/bureaucratic measures was considerable and unknown to well-meaning donors.

I landed in PNP and was greeted by my colleague Alain Mitzmacher, our Administration Officer. I was the only passenger, and no officials were around, so Alain suggested: "Let's go to the hotel." We intended to return later to present my passport with the proper visa to an immigration person.

When we returned some two hours later, we met an official who was quite furious because I had gone away into town without the blessings of an immigration officer.

I was a little scared when I was asked into a room. Alain was not allowed to go with me. A uniformed man interrogated me. This man was a Vietnamese political officer.

I did not know then, but later I learned the difference.

(You could spot Vietnamese people by their eyes. Khmers, the people in Kampuchea, had none of this but looked more Siamese).

His English was difficult to understand. He asked again and again whether I was an American spy. He was convinced of it when I told him I lived in NY. I was already quite sure this would end a short-lived assignment in Kampuchea.

Finally, he let me go. I think this time it was because I was German. Probably he thought I was East German, and perhaps he did not know that there were two Germanies at that time.

We drove back to the Hotel Samaki, where I was supposed to live and work. There was no choice. One could honestly say we were "confined" to the Samaki (translated as "solidarity") hotel. Nobody from Unicef, the ICRC, or all the NGOs could have private accommodation or offices anywhere else.

The hotel was previously the legendary "Royal Hotel." Nothing was left of its former glamour. It was dismal. One of the best rooms was occupied by Phillip Heffinck. He was there for two more days. I would be getting his room after that. Therefore I did not mind putting up with a small one in the meantime.

I met the small Unicef crew, all of whom I had worked with elsewhere. John Saunders was the Chief: his title was "Special Representative." Ian Hopwood, I knew from Africa. Then there was Alex Kukolevski, a Russian (USSR) who had been with Unicef for a long time. We traveled together in Nigeria. Philippe used his remaining time to hand over the business to me and introduce me to colleagues from ICRC and the NGOs. Particularly Oxfam (UK), with whom I had so much to do in the coming weeks.

The following morning. a Khmer came to us (We had one little room in the hotel as an office. Otherwise, we all worked out of our own rooms.) and introduced himself as Ngin Sok Lean. He told me he was my guide and would accompany me. Philippe had already warned me that an escort from the Foreign Ministry would always be with me, so I was not surprised. I remembered that we were in a communist state. It was ten years before the iron curtain fell.

Sok Lean, I called him, and he called me Ruttinger. Usually, I was glad to have him with me for communication purposes. Sometimes he got on my nerves because he was always standing behind me.

After the "liberation" of Kampuchea by the Vietnamese, Sok Lean was sent for several months to the Soviet Union, where he got his "true communist" training. He had just returned. Escorting me was his first job.

He pretended he did not understand English, but I knew he did. To me, and my colleagues, he spoke only French. Ordinary people in the country were not allowed to talk directly to foreigners. All conversations had to be via the official guide. If others were around, Sok Lean did not try to enforce that rule. Many Khmers spoke English or French and were keen to talk to us.

A few days after my arrival, the Khmer celebrated their New Year. On this occasion, Sok Lean wrote to me on a flimsy sheet of paper a letter as follows:

Phnom Penh le 7 Avril 1980

Cher Ruttinger,

C'est avec le meilleur de mon cœur que j'ai la joie de vous former me vœux fervents d'heureuse et lumineuse Année Nouvelle du Kamuchéa.

Je souhaite que "Chenam Vork" vous apporte pleinement de santé, de bonheur et ainsi que de sucés dans votre noble mission en République Populaire du Kampuchéa.

Votre sincère

Ngin Sok Lean

Département des Relations avec les

Organisations Internationales

Ministère des Affaires Etrangères

I thought that was rather nice, I had just met the man two days earlier, and he had written me such a cordial letter. So I learned my first lesson: the Khmer were friendly and kind. These days, however, they were under the absolute dictate of Vietnamese and USSR communists.

One "must" was to visit mass graves and other places where hundreds of skulls and bones of murdered people were stacked. A scary, frightful sight.

Here I learned the second lesson: in the three months I was in Kampuchea, no one ever suggested that this murderous regime, which can be compared with the Nazis from 1933 to 45, had anything to do with communism. Their present masters were communists. It was Pol Pot and his gang who did it.

In early 1980, many Western journalists were invited to Kampuchea to see the mass graves, bleached bones, and skulls of people murdered by the Khmer Rouge and Pol Pot. It is not that this didn't touch me, but I kept out of arguments as much as possible and stayed professional.

A lot was written in those days about Pol Pot and how the tragedy came about. Showcross' book "The Quality of Mercy" is one of the best I have read. I, however, was a logistics specialist, and there was a lot of work to be done. Although we all, the UN, ICRC, and the NGOs, had a lot of restrictions, we were still determined to do our work.

I was now in a position in Kampuchea where I could receive the logistics material I had ordered and bought as a procurement officer out of NY. One of my first "field trips" from PNP was to Kompong Som, the only deep-water port. There were three hundred impatiently awaited trucks, as well as conveyor belts from Japan, there.

I was just about to leave the Samaki Hotel with Sok Lean when Alex Kukolevski came up and asked whether he could accompany me. I said, "Why not. But do you have a permit to travel?" He said, "Don't worry about it."

We had to have a permit whenever we wanted to leave PNP, but usually, our guide took care of this. Alex was Russian, you remember. Rumor had it that he was a nephew of Leonid Brezhnev, then Prime Minister of the USSR, though he never confirmed this himself. Having Alex with me opened doors everywhere.

The Russians helped the relief effort by sending a boat full of stevedores to Kompong Som. They lived on the ship and worked in the harbor during the day. The Kampucheans, at this time, could not cope with all the deliveries, so the Russian help was beneficial.

When we were in the port, Alex said he wanted to go on a ship to take the opportunity and call his wife in Moscow. I knew his wife. I met her in Lagos, Nigeria, some years back.

At the ship, Alex was led into the radio room. I could not go with him there as a Westerner. A Russian officer invited me to the ship's restaurant and offered me a glass of Vodka.

Afterward, from far away, I took a picture of the ship. When I showed it to a navy man much later, he told me this was the silhouette of known Soviet spy ships, so no wonder Alex had first-class communication with his wife in Moscow.

STILL INSIDE KAMPUCHEA

Our trip to Kompong Som was to follow up on deliveries. The responsibility of the Kampuchean authorities, specifically the Ministry of Transport (MoT), was transferring trucks and other equipment to PNP or wherever needed. In addition, this Ministry was responsible for transporting relief supplies to the various distribution centers.

Our role was to monitor deliveries and distribution to beneficiaries. This was of great importance to the donors. John Saunders sent a SITREP at least once a week with all the details of what we were doing.

Regular meetings with the authorities, most frequently with the MoT, were necessary. These meetings were not always harmonious and friendly. With all due respect to our hosts, John Saunders pointed out discrepancies and inefficiencies. The authorities were sensitive to criticism. On the other hand, the donors wanted to know where their money was going.

The USA was the most critical, which, of course, was reciprocal. The Khmers, overseen by the Vietnamese and Russians, also mistrusted anything they thought was an American condition.

The Vietnam War, connected to the B-52 bombing of Cambodia before 1975, had only ended five years earlier. At this time, we had no American colleagues among our Unicef team. Still, there were American aid workers from NGOs in Kampuchea. Two organizations: Operation California and World Vision, come to mind. They had the same trouble on account of being Americans that we had.

Meanwhile, there was a change at the helm of Unicef in New York. Executive Director Henry Labouisse retired and was replaced by James Grant, both US citizens.

Grant came for a visit to PNP on May 1st, 1980. He had been in PNP briefly in January, but this time he stayed longer. He also visited various places in the field. I accompanied him to Prey Veng.

Grant was equally well and cordially received by Kampuchean Authorities and us aid peoples. His visit was highly opportune, as we were in a different operation phase. By now, trucks (logistics means) and food were coming into the country daily. They made it possible to effectively combat the famine. Various decisions on approach and strategy had to be made on the spot. Grant's authority was necessary to impress upon the Khmers that cooperation was essential for achieving positive results and saving lives.

The Khmers are great rice eaters; rice and fish are their staple diet. They also are great rice farmers, perhaps the best in the world. Before the seventies, their number one export commodity was rice.

I was at the PNP port daily to monitor food delivery. (I also like to be in ports and airports!) In April/May 1980, the arrival of food aid, seed, fertilizer, and other relief supplies was in full swing. The eight conveyor belts we bought in Japan were installed and used to their full extent. These foodstuffs were usually in fifty kg sacks.

Of course, there is always a certain amount of spilling. Sometimes a sack would burst and spill its content on the floor. When work was stopped in the evening after the unloading, Khmers with port access would come with little brooms and sweep every grain off the ground.

The Soviet Union sent maize (corn) of very crude quality. When this was offloaded, nobody swept the spills off the ground; it was left to the rats. My guide, Sok Lean, told me that people could not stomach maize; they would get sick when they ate it.

* * *

That time, April through June, was also the season

for planting floating rice. Hans Page, a countryman of mine, represented the Food and Agriculture Organization of the UN (FAO). Together with the Ministry of Agriculture, they established that more than 50,000 MT of rice seed was immediately required for planting.

There was a lot of political wrangling about how this quantity of seed could be brought into the country and distributed. Through their Ambassador in Bangkok, the USA wanted to have it "pushed" over the border, establishing a "land bridge" on the Thai border at Nong Chan. It was only forty km from there to Battambang, Kampuchea's main rice-growing area. This approach was opposed by the Authorities in PNP.

One has to know that in 1980 there were still many Khmer refugees living in camps on the Thai side of the border. They did not want to go back to their communist-ruled country. Thailand did not recognize the Heng Samrin government in PNP and still officially recognized the deposed dictator Pol Pot regime. (So did the UN in NY.) Pol Pot had withdrawn into the forests and mountains. It was obvious that he and his followers were getting help from Thailand. The ICRC also was concerned that rice farmers would use their scarce oxen and carts and waste time going to the border to collect rice instead of working in the fields.

In the end, the rice seed arrived more or less in time. Some sacks were pushed over the land bridge at the border, and more were received by two chartered DC-10 aircraft at the PNP airport, each loading fifty MT per flight. More seed was received by river-craft via the Mekong.

One thing was clear, the international community had done a good job during this first year of operation in furnishing sufficient rice for planting. Some reports in the global media suggesting that the farmers did not plant but ate the seed were absolutely not true.

My experience was that the Khmers are sincere and responsible people. In a remarkably short time after the collapse in 1979, they were self-sufficient and even started to export rice again. They could not have achieved this had they eaten the first shipments of seed sent by the international community.

I mentioned earlier that the GDR (East Germany) had donated one hundred fifty 5-ton, 4-WD trucks. They were called IFA and not known in the Western world at all. There was no "know-how" to maintain them in Kampuchea, nor were replacement parts obtainable anywhere. Therefore the GDR sent spare parts and four technicians from the factory in East Berlin.

Under the Ministry of Transport, these four engineers established a maintenance base. At this base, the IFA trucks and other trucks were maintained. There were at least eight hundred units in the relief operation by then. The engineers were rotated with others from the IFA factory every three months. I worked quite a bit with them. For instance, if they needed something for the maintenance base, parts, or tools, I could order it in Bangkok, and the items were in PNP in no time.

We became great friends. They took every opportunity to visit my room/office in the Samaki. In particular, I always had West German magazines (Der Spiegel, etc.), which I could ask for from our Bangkok support office. GDR personnel could not do such a thing. Their ambassador ensured they kept to the official East Berlin communist line.

They did not take the magazines away from my room but read them there. They also did not live in the Samaki Hotel but in the second hotel in PNP, then operational, called the Monorom.

On Saturday afternoons, we had friendly soccer matches with government officials in the great stadium in PNP. The East Germans were enthusiastic soccer players and were on our international side.

I remember we lost every single game. Against the Ministry of Foreign Affairs, we lost 7:3; against the Ministry of

Economy, we lost 5:3. I guess the heat made us poor players.

My room in the hotel had an air conditioner. Still, the electricity rarely worked, especially after 10 PM, so having an AC was useless. Often there was no water, which was even worse.

The Samaki had a swimming pool, but swimming was not advisable. There was no circulation of water, and it was green from algae. Once after they had just changed the water and cleaned the pool, I ventured in. Suddenly I found myself swimming in the same direction as a rat. That was scary.

KAMPUCHEA AFTERMATH

By the end of June 1980, when I left PNP after working there for three months, I was physically down. I was in Kampuchea during a very hot and humid time of the year. The temperature was something like New York in July or August but without the comfort of NY offices and apartments.

Furthermore, I spent most of my days at the port, warehouses, or vehicle maintenance facilities. When I returned to the Samaki Hotel, reports had to be written in the evenings. There were endless meetings with colleagues, the press, NGOs, and writers (William Shawcross, for instance) seven days a week.

There was no air-conditioning in the room and only cold water. Despite the heat, I would have liked a hot shower. There was often no water of any kind, so I was sometimes happy to get a cold shower. We had no choice where to eat, it was the Samaki Hotel, and the food was lousy. I had severe diarrhea four times in the three months I was there. There was no special diet when one got sick. The only cure was to not eat anything for two or three days. We could get medicine from our Red Cross colleagues.

Satisfaction? Yes, there was. I think we all in Kampuchea in those months after Pol Pot's ouster did a good job under difficult circumstances. Famine? The American Heritage Dictionary defines famine as "severe hunger, starvation." I have seen children with reddish hair, indicating "kwashiorkor" (severe malnutrition). But this was not widespread. I was not working in hospitals, so I may have missed something.

I have seen much worse in Sahelian Africa during droughts. The worst I have ever seen was in Ethiopia, where people literally died on the roadside. I know that many international officials who were in Kampuchea would disagree with me. No doubt there was "some sort of localized famine."

Kampuchea is not Ethiopia or Sahel region. It is an extremely fertile country with lots of rivers and lakes. There are fish and plants of many sorts. Besides rice, Khmers eat a lot of fish. They know how to catch and prepare them for conservation. Those who survived Pol Pot had a good chance of surviving the following year. After that time, Kampuchea was out of the most severe difficulties. International food aid came early and was efficient. I took part in this, and that makes me proud. The massive international assistance achieved its purpose.

Apart from killing millions of his people, Pol Pot and his Khmer Rouge almost wholly destroyed the country's infrastructure. Besides providing food aid, we helped to build up this infrastructure again. All these trucks, rivercraft, and bailey bridges. But we also assisted in building schools and reestablishing the education system. All this was to help the Khmers help themselves, and they have taken it up and done something positive with our help.

That must have been satisfying to donors and the many organizations involved. This is by no means always the case. I have seen international assistance money go down the drain many times.

Kampuchea is still a communist regime in the Chinese way. The problem then and now is still the politicians. One can say "despite" the politicians, Kampuchea is moving ahead.

Horst in Gaza

Doris in Gaza

The Equator

Horst in Syria

UN plane

Murchison Falls National Park

The funicular to Toni Nutti's island

Horst at a UN Conference

Horst at a Unicef well dedication

Horst & Doris

1981

KAMPUCHEA AGAIN

In April 1981, Unicef was still in the "Kampuchea Operation." In 1981, I was in charge of the Field Logistics Unit Supply Division at Headquarters in New York. In this capacity, I advised Unicef on all logistics matters. Furthermore, I was responsible for purchasing logistics items.

We did not provide Kampuchea with vehicles any longer. Still, we helped the Khmer maintain those we delivered the previous year. The government in PNP had no means to import spare parts or other things necessary to keep vehicles and river crafts in good repair from Western countries. They also had no convertible foreign currency to pay for spare parts.

I went to Kampuchea to research needs and survey the general transport situation. I traveled in a Red Cross (ICRC) Caravelle aircraft. I arrived in Phnom Penh one year after my first arrival. Unicef and other international organizations, and the remaining NGOs, were still in the Samaki Hotel, but many things there had improved. The pool was clean, and there weren't rats competing with the swimmers anymore. The food in the restaurant was edible.

East Germany still had technicians in PNP providing technical assistance. One of the GDR engineers from last year was in PNP for his second term. It was a big greeting when we met. I provided West German magazines again; they were still in demand.

Phnom Penh was a busy town. There were several restaurants where one could go and have a meal outside the hotel. In their own way, they had made progress. Schools were open. There were poor, but not hungry, people to be seen in the capital.

Pol Pot's Khmer Rouge was still holding out in the mountainous forests of Kampuchea. With sporadic attacks, they were a real menace to people in rural areas. But the Khmer Rouge was no longer a threat to the stability of Kampuchea.

My former guide Sok Lean was now a guide to another colleague. He was pleased when he saw me again. All the big trucks that we had provided were still running. The GDR technicians had done well, and Khmers are excellent mechanics.

Landmines were a big problem, also called "anti-personal mines." There were thousands in the fields. With topical rains pouring down during the rainy season, these mines were swept away and appeared in unpredictable locations. Thousands of people were killed or dangerously wounded. I have never seen so many young people with amputated legs.

1982

LEBANON EMERGENCY

For the Rüttinger Family, Lebanon is not just another country. We lived there from 1961 to 1964. Our youngest daughter, Andrea, was born in Beirut. Before we lived in Beirut, when we lived in Damascus and later in the Gaza Strip, we often visited the city and other places in Lebanon for holiday breaks.

In mid-June 1982, we lived in New York, and I worked at Unicef headquarters.

As in most emergencies, logistics was crucial when the "Lebanon Emergency" arose. For such events, we had a standing task force. We met on June 11th to discuss ways to get emergency supplies to Beirut as fast as possible and to other affected places in Lebanon.

In the summer of 1982, Israel fought heavily with Palestinians, who had practically taken over Lebanon. A civil war had been going on for several years in Lebanon. The Lebanese government was too weak to control the various Palestinian factions.

The civil war was not just Muslims against Christians; there were at least two groups of Muslims (Sunni and Shia Muslims). The Christians were also divided, and there was a sizable Druze population. Everyone fought everyone else, so from the early seventies onward, the county was divided into armed religious and ethnic enclaves, and Syria and Israel entered the conflict.

In June, in a surprise attack, Israel marched over the border to the north, up to Beirut. In just a few days, Beirut was encircled by Israeli forces. In the heavy fighting, as is usually the case, civilians, women, and children suffered the most.

It was summer, scorching in the Middle East, and the water supply was a problem. The infrastructure, including water mains and pumps, was damaged or could not be operated due to the lack of electricity. Many Lebanese and Palestinian families got displaced and looked for help, which undoubtedly they did not get from the warring factions. So again, the UN, of which Unicef is a part, the Red Cross (ICRC), and NGOs came to help.

On Friday, June 11th, in New York, we discussed ways and means to get emergency/relief supplies to the most affected areas. These were Beirut and Baalbek in the Bekaa Valley. We knew that other organizations intended to set up staging facilities in Cyprus.

I suggested we set up one for Unicef supplies in Damascus. Knowing the area well, I was sure there would be easier access to the Bekka and Beirut. Besides, in Syria, we could purchase many relief supplies locally and would not have to bring them in from the outside.

This proposal was eventually shared by all colleagues of the headquarters task force. Immediately our warehouse facility in Copenhagen (UNIPAC) was requested by phone and telex to prepare for loading supplies and charter an aircraft for Damascus. Our office in Geneva was asked to arrange Syria visas for Bent Aillaud, the Shipping Officer from Copenhagen, and me.

I flew to Geneva on Monday to pick up the visa, then to Copenhagen. I was on a B 707 freight plane on Tuesday morning, the second relief flight to Damascus. When I arrived in the Syrian capital, Bent, who had been on the first flight twelve hours earlier, was already on his way with a convoy and forty tons of relief supplies to Baalbek.

Our first relief convoy with emergency supplies direct

to Beirut left on June 21st from Damascus. I was traveling with this convoy, and we arrived there in the evening of that day. Other Organizations shipped their supplies to Cyprus, where they were stuck for some time because the port in Beirut was closed due to fighting in the port area.

Now, some statistics and information on relief/ emergency supplies. In these weeks and as a result of the fighting, it was estimated and later confirmed that some 300,000 Lebanese and 85,000 Palestinians required assistance such as shelter, medical aid, food, water, and sanitation. The needy people were particularly women and children.

We provided: baby food, medical supplies and vaccines, cooking utensils, kerosene stoves, blankets, large water tanks and jerrycans, tarpaulins and tents, mattresses, bars of soap and detergents, water purification tablets and insecticides, cooking oil and (important!) oral re-hydration tablets against diarrhea. Later we also provided water pumps and spare parts to repair damaged pumps.

In the first instance, these supplies were sent by four relief flights from the warehouse in Copenhagen, where emergency stock is always available. Later many of these things could be purchased in Syria. Many items from Syria fit local/regional specifications and could be bought at attractive prices.

Coming to Damascus was another sentimental journey for me. I lived there with my family from 1956 to 1960. Two of our daughters (Renate and Susanne) were born in the Syrian capital. I was with a German company in Damascus, just married. We met many people: Arabs and foreigners, some of whom are still our friends today. It was a good period in our lives. That was more than twenty years ago.

In June 1982, I had a memorable experience: one evening, my colleague Bent Aillaud and I went to the market, the famous "Souk-Hamedie." This is an interesting place to find everything, for instance, oriental jewelry, carpets, copper and brass pots, trays, etc.

As we strolled through the narrow, covered souk, we passed a shop I remembered from our days in Damascus. The owner sat outside the shop smoking his hubbly-bubbly (water pipe). When he saw me, he got up and said: "I know you." I know oriental sales talk and the strategies to get your attention.

However, before I could react, he continued, "Your wife has black hair and came regularly to my shop accompanied by a blond lady. They were both very good customers."

I was flabbergasted. The shopkeeper had indeed recognized me after more than twenty years. It was true, my wife's friend was blond, and they spent a lot of money in this shop. Of course, now I had to enter and buy some souvenirs. He also gave me a small ornament and asked me to bring it to my wife with best regards from his shop in Damascus. Bent was quite impressed with how popular I was with shopkeepers in the souk.

Speaking of the souk, we urgently needed about six hundred kerosene stoves for the emergency project in Lebanon. Such stoves are not found easily in Europe. Those used in our countries for camping are much too sophisticated to use in an Arab tent.

So we went to the souk and found a tinsmith with the right one. He had some, but not six hundred. He told us he would have the six hundred ready for delivery within an hour. He went around to all the tinsmiths in the street and got six hundred in total for a good price. That was impressive.

LEBANON II

One thing I don't do is discuss politics, except in very general terms, with local people, particularly not in a war situation. In my opinion, a UN official is unprofessional if he or she takes sides and discusses why something should or should not be.

Of course, having been involved in or following the news of the Middle East for a long time, we got a feel for what people thought, and sometimes they told us in no uncertain terms.

Lebanon has always had a problem with the balance between Muslims and Christians. The Christians say they are fifty percent of the population, but the Muslims say this has shifted and is no longer true. The President of Lebanon is always Christian, and the Prime Minister is always Sunni Muslim. Only when Iran became an Islamic Republic, due to the influence of the fundamentalists in Lebanon, did the Shias question this arrangement.

In our time, the Muslim population grew faster because of a higher birth rate. The Christians, with their President and control of the administration, made it easy for Christian Palestinians to become Lebanese citizens. Generally speaking, the Christians were better educated than the Muslims, particularly Palestinian Christians, so they got the best jobs.

Coming back to Lebanon and the emergency in 1982. In those days, the Israeli Army had encircled Beirut. You could easily tell one of their vehicles from an Arab one. They had red canvas at the back of their trucks and tanks. I guess it was for Israeli planes to easily spot their own vehicles and tell them apart from the enemy. In one incident I remember in East Beirut (the Christian part of the then-divided city), Israeli vehicles were among Arab civilian cars. Traffic was stopped at an intersection, and I heard an Arab shout: "Israel, you are welcome in Lebanon." None of the bystanders objected to this cry of sympathy for their, what should actually be, enemies. Now, this was in East Beirut. I am sure it could not have happened in West Beirut.

We international people traveled in white vehicles marked with the UN emblems. The Israelis were not friendly but correct to us. There were many roadblocks we had to pass. They gave us no preference over civilian traffic. They asked for identification but, when shown the ID, did not search our vehicles. I will have more on the relations between the UN and the Israel Army in those days.

LEBANON III

I want to say a few words about the personalities of the Unicef crew assigned to East Beirut in those days. Our office for Lebanon was in West Beirut. It's been there forever. But West Beirut was closed off in several ways, first by the various fighting Lebanese factions and secondly by the Israeli Army.

International personnel could cross over the "green border," as it was called. But this was always an unpredictable matter. For this reason, the second Beirut office was opened in Yarcee on the outskirts of town. There was only a handful of staff in this office. One of them was Gullmar Anderson, a police officer from Sweden and a proven manager in many emergency situations, bilaterally (Sweden) and internationally (Unicef, he was also in Cambodia).

Gullmar received our convoy at the Syrian/Lebanese border. I traveled there from Damascus in a UNDOF truck, but then I joined Gullmar in his Land Rover. He had a Radio in the car. UN vehicles in Lebanon at that time were equipped with this communication means for security. It was nice to see a colleague with whom I had worked previously in another part of the world. So we had quite a good talk. When our convoy was diverted off the highway into a Lebanese Army compound to be searched, Gullmar's radio came in handy. He was able to inform the UN in Beirut where we were.

When we finally arrived in Beirut-Yarcee, Abla Kadi, a locally employed Program Officer for health, received us. Abla Kadi was a Lebanese Druze. She was courageous and professional and always knew what to do next.

We stayed in her apartment in Ashrafie (East Beirut) with several colleagues. There was nowhere else to go. Abla later became an international staff member with Unicef and then served in Ethiopia (where I met her again) and Morocco.

I remember one incident in the early morning of this night we "camped" in her apartment. The whole night we heard cannon fire. It was scary. Just at daybreak, there was a lot of noise from the street below.

Local teenagers were engaged in a private but earnest and dangerous car race. Because of the narrow street, two cars contested against each other, then the winners fought it out for the first place. These were very young Lebanese, and I am sure their parents didn't just tolerate their escapades but were proud of their offspring. I was stunned and believed something like this could only happen in Lebanon.

Karl Larson of the South Lebanon Office had gotten married the day the Israeli Forces overran Qana. Now only a few days after his marriage, he was in the East Beirut Unicef office to report on the situation in the south and see what supplies he could get. He was accompanied by Morris Porter. Morris was British, a retired person who volunteered with Unicef in Qana. It is a special breed of people who spend their retirement helping mothers and children in a civil war situation. Those days were dangerous in Lebanon, and it wasn't a comfortable retirement.

After this two-day trip to Beirut, there were many things to do in Damascus. Bent Aillaud and I got office space in the Damascus Unicef Office. Of course, there was no war, civil or otherwise, in Syria. Life in the Syrian capital was quite normal.

The regular staff in the Unicef country office was busy with regular project work. Bent's and my role was to run the logistics operation for the Lebanon emergency project. We received two more charter flights with relief supplies from Copenhagen. Also, we searched the local market in Damascus for items needed in Lebanon.

There was the problem of a large refugee population in the Bekaa Valley, specifically in Baalbek. No fighting took place in this provincial capital. However, some fifty thousand people, eighty percent women and children, had fled from the South of Lebanon to Baalbek.

There was no shortage of food in Baalbek. But the newly arriving refugees had no money to buy food and other supplies. The local administration had no means to provide for these arriving refugees. They were housed in schools (it was vacation time) and tents; some found refuge with relatives.

Ancient Baalbek is just about 60 miles away from Damascus over the "Anti-Lebanon" mountain range. Baalbek is very well known for its tourist attractions. There are Roman temple ruins. When we lived in Damascus in the sixties, we came over to see concerts of the Berlin Philharmonics with Herbert von Karajan in the temple of Bacchus in Baalbek. That was a big social event. Time had changed dramatically. There were no tourists in Baalbek in the summer of 1982.

LEBANON-BEKAA

The third Unicef charter flight from Copenhagen, a load with 35 MT relief supplies, was received at the Damascus airport by Bent Aillaud and myself on 24th June 1982. We had hired three large commercial trucks with Syrian license plates. After loading the goods at the airport, we departed directly for Baalbek in Lebanon. The distance from the Syrian International Airport to Baalbek is just 80 miles.

I often traveled this route in the fifties when I lived with my family in Damascus. We traveled to the Bekaa Valley on holidays for many reasons.

Syria being mainly Islamic, Friday was our free day (TGIF!). Chtaura, just inside Lebanon, was a little town where we frequently shopped for groceries. Lebanese grocers had more items to our taste and liking at much better prices than in Damascus.

Between Chtaura and Baalbek is the experimental farm of the American University Beirut, Agriculture Department. We had very good American friends: Professor Steel and Professor Livingston, who were stationed in a beautiful setting with their young families on this farm. Their children and ours were the same age. We saw each other frequently.

When traveling in the Bekaa valley from Chtaura to the north, one could see this immensely fertile valley, about eight miles wide, guarded by mountain ranges, the "Anti Lebanon" mountains to the east and the "Lebanon" mountains to the west.

In ancient times, the Bekaa was called the "bread basket" of the Romans. There were a mix of Christian and Muslim villages on the slopes of these mountains. One could quickly tell which was which. Muslim villages had a mosque with a slender minaret in their center, and Christian villages had a church and a tower. There was also a monastery in a place called "Ksara." They had vineyards where the monks made the most delicious wine.

None of these basics appeared to have changed when we came with our convoy of three trucks and one white Unicef-marked Land Rover from Syria. We passed the Syrian border expecting to do immigration and customs formalities. When we came to the Lebanese border half a mile later, the customs and immigration houses were empty. "Why?" I thought. But the answer was simple: This part of Lebanon was occupied by the Syrian Army.

They confronted the Israeli Army to the South on Mt. Hermon. The Lebanese Army was not present here in those days. Thirty-five miles to the north of the border is Baalbek. We had no problems on our way. The roadblocks, manned with Syrians, just waved us through. I guess communication to these posts functioned, and we had our clearance from the border.

In addition to accompanying the convoy, Bent and I were assigned to investigate the general situation in Baalbek. Many refugee families were there due to the Israeli invasion of South Lebanon. In the Damascus Unicef office, we only had a vague idea and rumors about the situation there.

As mentioned in the previous installment, we found about fifty thousand refugees, eighty percent women and children. Later this number increased. Most of these refugees were Shia Muslims. It was common knowledge that in those days, Iranian agents came to the easily accessible Baalbek by way of Syria and established their questionable but important influence on these Lebanese and Palestinian Shia brothers.

In my opinion, that was when the "Hisbolla" gained importance and strength. Iranian agents in those days could not have gone to South Lebanon or anywhere else along the coast because there were Christian and Sunni Muslim factions, and nobody could pass these warlords unnoticed.

Northern Bekaa, however, was occupied by Syrians, who were sympathetic to the Iranians. (Syria always fought with Iraq!).

Initially, the Shia Muslims from the South of Lebanon were women and children. Later their husbands and young men followed. These destitute refugees were easy game for the Iranian agents: a gun, bombs, or other war material, a little money, and they were ready to do anything. Mainly they wanted to fight Israel. In addition, they were brainwashed and believed that this would be an easy matter.

Baalbek had quite an efficient administration, particularly an “Office of Social Development” (OSD). In no time, they had registered all the refugees. Thanks to this organization, the distribution of relief supplies was easy. There were also wounded Lebanese soldiers and civilians evacuated from the south in the general hospital in Baalbek. The Red Cross (ICRC) sent a German surgical team to help.

I remember one distinct observation that opened my eyes and understanding of the Bekaa Valley and Syria’s vital interests. We drove to a small village a short way up the hill, where we were told there were refugees and an OSD distribution center. From there, we had a beautiful view of northern Bekaa. There were endless fields, all green, a lovely green.

Innocently I asked what do they grow here? I was told it is all cannabis/marijuana. I was simply stunned. This vast area of marijuana. Can you imagine what they used the old Roman bread basket, the fertile Bekaa, for? So I thought, the Syrians are not just confronting the Israelis in the south. Their real interest must be in this stuff.

The Bekaa valley, going north, leads to Syrian territory and ends up in Latakia, the only Syrian outlet to the Mediterranean Sea. I had not read or heard about this marijuana-growing business before. It all made sense now.

As an outsider, when one hears about Lebanon, its civil war, and the Israeli invasion, one could think the whole country is in turmoil and flames. But several things were going on at the same time. Seemingly in perfect peace, farmers harvested fruit and vegetables in the fertile middle of the Bekaa, near Zahle, and marketed those in the whole Arabic region. While to the North of Baalbek, there were these endless fields of cannabis. Unbelievable.

We brought back a very realistic assessment of requirements in Baalbek. On the way home, we made several stops. Firstly we went to the farm of the American University Beirut. No Americans were left at this time, but the farm was still in business. Its head was Joe, an Armenian whom we knew. He was an assistant professor when we visited the farm in the fifties.

After that, I could not resist and stopped at the Ksara Monastery, where we bought a few bottles of their excellent red wine. My colleague Bent, a Dane from Copenhagen, soon grew fond of Ksara wines. Something else I could impress Bent with and show my knowledge of this part of the world.

In Chtaura, the Lebanese made a very special sandwich. It consists of a very thin flatbread, on it a sort of yogurt called "leban" and on this lots of spices. The flatbread was then rolled like a big cigar and eaten. It was delicious. An hour and one half later, we were back in our hotel, the comfortable Meridian in Damascus. From the duty point of view, I thought it was a successful mission to the Bekaa. For me personally, it was something as well; another sentimental journey.

SECOND TRIP TO BEIRUT

A few days later, sufficient relief supplies were accumulated, and Beirut was waiting. This time the UNDOF vehicles were not available to carry our supplies to Lebanon, so we hired four commercial trucks, each taking about fifteen MT, with Syrian license plates.

On June 28th, 1982, I led these trucks in a Unicef Land Rover with a Palestinian driver to Beirut. The direct route from Damascus to Beirut is only about 70 miles through the Bekaa and Chtaura, up the Lebanon mountain range, through Aley, and to Beirut. This short route was too uncertain and risky because of the different hostile factions in the Lebanon mountains. So, it was up to the north from Damascus to Homs, then to the west, passing the impressive, well-preserved crusader castle "Krak des Chevaliers" into North Lebanon.

Gullmar Anderson, Unicef Beirut-Yarzeh, was again at the border to receive us. He had done a good job in clearing our convoy as much as can be expected with the various factions. However, he had the bad news that the cargo had to be re-loaded onto local trucks with Lebanese license plates. Syrian trucks could not travel to Beirut. We re-loaded in Tripoli; there was no other way. Finally, we set off from Tripoli to Beirut along the coast, passing again through the various checkpoints manned by the Lebanese Army, the factions: Maradas (Muslims), Falangists (Christians), and finally, the Israelis on the outskirts of Beirut. All went well, and in the late evening, we arrived in Beirut.

Gullmar took me again to the apartment in Ashrafia for the night. Our cargo to Beirut was quite helpful, regular relief supplies like baby food, powdered skim milk, badly needed medical drugs for diarrhea control, kitchen sets, and kerosene cookers. But we also brought the critical spare parts for repairing water pumps. The restoration of the water supply to many communities and hospitals in Beirut and southern Lebanon was one of the most successful Unicef projects in those days.

A Lebanese engineer, Raymond Naimy, employed with Unicef, did an outstanding job. He was later officially commended by the UN Secretary-General in New York for his and his crew's excellent work. My involvement in this project was only to get some spare parts in Damascus and get them over to Beirut with this second convoy.

The following morning my driver and I set off for the return trip to Damascus. The coastal road from Beirut via Jounieh and Byblos to Tripoli was magnificent. Modern and sophisticated, Jounieh was the capital of the Lebanese Christians during these years of civil war. The exquisite "Casino du Liban" featured casino gambling and variety shows of Parisian standard. Jounieh also had a small port through which the Christians imported with suitable smaller vessels all their war supplies plus consumer goods, including luxurious items for high society Lebanese.

In Tripoli, we had a real scare. In this second-largest port city of Lebanon, there were mainly Sunni Muslims but also Christians. Generally, they lived together peacefully, each religious faction keeping to their area. But, on this day, when we traveled back to Damascus, there was fighting between the factions.

We stopped at a Sunni checkpoint and inquired whether we could use a particular road on the outskirts of Tripoli and were told that it was quite safe. However, while traveling on this road, suddenly, there was gunfire, and I saw the impact of bullets on the street. This was already unpleasant, but I thought they only meant to scare us. Then the driver stepped on the accelerator and drove like mad some two/three hundred meters until we were again in a "safe" zone.

I cannot now remember which frightened me more,

the gunfire or the driver's reaction and the speed we drove. We reached Damascus safely in the evening after a two-day, memorable second trip to Beirut.

Back in Damascus, I resumed what had become a regular duty, looking in the market (Souk) for items (spare parts for water pumps) that we needed for the Lebanon emergency program. On July 3rd, a cable came from New York, saying I had been nominated to represent Unicef in a "UN Survey Mission to Lebanon" that the UN Secretary-General had set up. Well, I thought, this is just about the most prestigious call I have ever received in my UN career. I should, the cable continued, instantly return to Beirut and join the team of Ambassador Anders Thunborg, who was named Chairman of this Inter-Agency Survey Team.

I took the direct route via Chtaura, Sofar, and Aley to Beirut this time. I thought I could risk the direct way without a truck convoy on my back, only me in a UN vehicle with a driver. Some four or five roadblocks were manned by warriors of different factions. It's always the same, Christians, Muslims, and, just before entering East Beirut, the Israelis. Nevertheless, it went without a hitch. I arrived safely in East Beirut, where the UN had set up a temporary office.

I met Ambassador Thunborg and the other mission members for the first time there. Edward Grunden, a Unicef colleague and education specialist, was nominated to reinforce our delegation. The other members came from sister organizations: FAO, WFP, WHO, and UNHCR, so we had specialists in all fields. We were twelve in all. Due to the insecurity in the present UN building, we moved up to the resort town of Bromana, high up the mountains above Beirut. There we stayed in the Al Bustan Hotel, where we could organize the implementation of the mission with the following objectives:

"On June 25th, 1982, in response to a request from the government of Lebanon, the Secretary-General set up an Inter-Agency Survey Mission under the Chairmanship of Ambassador Anders Thunborg of Sweden, which was to conduct a survey of the relief, rehabilitation, and reconstruction needs of the country. Based on its assessment, the mission is to recommend the type, scope, and priorities for international assistance."

Given our short time and the several places we had to assess, we split into three groups, each visiting a different area. I was with the group visiting the Bekaa Valley and Northern Lebanon. Partly because I had recent experience in the area.

I will never forget the evening before we left, each group to somewhere else. We had the most extraordinary experience in this luxury hotel.

Shortly after the Israeli invasion of Lebanon, the warring factions began fighting heavily. It was difficult for me or any of us to judge the military situation. Still, it appeared that the Israeli Army was not much concerned with this fighting between the Lebanese and Palestinians as long as they were not attacked. They weren't attacked because they were much too strong.

We were sitting up in the mountains in the Al Bustan Hotel. And had a very good dinner. There was no shortage of anything in this Christian part of Lebanon. We had a magnificent view of the city from our beautiful dining room. Up to Jounieh to the north and the airport to the south. While we were eating, suddenly, heavy cannon fire began. For at least two hours, we could see the most bizarre fireworks one could imagine. Cannon fire came from the inside of Beirut to the east side, and they (Christians) retaliated by the same means. Really weird. We were in splendid luxury; a few miles down the hill was destruction and death.

The following morning the four of us, the Bekaa group, left Bromana and took a small road over the Lebanon range down to Zahle in the Valley. This was a little scary because I do not think anyone except military personnel had traveled on this road since the outbreak of hostilities ten years earlier. In Zahle was our first contact with local authorities, but there was nothing for us to see or report. The center of our investigation was Baalbek. That was where there were displaced Lebanese and Palestinians from the South of Lebanon.

The Unicef inquiry I had done just a few days earlier was helpful. Soon we had all the information we needed. The figures had not changed very much; there were about fifty thousand refugees, mainly Lebanese but also Palestinian refugees.

We had to stay overnight in Balbeeck. There was a good hotel used in the good old days by tourists called the Palmyra Hotel. Its staff was pleased to have something to do, none had been dismissed, but tourists did not come in those days. They were all ready to serve us poor UN people. We had an excellent dinner and, of course, "Ksara" wine from the monastery.

The following morning we departed for northern Lebanon. We went up over the mountain range towards Tripoli. The first stop was Ehden, where we met the previous President of Lebanon, Souleiman Frangieh. He received us like royalty. He did not have many international visitors in his mountain village in those days.

Mr. Frangieh gave us a good appraisal of the situation in northern Lebanon. His village was not affected by current events. Some refugees had come from the south, but relatives absorbed these. The former President suggested we visit the former Prime Minister Rashid Karami in Tripoli. He gave him a call to advise him of our visit.

The Sunni Karami was Prime Minister when the Christian Frangieh was the President of the Republic a few years earlier. Both were, it seemed, friends. Rashid Karami also gave us a good idea of the situation. He was still very involved in the politics of his constituency. About seven thousand five hundred refugees had come to Tripoli from the south. Most stayed with relatives or were otherwise self-supporting.

I told Mr. Karami that I had been shot at when I passed Tripoli a few days earlier. He regretted this and said that these things could not be avoided. At the moment, he said, everything is quiet. Rashid Karami lived on one of the upper floors of a ten or twelve-story building. He received us in his study.

What impressed me most was his gallery of photos with signatures of the most famous people of that time. He had met them all in his long political career. There was Nixon, Carter, Wilson, our German President Heuss, you name them; their photos were in Karami's study.

Back in Beirut, the three groups of our survey team compiled their findings. This report was then combined with Ambassador Thunborg's report to the Secretary-General. Our findings allowed realistic fundraising and reconstruction projects to be planned.

That evening, we all sat together and spoke of our adventures. The group that went to the south had to contact the Israelis, not just the military. That must have been quite interesting. Israel had an "Inter-Departmental Coordination" section in the Ministry of Economy. They did not always see things as our people saw them.

Of course, it was difficult to tell whether the damages and refugees were caused by the Israeli invasion or civil warfare. Anyhow, I think our figures were quite realistic. After all, we were only interested in people in need; guilt was not our concern. We found that these events affected some 300,000 Lebanese and 83,000 Palestinians. These figures were accepted by the international donor community.

Well, after some more days in Beirut, and finally some days in Damascus, just a month after I left the Big Apple, I departed from the Damascus International Airport. I was returning to my family in New York City.

Seventeen years have passed since these events in Lebanon. Somehow the Lebanese have found a modus to live without shooting at each other. But the whole region, of course, has no peace, and this is a pity. With these potentially rich lands and industrious people on all sides, if there were peace, trade, and just living together, this region could be a formidable competitor, economically speaking, to Europe.

Fifty years of confrontation with many large and little wars should be enough. Perhaps now, as the Yugoslavian war comes to an end, Jews and Arabs will come to the conclusion that there is more to life than hating each other.

1983

SUPPLIES AND CHINA

Unicef spends a considerable amount of money on project supplies. In fact, at one point in the old days, Unicef was unfairly called a "Supply Organization" because more than seventy percent of funds are spent on program supplies.

In Unicef, countries are not assessed but donate voluntarily after pledging their contribution for an upcoming budget cycle. In addition to contributions to the general budget, states finance special projects they consider worthwhile implementing. Furthermore, funds from national committees worldwide are collected through fundraising activities, like selling the famous Unicef greeting cards.

In principle, no strings are attached to a donation, except in the case of specially financed projects, where the nature of the project is agreed upon. A donor country cannot demand that Unicef spend their donated money purchasing supplies in their country.

Generally speaking, purchases are made after public, international bidding, and only the best suitable item at the lowest cost is considered. "Suitability" is a significant factor. There is no use sending something to a country that cannot be used efficiently only because it is cheap.

Standardization also plays a role. This is particularly true for vehicles. One cannot send different makes and models each time transportation is needed, which might result from bidding. Maintenance and spare parts would be unmanageable. Countries and individual suppliers can legitimately contact Unicef and inform the Supply Division of their products and possibilities.

After this long introduction, I want to write about how

and why we were in China. China is a relative latecomer in UN development efforts (At least fifteen years ago when this story occurred!). On the one hand, it is a recipient of Unicef assistance and "know-how; on the other hand, it is also a potential supplier of a whole range of suitable project supplies.

The Ministry of Trade invited Unicef to come to Beijing (Peking) to teach government officials about Unicef's supply procedures in a workshop. Furthermore, we were invited to the International Trade Fair in Guangzhou (Canton) to learn more about China's capability to supply suitable items to Unicef.

In April 1983, five Supply Division staff, including myself, traveled to Beijing and conducted a one-week supply workshop with keenly interested Chinese government counterparts. After that, we flew to Guangzhou, formerly and better known in the Western world as "Canton."

This China airline plane was a Russian Ilyushin with a very narrow cabin. This flight was full up to the last seat. Even the jump seats were occupied.

I was squeezed into one of the seats. Once seated, it was impossible to get out again. Going to the bathroom during the flight was out of the question. My neighbor was a French-speaking Chinese businessman from Shanghai. We had a good conversation, and the flight lasted less than four hours.

During this time, I was absolutely pinned down in my seat. Service was not too bad; we were served food and drinks. On arrival in Guangzhou, I was anxious to find a bathroom. Still, we were received by an official delegation of the Trade Ministry, so I could not disappear immediately.

Finally, we were about to board two mini-busses waiting outside the terminal building. There I noticed, to my relief, toilet facilities. They were even marked in Western letters. I put my briefcase and jacket on one of the buses and told one of my colleagues that I was going to the restroom and would be back in a moment.

I was not away for more than, say, three minutes. Nevertheless, when I returned, both buses and my briefcase were gone. I was in an almost total state of shock when I realized I was alone at the Airport in Guangzhou. I had no ID or money, nor did I know where we would be staying. I went to the airline counter. Nobody spoke or was willing to speak a word of English. I tried everything to find someone with whom I could communicate in English, French, or German. No luck; nobody understood any of these languages.

Soon I had the feeling that nobody wanted to, or was allowed to, speak to a foreigner. There were so many people around, but I was the loneliest person in all of China. Finally, I just sat somewhere in the arrival hall and thought somebody would have to come and collect me.

That took a long time. I later learned that the airport was twenty-five km from the hotel on a bustling road with many traffic jams. More than an hour later, as I was sitting like an abandoned child on a bench, an official came back and looked for me.

The colleague to whom I said I would be back in a moment had forgotten about it and thought I was on the other bus. My friendly colleagues noticed my absence when my briefcase and jacket remained on the hotel bus. Only then were the officials alarmed. One bus rushed back to the airport. The official of the Trade Ministry greeted me with many apologies. I was genuinely relieved and pleased when I arrived at the Tong Fang Hotel and saw everyone else again.

Now that was in 1983, seventeen years ago. But we had another experience that shows how China was in those days. I hope things have changed since then; at least I know many tourists are now traveling to the country.

We got the program for the four days of our stay in Guangzhou. Apart from visiting the International Trade Fair, the government also wanted to entertain us. We were invited to the Great Hall of the People to see Peter Tchaikovsky's Swan Lake on the second evening. I like that ballet very much, and Arne Jensen, our director, also enjoys ballet.

When we went there the following day with our official

escort, there were a few other Western guests, but not many. When the curtain finally rose, the music started to magnificent stage scenery. But the Chinese spectators were not quiet but chatted away and noisily unwrapped foodstuff for at least fifteen more minutes. That was very unusual for us. The performance was of a very high standard and compared with what I have seen at NY City Opera.

We noticed that nobody, except us Westerners, applauded. When the performance ended, people just stood up and left with no applause whatsoever. But we, about thirty Westerners, gave them a standing ovation for ten minutes, and I think the dancers and actors were pleased. They deserved it.

The next day, we had a free evening. Arne Jensen and I thought we would like to see the ballet again, as we liked it so much. So we walked to the Great Hall of the People to buy tickets. And here is my second experience: nobody sold us tickets or wanted to admit us to the theater.

Nobody spoke English. They just pretended not to understand what we wanted. We were sure that there were unoccupied places as there had been the previous evening. It seemed that even fewer people were present that evening. Very frustrated, we left the Great Hall of the People in Canton.

* * *

The international Fair was interesting in several aspects. There were state companies with Western standards in presenting their products. Very professional salespeople demonstrated what they sold. They spoke English, French, or German, and one would not think of oneself as being in a communist country that had just opened to the West. These were, in particular, textile, paper, and pharmaceutical product firms.

Then again, others could not sell a thing to visitors from the West. For instance, there was in the fair yard a jeeplike 4-WD utility vehicle. As this was my line of business in Unicef, I went and had a look. There was nobody around whom I could ask about it. The vehicle was closed and very dusty.

Finally, somebody came. I tried to explain that I wanted to know more about that Jeep. The person did not speak English, and bystanders had to translate. Finally, he went to get the key. It took him half an hour before he was back. Well, you can imagine that the manufacturer of this Jeep never appeared on our list of suitable bidders.

TO SOMALIA BEFORE CHRISTMAS

In December 1983, I was posted at headquarters in New York. I was in charge of the "Field Logistics Unit." There were only two of us and one secretary. We were general trouble shooters on all supply matters. We also provided advice on program logistics and supplies to our field offices worldwide.

Having traveled extensively that year, Doris and I looked forward to some quiet holidays. We were supposed to be united with our daughters for Christmas. On December 9th, Arne Jensen, our Danish director of the Supply Division, then my boss, came into my office and said he had bad news.

"You need to fly immediately to Mogadishu, Somalia. On the way, you should also see about some business in our Regional Office in Nairobi."

"Why me?" I replied. It seemed to me that some people in the Division never traveled. "Would I be back for Christmas?"

It turned out that there was a program preview meeting in Mogadishu commencing December 18th. Somebody from Supply/Logistics needed to participate in that meeting. The other HQ divisions and the Regional Office in Nairobi would also send support staff.

I never said no if asked to do even an almost impossible thing. So, I said "OK, I will go." I did some calculations. How could I be back by December 24th, considering that flights in and out of Mogadishu were not frequent and the meeting only started on December 18th? I went to our travel office in the building. And sure enough, air connections from Somalia were as difficult as I thought they would be.

However, it was possible to fly on a Thursday (Dec.22nd) from Mogadishu to Jeddah by "Saudia-Airline," from there take a Lufthansa flight to Frankfurt, and the following morning another Lufthansa to New York. It seemed OK. The problem was that I did not have a visa for Saudi Arabia, and there was no time to obtain one. I thought I could get a transit visa in Mogadishu at the consulate there. Our office there could arrange this for me. So I left New York on Sunday evening, December 11th, for Frankfurt, from there to Nairobi and later, together with other colleagues of the Regional Office, to Mogadishu. From Nairobi, only two and a half hours.

Somalia became only known to many people in America and Europe in the early nineties when things went completely out of control. Somali Militia tribesmen went berserk and dragged a dead American soldier tied by his feet to a jeep through Mogadishu. That was terrible, but Somalia existed before that event, and it was not unpleasant to visit that country in the past.

Even then and more nowadays, it is a very poor county. The UN has classified some 22 countries as "LDC," meaning least developed countries; Somalia is one of them. For that meeting, the Unicef colleagues from other countries and I stayed in the "Al Aruba" Hotel near the port, with a lovely view of the Indian Ocean. The place was a nice hotel but, like everything else in Somalia, "a little run down."

We had a good, productive meeting and, in the evenings, pleasant get-together parties. Most of us had known each other for many years, having met elsewhere and even being stationed together in other parts of the world. We were a big family in Unicef.

Mogadishu was, and still is, what is known in the UN as a "hardship duty station." Food, accommodation, schooling, and health services all are a problem. On an event, such as the program preview meeting described above, when colleagues and friends from outside the station, New York, Nairobi, etc., came, that was really something stimulating for the colleagues stationed there. And all this just before Christmas.

We had serious meetings and hard work, but we also had a good time. With us was Mary Racelis, the Regional Director for East Africa. She was from the Philippines. (Unicef has a good “gender” record, with an equal percentage of highly educated and qualified women in higher positions.) I knew Mary from many years of working together, particularly when she was at headquarters in New York. So, despite the “hardship station” and work, we had a good time just before the holidays.

Then I remembered my Saudi Arabia visa situation and went to the Saudi Consul, who conveniently was also the Saudia Airlines agent. He said he could not issue me a visa in that short time. He would have to refer back to his government to do so. But he continued that it was not required for direct transit, meaning not leaving Jeddah Airport. That was fair enough for me, I did not intend to leave the airport anyhow, but at this point, I did not know how complicated the airport in Jeddah was.

With the meeting over, and work done, I left Mogadishu on December 22nd for Jeddah, a relatively short flight. Given Somalia postal service, I carried season greeting letters from colleagues by the dozens to Frankfurt and New York. No business travelers were on board. It was mostly Somalis, bound for the Gulf States, not necessarily Saudi Arabia, in search of work. There were no other air connections to the Arabian peninsula. Later it turned out that none of my travel companions had a visa.

We arrived in Jeddah at a terminal for local flights, not the international one from where I was supposed to take my connecting flight to Frankfurt. They had the most strict immigration procedures and baggage checks I had ever experienced in an airport. The officials were extremely unfriendly. Of course, they searched for alcohol, but I expected this. I definitely would not, even in transit, carry a bottle of whiskey in my baggage.

Having no visa, I was placed under guard and felt like a prisoner. I was driven in the company of heavily armed men in a military Land Rover to the International Terminal. My treatment was rough but still relatively decent compared to the treatment of the Somalis that were with me on that flight. They were treated like dirt. I had not seen this in my life. I am particularly bothered if I see racial discrimination. That was definitely not "typically Arab." We lived in Arab countries for a long time and never had reason to complain about bad treatment.

The International Terminal might almost have been called normal. I checked my baggage with Lufthansa and went through the security arrangements. Of course, there was no lounge in the departure hall where one could have an alcoholic beverage, and I still had plenty of time.

There were the gates for several international departures. One of the airliners parked out there was a Pakistan International plane. At this gate, I saw another example of uncivilized Saudi Arabian behavior. About twenty oriental-looking men, handcuffed and heavily guarded, were driven like cattle to the gangway. I was told that these were foreign workers in Saudi Arabia who had somehow "sinned" and were now being expelled from the country (perhaps they drank "Eau de Cologne" for alcohol or looked at a Saudi woman?) Well, I had had enough. What I saw at the Jeddah Airport reminded me of the old slave trade.

By now, it was almost midnight, and my flight was called. The plane was full to the last seat, all German businessmen, technicians, and specialists working in Saudi Arabia. Everyone was, at this time, heading home for the holidays.

The plane was still rolling on takeoff when all hands went up for the service call bottom. Apparently familiar with this particular route, the stewardess laughed and shouted, yes, yes, we are coming. Well, these travelers, mostly men, had been in dry Saudi Arabia for months, and now that they were on a German airliner, they needed a drink. Earlier than usual: the stewards opened the bar for these poor souls during takeoff.

Nobody asked for food, which we later got anyhow. The traveler beside me, who had lived in Saudi Arabia for several years, confirmed my observations. Western technicians and business people, unless they bring in drugs and/or alcohol, have nothing to complain about in Saudi Arabia and earn very good money. But domestic and other lower-grade workers, usually from Asian countries, have a much more difficult life, although by the standards of their home countries, they, too, earn good wages.

I had a delay of several hours in Frankfurt. Finally, I was on another Lufthansa airliner to New York, where I arrived in the afternoon. After all this travel, change of climate and time, and sitting for hours in a narrow airline seat, I was dead tired. The next day was Christmas Eve. The whole family was together for a lovely dinner, and we were all pleased.

However, I did not last long. I fell asleep under the Christmas tree. They let me sleep and did not wake me up.

1984

COCKROACHES

I encountered the "German" cockroach in New York, a little bigger than a fly. (Notice how Americans call these roaches, which we sometimes saw in Waterside, the "German" cockroach, and there is also "German" measles, but there is, on the other hand, the "American" Eagle. Well, I must be fair; there are "German" shepherds too).

If you were the kind of person to do this, you could crush one under your thumb. I would like to see someone crush one of those huge Ivorian cockroaches under their thumb.

We always tried to keep them under control in the house. It worked by sprinkling "Baygon" powder on the threshold. That worked most of the year, but there was a period in the spring when cockroaches, an inch long or more, did not crawl over the threshold but flew.

Inevitably they came into the house, hiding somewhere, laying thousands or more of those jelly eggs, which breed new cockroaches. A constant battle.

Doris could never step on a cockroach, but she could kill it by taking off one shoe, using it like a hammer, and hitting the roach with the heel (She was good at aiming, keeping a little in front of the roach's path). We had our share of experiences with these insects. None of us gets overly excited seeing one.

They live in humid climates. We battled them mainly in Beirut, Gaza, and Abidjan. They are rare in Damascus and Kampala.

ANDREA IN KENYA

As you may expect, our daughters grew up protected. In a clean and comfortable environment. In the Middle East and in Africa, we were always a "minority." Being a "minority" could be quite different in different locations. For example, being Hispanic in New England or Turkish in Germany.

We were better off than the majority of citizens. We always had a proper house, air-conditioned, where it was hot and protected against mosquitoes. We always had running hot and cold water. We had sufficient food, a housemaid, or male help.

We did not particularly overprotect our daughters. They got the feeling of poorer Africa too. My previous story on the trip by car to Mali is an example.

When we were in the US (stationed at Unicef headquarters), Andrea, our youngest, went to a college in Vermont after attending the UN International School in New York. In the fall of 1984, she signed up for a "Semester Abroad." She went to Kenya for five months with the School for International Training in Brattleboro, VT. They were some twenty students in this semester abroad program.

Andrea was the only non-American girl with African experience. There was one Egyptian student. The program was hosted by the University of Nairobi. Activities were studies in Swahili; Work camp in which they dug a water well; living for some weeks with a Kenyan family in Nairobi; working for some time on a coffee farm.

It so happened that I was on an official mission in East Africa while Andrea was there. I spent some days in Nairobi, where she lived with a Kenyan family.

Independence Day came up, and for this festivity, the lawn of the Jomo Kenyatta Stadium had to be in perfect condition for the parade. It was irrigated for weeks before. That was of national importance and had the highest priority.

Because of the water shortage, the water supply for houses near the Kenyatta stadium was shut off. Andrea's host family lived just next to that Stadium and had no water for days.

It was handy that Daddy was in a good hotel in the city. Andrea came and took showers in the hotel as long as I remained in Nairobi.

During that semester in Nairobi, the students used public transport: crowded minibusses called "matatus" (general matatu-rule: there is always room for another person!). They ate local food.

Andrea was given a simple room in a farmhouse when she worked on a coffee farm for the program. After some days, an African lady came in a flashy Mercedes. It turned out that she was the sister of the previous Kenyan President, Kenyatta. She owned the coffee farm and managed it herself.

She took a liking to Andrea and took her to various places, including the coffee auctions. That was very interesting for her. She might not otherwise have seen it.

Andrea came home to New York just before the Christmas holidays. She was very excited and told us about her experience. One thing, in particular, made us think. She said: "Although I lived with you for eleven years in both East and West Africa, I never saw Africa the way I did during these five months when I was on my own in Kenya." (Baring the showers in Daddy's hotel room!)

AFGHANISTAN II

My second visit to Kabul was in the autumn of 1984. It was a short mission on routine supply matters. In December 1979, the USSR marched into Afghanistan and was soon in Kabul. President Hafizullah Amin was killed, which is quite customary in this country. Presidents in power during a coup d'Etat usually did not survive.

The Russians brought their own man. Babrak Karmal was installed as the President of Afghanistan. The Russians found themselves getting more and more isolated. Recall the boycott of the Olympic games in Moscow in 1980, when Western countries did not send their athletes because of the Soviet invasion of Afghanistan.

During my visit in 1984, the USSR still occupied the country. They had difficulty fighting off the Mujahideen freedom fighters, who they called rebels. With all their military might, the Russians could not win against them. The fighting and rocket attacks on Kabul caused damage to the capital. Many houses were destroyed.

We needed to rent warehouse space for storing supplies temporarily before they could be distributed. I was shown a military installation that the Russians had left shortly before, a hangar where soldiers had lived.

I never saw such a mess, the whole place was vandalized, and I was told it was the way the occupation forces used to live. Shocking. The mood of the Afghans was somber and depressed. I was pleased when I could leave after only three days. More than nine years after the invasion in February 1989, the USSR troops left Afghanistan. It was their Vietnam, no doubt.

1985

ETHIOPIA

It was different when I landed at Addis Ababa International Airport on October 8th, 1985. I had been to Ethiopia on shorter missions many times before, but this time I came to stay for quite a while. Addis was my new duty station. The organization transferred me out of New York to Africa.

Being an international civil servant, one must expect to be posted at any time, anywhere in the world. Doris and I had our share of transfers and changes of living place many times, but now we were well settled in New York and did not want to move again. We had two of our daughters with us in the USA. Doris had found a good job with the German Information Center. Our life had become somewhat "normal."

Also, we had heard about an extreme shortage of accommodation in the Ethiopian capital. Where would we stay? We decided I should go to Addis alone, and Doris would remain in New York.

Unicef sweetened my transfer by giving me a handsome promotion. I had been on a mission to Ethiopia only in January of that year and had made several recommendations on program logistics, so Unicef probably thought: "This man knows logistics, let's send him there to implement his own recommendations."

The emergency situation in the country had gone from bad to worse. There were several reasons for this: first, an extreme drought, particularly in the rough, mountainous part north of Addis Ababa. Secondly, the socialistic regime of "the leader" Mengistu Haile was not helping overcome food shortages and other problems. Third, the war with Eritrea was draining the last resources from the country.

* * *

I moved into the Addis-Hilton. It was full of international aid people. Everybody lived in a hotel, as other accommodations were unavailable in the city. The choices were not great, as no tourists were in the country in those years.

My new assignment was to the special office of the Assistant Secretary-General for Emergency Operations in Ethiopia. Emergency supplies, particularly food aid, came to the country from all over the world. Our function was to coordinate the arrival and distribution of this aid.

There were some spectacular pictures shown on the television news. Planes arrived at Addis Airport with medical stores and food. Much as this was appreciated, an aircraft full of supplies is just a drop of water on a hot stone. There were nine million people affected by the drought and hungry. Only surface transportation could bring sufficient quantities of food to cause an impact.

There were only two harbors in Ethiopia: Assab and Massawa. Both are now in Eritrea, but this province was part of Ethiopia then. A third possible port of entry was Djibouti, an independent country, from where a rather inefficient railroad, "Ethio-Djibouti," connected to Addis Ababa.

From June 1985 to July 1986, about 1.2 million MT (metric tons) of emergency supplies (mostly food aid) arrived in the port of Assab. To imagine the magnitude of this tonnage, one would have to consider that a truck/trailer combination carries about 22 MT and that the most affected drought region was north of Addis, more than one thousand kilometers away from the coast, over rough and mountainous roads. This tonnage amounted to 55,000 truckloads, and therefore 152 trucks had to leave the port daily just to transport emergency supplies. That is not counting regular commercial supplies. The whole country was not in an emergency, and life continued.

The road from Assab to the most drought-affected areas is formidable. Every truck carrying twenty-two tons had to navigate the distance, some via Addis Ababa. Others turned east at Eloha to Bati, Desi, and on. The second choice was shorter, but the road was worse.

Nevertheless, both ways are of great diversity as far as physical configuration and climate are concerned. Shortly after Assab, a steep climb up to Mt. Musa Ali, then equally sheer downhill into a deep valley and up again. This terrain compares in size and features with the great canyons of Arizona.

Imagine standing on the North Rim of the Grand Canyon, looking down to the Colorado River, and then up to the South Rim. Now you have to drive a big truck through this valley. Admittedly there are no roads but hiking trails at the Grand Canyon. The roads through this valley in Ethiopia are tarred but narrow and have many potholes. It is tremendously hot down in the valley.

My respect for the Ethiopian truck drivers grew each time I drove in a Land Rover through the valley. In addition, I admired the few private transport entrepreneurs who remained in the then socialist/communist Ethiopia of the 80s. Many of these transporters performed more round trips to the port than the trucks of the state-owned modern transport fleet. Unlike the latter, private truck owners had no access to spare parts and tires. I saw thirty year and older Fiat trucks and admired the drivers and also the mechanics who managed to keep them on the road.

Here is an interesting story concerning birds. I am not an ornithologist, which is a pity because Ethiopia has beautiful and exotic birds. There were hundreds of fat birds sitting on the Assab road. They looked like gray pigeons. Unfortunately, I hit quite a few when I drove the Land Rover over that road. I felt bad about it. I thought, why don't they fly away like other birds do when a vehicle approaches.

Reflecting on this and discussing it with other road users, it transpired that because of the thousands of tonnes of grain transported by hundreds of trucks daily over this road, there is naturally some spilling from the sacks. There was good food for the birds to be found on that road. Being well nourished and fat as these pigeons were, they lost speed and flexibility. They were fast enough to fly away when a slow truck approached but too slow to take off quickly when a much faster Land Rover came along. There were very few passenger vehicles traveling on this road in those days.

One of the mandates of the Assistant Secretary-General for Emergency Operations in Ethiopia, particularly the duty of his Logistics Officer, was to monitor arrivals, food requirements, warehouse holdings, and distribution. Not an easy task in the vast country of Ethiopia. One of the most drought-affected areas was the mountains about one hundred miles north of Addis Ababa. Roads to these mountain villages were so bad that only small 4-wheel drive trucks could be used. During the rainy season, surface travel was impossible. In the dry period, a vehicle would take one week to complete a round trip.

There were people in desperate need of food. At the beginning of 1985, the Assistant Secretary-General for Emergency Operations, Kurt Jansson from Finland, proposed a food airdrop operation for the mountain people. This airdrop operation even got a name, *"TESFA,"* which in Amharic means: "Hope." Multi-agency and bilateral efforts began to get *TESFA* on its way. On January 26th, 1985, a Royal Airforce Hercules dropped the first sixteen MT of food at three pm.

In the autumn of 1985, the British Royal Airforce (RAF), the German (West) Luftwaffe, and the Polish Airforce, with several helicopters, were engaged in *TESFA,* the airdrop operation in these mountains. The pilots and crews had surely done airdrops elsewhere. Perhaps it was even part of their military training. But I was told every terrain is different, and the material being dropped must be considered.

TESFA called for dropping bags of grain on a very

rough target not larger than a soccer field. Experience had been gained in the past months. However, with the changing situation and particularity of drop sites, it was still learning by doing.

The Royal Airforce flew the Lockheed C 130, a 4-propeller craft called “Hercules.” The Hercules carried some sixteen MT of food on these missions. The Luftwaffe flew 2-propeller Transall aircraft carrying ten MT of food. Both types had tailgates by which the food was dropped. The RAF dropped from about six to eight meters, and the Germans managed to descend to only two meters.

It is hard to believe, but the British results, as far as breakage was concerned, were better than the German results. The RAF and the Luftwaffe shared one camp. A big tent at the Addis Ababa Airport, and one can imagine their disputes about these results.

Various techniques were tried. Food was repacked into twenty-five kg bags at the Addis Airport. Great attention was given to packing. Each bag consisted of two sacks, an inner and an outer one. They were not too tightly filled, and sufficient free space in both bags allowed the contents to expand on impact. The sacks were stacked on wooden pallets, usually thirty-six bags per pallet. These were destroyed on impact but dampened the shock like a cushion.

There were always disputes between pilots, loadmasters, and those packing. In the end, techniques were so refined that not more than five percent of bags burst on impact. But there was no wastage. After the dropping operation, hundreds of men, women, and children rushed to the field and swept every grain from the ground.

The Polish helicopters flew ahead of the large transport planes. They carried a crew to prepare the ground and set the markers to indicate the airdrop zone. The helicopters also had a medical team of one doctor and two nurses to provide services to the population while the craft was on the ground. The locations were difficult to reach for the national health service.

One Thursday in October 1985, I had an opportunity to fly with an RAF Hercules on an airdrop mission to Lemi in the Wollo province, 120 miles north of Addis Ababa. The captain invited me to sit behind the two pilots on the flight deck of the big plane, the best place to watch the takeoff from high altitude at Addis Ababa International Airport.

I set my stopwatch, and after exactly twenty-eight minutes in flight, we were over the drop area. As we circled the site, I observed the white helicopter from the Polish Airforce. The co-pilot pointed out the markers. Critically, the field needed to be kept clear while the dropping was done. People were quite disciplined and remained outside the area, waiting for what would fall down from heaven.

Then came the approach for the first "life run." The co-pilot lay down and looked through some sort of an aiming device. By radio, he issued instructions to the cargo bay of the Hercules.

The plane made a total of four runs. Four MT went through the open tailgate on each run. I remained on the flight deck for the first two, watching the impressive approach to that high plateau coming over a steep valley towards a wild cliff. The plane flew approximately twenty-five feet over the field, then made the drop. Circling the drop site took about five minutes.

For the last two runs, I went to the aircraft's rear. Of course, like the rest of the crew, I had to put a harness around my waist and was hooked to a steel cable that ran alongside the cargo room. The rear door was open. It was a little frightening. While the plane was circling, the four airmen prepared for the next drop. They moved four stakes on pallets to the very rear of the aircraft. This was hard work, and they had to do it fast.

The loadmaster directed the men. He was in radio contact with the aiming pilot, and when he got the signal, the airmen pushed the pallets through the gate and out of the aircraft, using all their strength. It was good that they were hooked to that steel cable.

Though scared, I ventured to the rear and looked down while the plane circled over this roughed, wild canyon. About eighteen minutes over the dropping area, the Hercules headed South towards Addis, where we landed after about an hour and a half in the air. Mission number one was completed for the RAF crew. They would make another three flights that day, dropping sixty tons of food for the needy people of Lemi. I was genuinely impressed by the operation and thought it was commendable for military aircraft to be used to drop food. Much better than dropping bombs.

One afterthought: 1985 was the peak of the Ethiopian famine. The cold war was still on, but, at this time, there was absolutely no problem for the RAF, German Luftwaffe, Belgian military people, or us UN staff communicating and working together with colleagues from the USSR, the Polish Airforce, East Germans, etc. We had one mutual job to do: bring relief to drought-stricken Ethiopia. A year later, relations became difficult again when the worst emergency was over. Coffee with a Polish helicopter pilot in an RAF tent was no longer possible.

ETHIOPIA AGAIN

Many of my stories are about Ethiopia. It is one African country I have been to more than many others. I was very actively involved in the 1985/86 drought. It is said that eight million Ethiopians are presently affected by famine. During the previous famine, nine million people were affected.

The basis for logistics is different this time. Ethiopia no longer has access to the sea. During the 1985/86 campaign, Ethiopia and Eritrea were still one country. Consequently, Assab, in Eritrea, was the main port of entry for all relief supplies.

Eritrea is now separated from Ethiopia, and the countries are at war. Therefore the port of Assab is no longer an option for landing food for the needy. The UN is debating, at this time, where aid should enter. There is, of course, Djibouti, the traditional port for the "old" imperial Ethiopia. Djibouti is linked by rail to Addis Ababa. Still, neither the port nor the railway has sufficient capacity for a big food import operation.

So the UN is now considering the port of Berbera in Northern Somalia as a port of entry for relief supplies. Roads from Berbera to drought-affected areas in northeastern Ethiopia are partly nonexistent. Fifteen years ago, we had a good infrastructure, with an efficient port in Assab and a tarred road up to Addis Ababa. There is nothing of the sort from Berbera. That is a mindboggling challenge, a shocking road over desert tracks through a wild, lawless country (Somalia). I was there and can testify to it.

But on the other hand, a little honesty might be appropriate. The donor community is responding to emergencies made by nature. It is unfair to say the world is standing idle while people are starving from famine. During the last fifty years, Ethiopia has received a fair share of money spent by donors.

What have the Ethiopians done in the last fifteen years since the previous drought? Have they prepared for the next one, sure to come? No! Have they built up food stocks for new droughts, which occur inevitably in this part of the world? No! Have they negotiated a necessary treaty with Eritrea for the use of Assab as a port of entry for commercial and relief supplies? No!

Even now, when relief organizations rush to bring food to hungry Ethiopians, they fight another senseless, stupid border war with neighboring Eritrea, which is said to cost one million US dollars daily. This border war over an infertile piece of land kills thousands of people. In contrast, the donor community is trying to save lives. Isn't this ridiculous? They fight a senseless, costly war with Eritrea and expect the world community to feed their people.

There are many other emergencies, mostly natural calamities, but also some man-made disasters. There was a flood in Mozambique recently, which left large portions of the harvest destroyed. Also, the Sahelian countries Kenya, Somalia, Sudan, Eritrea, and Djibouti need help. New fighting is going on in the Eastern part of the Congo. So, plenty of opportunity for donors to spend money on relief operations.

THE ROAD TO ASSAB

Many stories could be written about the highway that connects the Red Sea port of Assab to the very core of Ethiopia with its large populous centers of Nazareth, Debre Zeit, and finally, Addis Ababa. Almost 600 miles long, the road is not too bad by Ethiopian standards. Its surface is tarred throughout. However, it is a narrow road, and some sections are dangerous.

I wrote about this road in my story entitled “Ethiopia.” I want to add a further bizarre episode to the saga. Assab was Ethiopia’s main port of entry in 1985 when this story took place. However, Assab was in Eritrean territory, and with the separation and independence of Eritrea from Ethiopia, the latter no longer had an outlet to the sea. It was now a landlocked country surrounded by hostile neighbors.

I believe this fact is the real reason for the fighting between Eritrea and Ethiopia over the last several years.

In 1985, after Emperor Haile Selassie had been ousted, Ethiopia was a socialist (say communist) country. The whole infrastructure was nationalized and accordingly inefficient. The bureaucracy was tremendous, which did not help combat the country’s drought situation.

At that time, Unicef was supplying some utility vehicles for the mobility of assisted projects. I remember there were twenty Toyota vehicles, some pick-up trucks, and some Landcruisers to transport project personnel. Theoretically, the principle was that Unicef’s responsibility ended at the ship’s tackle at the port’s wharf. As all commercial forwarders were nationalized, they had an Ethiopian state forwarding agency that was supposed to do the port clearance and forward these vehicles to Addis.

It took weeks. The vehicles were needed to begin a national vaccination campaign at the Ministry of Health in Addis. Besides inefficient procedures, money was missing for clearing charges and hiring drivers to drive the vehicles over the Assab road to their destination in Addis Ababa.

It made no sense to delay a campaign because a relatively small sum of money could not be obtained. Everything else was ready to extend this campaign to rural areas, but vehicles were needed. So as many times before, Unicef paid the national forwarding agent the port charges and hired the drivers.

As our payment was theoretically only a reimbursement of expenses, it could not be construed that the drivers hired by the forwarder were Unicef employees. Nor had we anything to do with selecting them and checking their ability to drive a motor vehicle. All this was done by the government through their nationalized forwarder.

Later it occurred to us that they checked the Communist party identity cards, but not the driving licenses, of the men. There are excellent drivers in Ethiopia, and I highly admire them. I have written about it in other stories. Those hired to bring these new Toyota vehicles to Addis didn't have the required skills for the Assab road.

On the first escarpment, one of the Toyotas left the road and dived into a deep precipice. This accident killed the driver and made the vehicle a total write-off. A second driver recovered the body of his deceased comrade and put him on the back of his new Toyota pick-up truck.

On the next escarpment down, some 120 miles further, this pick-up also had an accident. The driver drove it into a deep ditch. He was thrown out of the vehicle and was severely injured. Soon it turned out that he was paralyzed from the waist down.

All this was tragic and shocking for us when we heard it. These drivers were not qualified to drive at all, particularly not on the dangerous Assab road. The saga went on. Only a few days later, the families of the deceased and the injured drivers came to the Unicef office in Addis and claimed compensation. They made the point that their loved ones were Unicef employees. What followed were lengthy negotiations involving the two families, Unicef, and the government (They should have known better, but they took the side of the families).

Eventually, the case was submitted to the UN Legal Department in New York. The UN did not recognize any responsibility for the grave results of these accidents. After lengthy discussions on a humanitarian basis, Unicef paid a certain sum (I think it was five thousand US dollars each) to help the families without accepting a legal responsibility. It was then expressively only a voluntary contribution for their losses.

Considering the dangerous narrow winding Assab road and crossing two valleys similar to the Grand Canyon in Colorado, there were not too many accidents because, as I said above, the regular Ethiopian drivers are excellent and solid professionals.

GIRL IN THE ELEVATOR

When I was in Ethiopia in 1985/86, the country was run along socialist lines by a "Provisional Military government." The head of State was the arch-communist Mengistu Haile Mariam. So everything went the socialistic, highly inefficient way. Nobody dared to decide anything.

When I arrived in Addis Ababa in October 1985, I took a room in a hotel. I immediately applied for an apartment. These were scarce in the city. All housing was centrally administered and allocated by a government housing committee. I stayed for more than ten months in the hotel.

Finally, I got a two-bedroom apartment on Churchill Road, which is not a bad location. The house was not new, but the apartment was renovated. I was content.

The apartment was on the fourth floor, which was the top. There was an elevator, but I never trusted the thing and usually just walked up and down the four flights, which gave me a little exercise.

I was the only "Ferenji" living in the house. My neighbors were all well-to-do Ethiopians by socialist standards. Foreigners were called "Ferenji," it was not meant to be discriminating; supposedly, it was a friendly pet name.

Beneath my apartment on the third floor lived a nice couple. Both were with Ethiopian Airways. He was the captain of a Boeing 707, and the missus was a stewardess with this prestigious state airline. There was a twelve-to-fourteen-year-old girl with them, obviously their housemaid.

It was common for poor young girls from the countryside to be given away as servants to a family, even in this socialist country. Actually, we would call it "child labor" or child abuse. In Ethiopia, it had been traditional for hundreds of years. Now, I think that the young girl with my downstairs neighbors was, in a way, lucky. "Her" family was probably a "good" one and did not abuse her.

One evening I left the apartment on my way out for a meal in a restaurant. In the stairway were many people. The whole house was there, all chatting at the same time.

What was this all about? Somebody told me the elevator got stuck between the second and third floors, with the housemaid of my airline neighbors inside. This old-fashioned elevator was the open type with only a steel trellised gate. One could see inside the cabin. I saw the girl, she was very frightened.

One of the spectators told me they had already sent a message to the head of the "kebele" (the lead official of the neighborhood) and asked for an elevator man to come and get the cabin moved and opened. There were not too many elevators in use. Consequently, an elevator repair person was difficult to find. Not just any technician could rescue the girl; in the socialist way, it had to be a "comrade technician" approved by the party.

There was no use for me to stay. I went to the restaurant and met a few people. We had a nice dinner and conversation. It was about 10:30 PM when I got home. All the people were still in the stairway, and the girl was still stuck in the elevator.

The neighbors told me that two men sent by the "kebele" were already there, and they could do nothing. Tomorrow morning a real elevator specialist would come and get the girl out. I felt very sorry for the girl; she was very unhappy. I wanted to help her get out.

I was not too knowledgeable about how an elevator functions. However, I thought there must be a way to manually crank the elevator to the next stop, where the gate could be opened.

The airline neighbor spoke English, and I asked them for a flashlight. We went together upstairs to the little machine room. There I found what I was looking for, a wheel obviously for manual use. I turned the wheel carefully. Suddenly the electric motor started to run, the elevator moved, and that was it.

When we came down to the elevator, the girl was free, with tears in her eyes. She kissed my hands. The joy of my fellow tenants was unbelievable. I, the "Ferenji," was their great hero. The airline captain and his wife invited me for a drink (Normally, Ethiopians had no good (imported) liquor in those days. Still, airline people, even in socialist Ethiopia, were an exception). We became quite good friends.

Well, on the following day, the elevator specialist did not come. Still, the elevator was working anyhow and gave no more trouble. I still did not use it. I walked up and down the stairs. I did not trust the thing!

VOLUNTEERS

I have written a bit about "volunteers." This is important because, in my experience, it is often not understood by those officials requesting volunteers nor by the volunteers themselves where their services are helpful and where they are counterproductive. Furthermore, many underestimate the costs of volunteering in a foreign, faraway country.

Although these countries are called "underdeveloped," that does not necessarily mean that individuals of such a country are any less educated than many of the volunteers are. Governments with whom we cooperate in assisted programs know, of course, who of the expatriates provided by the organization is a volunteer and who is a professional. They want the professional but do accept, under certain circumstances, a volunteer.

Missing the required qualifications and experience, a young volunteer who just finished college cannot do the work of a professional. The officials of recipient countries know this. So there is the question of whether they accept the advice they are given, which is essential. Many local, qualified women or men in a project know more than the foreign expert.

Two things get in their way: Firstly, their pay is much less than the pay of a foreign expert, even less than the "pocket money" of a volunteer. Therefore the motivation of locals is low. Secondly, there is a saying: "The prophet is not listened to in his own country." I have repeatedly experienced a qualified local transport officer making a proposal to his superior in a government ministry and not being listened to. If I made the same proposal as a foreign "expert," it was accepted.

It is mindboggling if one considers the waste of

resources: money, and people, because of this attitude in high government officials. That reminds me of a quiz recounted among colleagues; Question: "Do you know who is an expert?" Answer: "Anyone who is five miles away from home!"

In this connection, I include the story "Pop Singer" below. It really happened and proves, at least to me, that you need knowledge and experience. Good intentions and willingness to help are not enough.

BAND-AID

In Ethiopia, in 1985, a severe drought struck the country. Because of the secrecy the socialist government had introduced after Emperor Haile Selassie was ousted, the rest of the world did not note this drought. The government of Ethiopia was too proud to ask for help until a British TV team was allowed in and produced a hair-raising horror film report of people reduced to skeletons, dying by the thousands, because of hunger and disease.

The reaction that this TV report produced was phenomenal. Aid organizations from the UN and bilateral and non-governmental organizations (NGOs) scrambled to help and rushed to Addis Ababa. I was immediately sent from Unicef and stayed for two years.

At that time, there was a well-known Irish pop singer, Bob Geldorf. He was rich, a philanthropist. And I might say a little arrogant. He flew to Addis Ababa and went straight to the government, announcing he had come to help.

"What do you need?" he asked.

"We need as many motor vehicles (trucks) as possible," they immediately told him. (In my opinion, this was not a priority!)

The setup in Ethiopia at this time was, on the government side, there was the Relief and Rehabilitation Commission (RRC). The UN Office of Emergency Operation (UNEOE) was on the donor side, headed by a special coordinator. I was put in second place in UNEOE by Unicef. The coordinator at that time was Kurt Jansson, from Finland, with whom I had worked in Cambodia.

UNEOE was recognized by all donor organizations

as the emergency coordinating body. We held regular meetings with donors to avoid duplication of efforts. RRC often requested assistance from different organizations. In particular to get more motor vehicles.

Bob Geldorf met briefly, and reluctantly, with Jansson, probably thinking: "Why should I bother with UN bureaucrats?" I was present at part of this meeting. He told Jansson of the creation of "Band-Aid" ("Band" meaning band of musicians) further that he was going to immediately provide one hundred heavy-duty trucks.

We told him that several donors already intended to donate heavy trucks. And also, it would be advantageous if fleet standardization were considered. ("Standardization" means trucks of the same make and type, size of tires, etc.) That would facilitate serviceability and provision of spare parts. In socialist Ethiopia, spare parts were in extremely short supply and only available for a limited number of trucks.

I told Geldorf that Unicef had a large procurement section with professional purchasing agents. And offered to assist Band-Aid in getting the right trucks to fill his promised donation. He thanked us but said Band-Aid was quite capable and could buy the trucks needed at an excellent price.

Well, with all my knowledge of procurement and transport experience of some eighteen years in Africa, I felt a little inferior to this pop singer who seemed to know it better than I did. As I wrote above, Bob Geldorf was a bit arrogant. Next, we heard Band-Aid apparently secured a real bargain. Now I started to feel even more inferior.

Here it comes: there was an opportunity to buy some 80 trucks from a Saudi Transport Company in Saudi Arabia, not even 300 miles away across the Red Sea from Ethiopia. "Very little used," "In good condition" (by Arab standards), "Ready for immediate delivery," and best of all, only half the price of new trucks. The make of the trucks was "Magirus," a German manufacturer. There were no other Magirus trucks, spare parts, or service facilities in the country.

Weeks passed. New trucks from other donors arrived in Ethiopia. They were immediately used for food transportation from the port of Assab to the drought-stricken area North of Addis. "Where on earth are the Band-Aid trucks?" was a daily question in UNEOE. Shipping them across the Red Sea to Assab should not be too difficult. Cables went forth and back to Band-Aid in the UK. No trucks in sight!

As the time passed, I got my satisfaction. I was fully restored as a transportation expert among my colleagues who, I am sure, had earlier thought that Bob Geldorf knew more about heavy-duty trucks than I did.

Several things were revealed. The trucks were, in fact, "Very little used" but had been parked for some three years in the open, exposed to sand and sun in Saudi Arabia. They were not in running condition to be driven to a port for shipment.

The manufacturer, Magirus in Germany, was alerted and sent, at Band-Aid's expense, a team of service engineers to Saudi Arabia to get these trucks back in operation. That took a lot of time. Then, the trucks were shipped with several small vessels to Assab. That, too, took time.

On arrival, the Ethiopian customs demanded quite a substantial amount of customs fees. It took weeks. The vehicles were standing idle until the matter was cleared. I am unsure whether the fees were paid in the end. This hassle could have been avoided altogether had the trucks come under the UN umbrella.

Finally, the trucks were loaded in Assab for their first trip up north. Several Magirus trucks left the town of Assab in convoy. The big day had come. As they reached the Danakil Depression, one tire after the other blew out. The spare tires were soon all used up, and the convoy halted. The tires, having been mounted unprotected on trucks parked for years under the Saudi Arabian sun, were brittle and unsafe, as can be imagined. Those tires could not withstand the heavy load and renewed heat of the Danakil Desert.

The saga goes on. With their original specifications for

Saudi Arabia, these trucks were equipped with special tire sizes specifically useful for operation in that country. Tire sizes for trucks do not necessarily depend on the vehicle's make. But, those to be replaced now were nowhere to be found in Ethiopia.

Again cables went to Band-Aid in the UK. New, non-standard tires were bought and sent by air to Ethiopia. Later there were endless troubles with these second-hand Magirus trucks, and no expertise was available in the country. The manufacturer in Germany assigned, at the account of Band-Aid, a crew of German servicemen to Assab to keep the trucks running.

That was the story of a pop-singer philanthropist. Who tried to be a transportation expert and dropped the ball.

COMPUTERS

I have had a lifelong interest in the technology of computers. My first "computing device" was an electronic calculator in the sixties, when other people still used mechanical calculating machines. Apart from an early specialized computer in the Finance Department, Unicef started to get computerized in the late seventies and early eighties.

NY Headquarters were, of course, the first to put the old typewriters away and install workstations hooked up to a WANG mainframe computer. In those years, there were no PCs available.

Secretaries (in UN terminology: "General Service Staff") were the only ones given the machines initially. (The others, including myself, were "Professional Staff." I personally never understood this distinction.) I thought from the beginning that this was a waste of resources. Given the power of modern computers, why should these only be operated by secretaries.

Soon, however, management realized that professionals, too, should be computer literate. I applied for and was among the first professionals in headquarters trained to use a workstation. I used it extensively and had a good arrangement with my American secretary. I drafted every memo, report, and letter on the computer, saved, and gave them to the secretary for editing (Unfortunately, I was never a good writer, and spelling was my weak point).

There was quite a resistance by professional colleagues, I should say older colleagues, to sit at a workstation and operate the computer. Some were afraid of the new technology, which they knew nothing about. Others simply thought it was beneath their dignity to sit at a keyboard and type. I guess they had sworn to themselves never to go back to a typewriter and mistakenly saw the computer's keyboard as one of a typewriter. It was hard to convince them that using a computer did not mean returning to general service work.

In Supply Division, some professional colleagues, usually women, who originally started in the organization in the general service category as secretaries or clerks, earned a reclassification into the professional category. They did this with hard work, including obtaining a degree in evening classes. They were rightly very proud of this achievement.

Then came the PC and, with it, the possibility to also computerize Unicef's field offices. The beginning was difficult and depended more or less on whether or not the particular office had someone interested and skillful enough to install and make themselves familiar with the machines. And further to train the staff in the use of computers. Regional offices, such as Nairobi, employed knowledgeable staff, but smaller field offices could not do this.

When I arrived in Addis Ababa in the summer of 1985, there were lots of WANG-PCs still in their shipping crates. They had arrived several months earlier. Nobody opened the boxes and installed the PCs. I spoke to the representative, a lady from India. She told me they were waiting for someone from the Regional Office to set up the PCs, and she did not know when this would happen.

I suggested we do it ourselves and presented myself as a "computer expert." (Remember the definition of an "expert": anyone more than five miles away from home is an expert.) She agreed, and we unpacked the machines. In those first years, Unicef standardized on WANG computers. Wang had its own operating system, WANG-DOS, incompatible with IBM DOS. At that time, WANG had quite an advanced, efficient word-processing program and a Lotus spreadsheet program.

Soon I found several Ethiopian employees in the Addis office who were extraordinarily talented and enthusiastic about learning to use a PC. There was Tserha, a mother of four children. She worked in the field office's Finance Section and had never seen a computer. It was amazing to watch her rapid progress and the logic with which she handled this new technology. We created a computer club called "WUG" (Wang User Group) and even met outside office hours. Anyone could participate.

Even our Ethiopian drivers wanted to learn word processing and how to use a PC. Tserha soon became our chief instructor. She was very good at using the Lotus spreadsheet program, which was particularly useful in finance.

About six months later, a lady computer specialist came from Nairobi to introduce the Addis office staff to the use of computers. We all already knew more than she did. She could not teach us anything we did not already know by self-teaching.

Later in my travels around Unicef field offices, I made similar observations about the "local" staff. Some twenty years ago, many arrogant snobs thought computers were only for Western-educated people. Not so, Africans and other young employees of developing countries were keenly interested in this new technology.

1986

ERITREA

Eritrea is now an independent country. It was not when I was there on a mission in January 1986. During the last hundred years, Eritrean history was an example of what could go wrong in an African country when foreign powers dictate what they think is right.

In 1890 Eritrea became an Italian colony. They possessed the two Red Sea ports of Massawa and Assab. In 1935 the "Duce" Benito Mussolini built up a powerful military force and marched from Eritrea into Ethiopia.

With his troops mainly armed with spears, bows and arrows, and some shotguns, the Emperor, Haile Selassie, could not resist the modern Italian army. He fled into exile in Britain. After six years of occupation, the British threw the Italians out of Ethiopia in 1941. The Emperor returned to his homeland.

After WWII, the British put Haile Selassie back in power in Eritrea without asking its people. He integrated Eritrea into Ethiopia, again without the people's consent. Shortly after that, the Eritreans got together, founded the ELF (Eritrean Liberation Front), and fought Ethiopia, first the Emperor, and later Mengistu, the communist, for thirty years.

During the last phase of their struggle for independence, the ELF found an ally, namely the rebels of the Tigre Province. Finally, they gained their independence in 1989.

With Eritrean independence, the two Red Sea ports, Massawa and Assab, were lost to Ethiopia. With the only other port along this shoreline, Djibouti, a (small) sovereign state by itself, Ethiopia now has no access to the sea. I venture to say that this is one of the principal underlying causes for the present stubborn fighting between Eritrea and Ethiopia.

However, Ethiopia maintains it is about a piece of desert land.

After this rather lengthy introduction, I would like to write about my visit to Eritrea in January 1986. Again a worst-case scenario: extreme drought combined with the long war against Ethiopia and widespread famine. In the mid-eighties, Ethiopia was only partly affected by dryness. Southern Ethiopia was not. But Eritrea was totally crippled by the drought. Ethiopian forces controlled the big towns like Asmara, Adigrat, Massawa, and Kerem, and the ELF held the rest of the country.

The "lifeline" for Asmara was the road from the port city of Massawa to Asmara, about eighty miles. During the day, this road was "open," meaning military escorts protected convoys of trucks making their way up the steep winding road from the port to the capital. Convoys to other government-controlled centers were also protected by the Ethiopian army.

I traveled with a UN Landcruiser, a Unicef driver, and an Asmara-based colleague along this road to Massawa. Leaving after daybreak, we traveled in an escorted convoy of vehicles. The countryside is overwhelmingly beautiful. During the Italian time, there was a railroad from Asmara to Massawa. The track is still visible; even the rails are partly in place.

In Massawa was the small private Luna Hotel, owned by Sen. Mario, a left-behind Italian. We were lucky to find accommodation there. The state-run hotels are terrible. Sen. Mario was renowned all over East Africa for his excellent cuisine. The hotel was situated on the fish-rich Red Sea. Naturally, the main dishes were fish of all sorts. Except for some international aid officials like us, no foreigners or tourists were in town. So we had the royal treatment.

Our mission was, of course, not to test Sen. Mario's cuisine. There were problems with the offtake from the port. UN agencies, the ICRC, and NGOs had insufficient trucks to transport all the delivered food. We had to rely on transport from the National Transport Corporation (NATRACO) to transport food aid for their hungry population.

However, the Ethiopian army often requisitioned NATRACO trucks to transport military hardware. The port had an “off-limits” section where USSR ships endlessly delivered war material. NATRACO trucks often stood by for the army, creating a backlog in the port offtake. Although a civilian “coordinator” was responsible for negotiating between the military and international aid organizations, we could do nothing to improve this situation.

Back in Asmara, I stayed in an old Italian-style hotel called the “Ambasoira” The owner was an elderly Signora. I felt like I was in Italy, which certainly left its stamp on Eritrea, particularly Asmara. Italian is the language mainly spoken to foreigners. If you cannot reply when being addressed, they switch to English.

I stayed at the Ambasoira for three nights. The ELF rebels penetrated the town every night, and one could hear gunfire and sometimes explosions. It was a bit scary lying in bed and hearing these war noises. I am not a brave man.

Here again, we had problems with the offtake of food aid from warehouses in the capital and transportation to Eritrea’s interior. Truck convoys depended on escorts by the army. The road to Keren, sixty miles north of Asmara, was relatively safe during the daytime. This road was also open from both ends between eight am and two pm. It was less well maintained but caused no problems for the trucks.

There is a catholic mission, a hospital, and a large catholic school, run by missionaries, including some Italians. They also took care of food distribution and could do so relatively undisturbed. We thought they were protected by the EFL. In turn, of course, the EFL got food. I noticed this in other places, too; the valid currency for protection is food. Soldiers and rebels alike cannot fight on an empty stomach.

Back in Asmara once more, we visited the ICRC installation. A convoy of sixteen trucks had returned from Mekele, two hundred miles each way. The convoy delivered 340 MT of food to this center in the Tigre Province. They were escorted by the Ethiopian army and needed twelve days for the round trip. Even longer delays were experienced by a World Vision International (WVI) convoy, which had been held up for three weeks in Adwa, Tigre Province, on the way to ancient Axum.

At this point, I want to mention and pay tribute to the hard work of the truck drivers in this operation. Being on such trips through hostile territory by convoy is certainly no fun. They are bossed around by the army escorts, and threatened by rebels and/or government soldiers, in hot weather on dusty bad roads. These drivers most likely can't even appreciate the beauty of this mountainous, wild part of East Africa.

PERSONAL CAR

One story on Ethiopia I wanted to write. This happened when I collected my new Volkswagen at the port of Assab and drove it to Addis Ababa. As a member of a UN Organization, I was entitled to bring in a personal car free of customs and other taxes.

I ordered a new VW-Golf Diesel (VW-Rabbit in the US) at the factory. After three months, I was told the car had arrived in Assab. I decided to go there myself and collect it. I had to inspect the port operation twice a month anyway.

At the same time, there were two delegations from donor countries, one from Australia and one from the USA. They wanted to see the port situation, in particular, because there had been press reports about inefficiency and waste of food aid.

I remember Senator Kerry Sibraa was a member of the Australian delegation; his views were critical but fair. We were some fifteen people, so the Australian and the United States Embassy decided to charter a De Havilland Twin Otter from Ethiopian Airways to make the journey.

I represented the UN Emergency Operation. After two and a half hours flight, we reached Assab. It was hot. As a significant international donor delegation, we were received by the port manager and some other officials. After the usual welcome formality, we were driven to the port.

I knew there were no surprises to be expected because I had the arrival and departure figures. Ethiopians are not always efficient, but they are honest. Assab had, due to the influx of emergency shipments, about three times its usual handling. The port worked twenty-four hours, seven days a week.

The Ethiopians managed reasonably well. There is a certain amount of spillage in any offloading operation of bulk grain. That was not different in Assab. They had swept this into a corner.

Several weeks ago, there had been a heap of spilled wheat when a TV team came and visited the port and took pictures of it from all angles. These pictures were shown in several Western countries. Naturally, donor countries were worried about the "waste" of food aid in Ethiopia.

Hence the visit of the donor contingent to Assab on that Monday, February 3rd, 1986. Members of the delegation were critical and even criticized some aspects of the port operation, particularly the bureaucracy involved with the dispatch of trucks. However, they were satisfied that there was no unusual spillage or waste of food aid.

* * *

NOTE: Here is a development: as I write this story on the inspection of the port situation by donor representatives, radio reports say that Ethiopian military planes have bombarded the airport in Assab just today. At this point, I recall the installment entitled "Eritrea," in which I ventured to say that the principal underlying cause for the present (June 99) renewed fighting between Eritrea and Ethiopia is that Ethiopia lost access to the sea when Eritrea became an independent country.

Assab is on Eritrean territory. Only a modest strip of unpopulated desert land connects Assab with the rest of Eritrea. When they gained independence in the early nineties, they signed an agreement for the usage of the port by Ethiopia. With the present fighting between the two, this agreement seems dead. I would not be surprised if next, we hear of an impending attack and takeover of this port by Ethiopian forces. Mark my words!

Bombing this airport by itself is a joke, but it could also mark the beginning of a takeover. This airport consists only of a runway and a shack, surrounded by sand dunes. I landed many times on this airfield and know it. The runway can be repaired within hours, and I do not think Eritrea has any air force to speak of.

* * *

Now let us return to February 3rd, 1986, when I collected my car in Assab: In the early afternoon, the delegation returned by plane to Addis Ababa. I had some more business to do, but then, with the help of our port clearing agent, I started formalities to get my VW Rabbit out of customs bond. Karl Marx once said: "trusting someone is good. Controlling him is better."

In Socialist-Ethiopia of the eighties, an enormous bureaucracy had developed, almost crippling the country. Nobody trusted anybody, and no decisions were taken by anybody. Stamped papers were required for the most trifling thing.

I learned my lesson when I cleared that car in Assab with the idea of driving it away from the port, thus saving time and money. Most UN and other international people ask the state clearing agent to bring a newly shipped personal car from Assab to Addis. That took a month and more and was costly.

It took me only(!) two days. I had to go through countless port/customs officials. I got many rubber stamps, which had to be certified by other officials. The car had to be repeatedly inspected. The chassis number and engine number were verified three times.

Finally, I had to get fuel for the trip to Addis. Not only did I have to get the car's tank filled, but I also needed a spare fuel container because refueling on the road to Addis was impossible.

When I flew to Assab, there was a free seat on the plane. I brought my Ethiopian driver along. His name was Ato (for Mr.) Kiefle. He was a tremendous help, not just in driving the car to Addis but in clearing customs at the port as well.

Two days after we arrived, we left Assab at five am.

We wanted to travel early, in any case, before the daily truck convoys with food left the port because, on this road, it was almost impossible to overtake a single truck, even less a convoy of trucks.

Some fifty miles out of Assab and after we had crossed a mountain range, we reached the "Danakil Depression," a desert similar to "Death Valley" in California: low, hot, and dry. Now it paid off that we had left early. We crossed part of this desert in the cool morning. Once the sun rose, temperatures of 110-120 F were soon reached. Anyhow, my new VW Diesel performed excellently. We were two and could alternate driving.

On this road, there was one thing I will remember for a very long time. It is the tremendous hospitality an ordinary Ethiopian woman extended to the driver and me. We knew this road would not have exciting food or refreshment facilities. There were little "truck stops" where one could at least have a coffee or a Coke.

Coffee originally comes from the "Keffa" province south of Addis Ababa. From there, it reached Europe, the US, and the rest of the world. Coffee is one of the exported goods of Ethiopia. Even during the socialistic time of Mengistu Haile, coffee was shipped worldwide. Preparing coffee in Ethiopia is a solemn ceremony. It takes time. Women mainly do it, and with such grace, it is unbelievable. When finished, it is served like "espresso" in small cups and sweet.

So much for the introduction; now for the story. At one point on the trip, we stopped near what we thought was a little restaurant where truck drivers got their refreshments. However, we must have made a mistake when we entered the restaurant.

We entered a small house and sat down at a low table. When a woman came, we asked for coffee. The woman said nothing but went to her fireplace in the hut, where a charcoal fire was burning. She prepared two cups of coffee for us in the authentic ceremonial way of the country.

It was a joy to watch her do it. We had the coffee and got

a glass of water, customarily drunk with coffee. (For obvious reasons, I did not drink the water.) I wanted to pay when I finished, but the woman refused to take the money. We then realized that this hut was not part of the truck stop.

I was embarrassed that I had taken her coffee and could not pay, but this was out of the question. My driver advised me I should not insist. Anyhow there were some stores in that village. With the driver's help, I got two pounds of sugar, a commodity much in demand. She accepted the sugar with many thanks and kissed my hand. This incident made me feel very warm toward the ordinary people of Ethiopia.

We drove six hundred and fifty miles. Most of the road, except for the last eighty miles, is desert and hot. There are two deep valleys to cross, a scenery as spectacular as the grand canyon. The road was narrow and long stretches were in poor condition. At about 5:30 pm, after twelve hours of driving in adverse conditions, we reached Addis Ababa. It was raining, and I loved it.

SUSANNE'S VISIT TO ADDIS

I had been in Addis Ababa for a year when I got the good news that daughter Susanne was coming to visit her poor lonely father. She came in October 1986. At that time, I had just moved out of the hotel and settled into my apartment.

Susanne can tell some of her own stories about her visit to Ethiopia. Africa was not new to her. She had been with us in Kampala, Uganda, for six years. When we were posted in Abidjan, Ivory Coast, she had come twice a year from her boarding school in Germany.

During her visit to Ethiopia, I had to travel to one of our Unicef projects in Arba Minch (Amharic for forty springs!), the provincial capital of the Gama-Gofa province. I asked permission from the office for Susanne to accompany me on this duty trip.

We set off in a Toyota Landcruiser for the five hundred and ten km trip to Arba Minch. Half of this road was asphalted; the rest was dirt, in not too bad condition. After some flat tires and a vehicle brake problem, we arrived at the Becala Mola Hotel. Our trip took about twelve hours.

Dinner was, of course, fish. This was a change, as there is no fresh fish in Addis. There are eight big lakes near Arba Minch, two of the biggest being Lake Abaya and Lake Chamo.

The following morning I had discussions at the health department. Susanne and our driver went down to Lake Chamo during this time. They got a boat and ventured out onto the lake. It must have been quite an adventure. There were literally hundreds of crocodiles, and they, with a local fisherman, were very vulnerable in a small wooden boat.

I was scared when I heard about it afterward, and I blamed the driver. "You should know better," I told him.

From Arba Minch, I had to visit a hospital some forty km away, which participated in the Unicef-assisted basic health services project. It is high up in the mountains at a place called Chencha. It was about the smallest hospital in Ethiopia, with only twelve beds. The doctor in charge was assigned from the German bilateral aid program.

He invited us for a cup of tea. He was a bachelor, and his house was, mildly speaking, a bit messy. But he was very nice. Apart from being a medical doctor, he was also a mechanic, an electrician, a gardener, and a cook. Being a doctor in a mountain hospital, one has to be

Another thing about Susanne in Ethiopia, we played a lot of tennis, and she always beat me. Not once did she let me win, ungrateful girl. When she left, she sold the tennis racquet she had brought from New York to a Swede. For him, it was an opportunity to buy a high-quality racquet. For Susanne, it was easy to replace it when she returned to the States.

WAR AND PEACE

Several happenings these days are occupying my mind: Reports of heavy fighting between Ethiopian and Eritrean forces at their border, The G-8 summit in Cologne, and, of course, the crisis in Yugoslav over Kosovo.

The seven biggest industrialized nations, and Russia, are having their annual meeting in Cologne, Germany. One agenda point is waiving repayments of debts from the least developed countries (LDC), thus giving them a chance for a new beginning. I am all for this. This proposal has my wholehearted support.

Having said this, I believe such renunciation of debt repayment must depend on conditions. For example, Ethiopia and Eritrea are among the poorest countries in the world. Their present fighting for a piece of desert land is idiotic. More seriously, it's irresponsible toward their own population. Any plans for aid to the two countries and debt repayment questions should be on hold until they come to their senses.

Furthermore, both countries' UN membership should be suspended. Nothing, nothing whatsoever, justifies their present war.

Interestingly the current president of Ethiopia, a Tigrean, was formerly a rebel. In the eighties, when I was in Ethiopia, he fought alongside another rebel leader from Eritrea, now that country's president. Both, so I heard, were good friends. Now fifteen years later, both of them are presidents of poor countries. And they fight each other and cause death to many young soldiers.

Could anyone explain to me how the human brain works? Equally guilty, of course, are those who supply them with weapons. The same applies to India and Pakistan. They, too, fight each other now but can hardly afford a war. At least they manufacture their own weapons, including nuclear bombs.

The present Ethiopian / Eritrean skirmishes remind me; in July 1986, I was on a humanitarian mission not far from where they are now fighting, in Sekota, in the Province of Tigre. At that time, Sekota had the worst-case scenario happen. A severe drought crippled the whole country.

Eritrea and Ethiopia were formerly one country, but Eritrea fought for independence. This "civil war" lasted 30 years. The (Ethiopian) Tigre Province was rebelling, too. They fought together with Eritrea against the communist regime of Mengistu in Addis Ababa. There were daily fights in and around Sekota. In between all this mess, the UN, the Red Cross (ICRC), and particularly one (American-based) NGO, "World Vision International" (WVI), were struggling to keep the population from starvation and, in the case of the ICRC, treat their war wounded. A classical case where warlords of all factions used humanitarian aid agencies in their fighting strategy.

Sekota is high in the mountains north of Addis, fifty miles off the principal highway to Asmara (Eritrea). The nearest storage place for international food aid was Korem, but the road to Korem was shockingly bad. In fact, it could only be negotiated by smaller (up to 5/6-ton) 4-wheel drive trucks. An estimated 200,000 people lived in the surrounding hills, mainly in Sekota. They needed at least 1,500 MT of food monthly to supplement their meager stocks. Most of this food aid had to be flown to Sekota and dropped from big transport aircraft on the airfield, which was too small for them to land.

On July seventeenth, 1986, I had an opportunity to fly from WVI from Addis to Sekota. The aircraft was a De Havilland Twin-Otter, the largest plane that could land on this mountaintop airstrip. After a two-hour flight from Addis, we arrived over Sekota but could not land because a Belgian Airforce Hercules, on charter for ICRC, had just dropped 12 tons of wheat on the airfield. This had to be removed to clear the airstrip.

When we finally landed, it was not fun for a nervous passenger. The plane needed the whole length that the mountaintop could provide.

Our WVI aircraft could not remain at the airstrip but had to fly to Korem. Another Hercules airdrop of food was expected. There was no sufficiently safe place on the airfield to park the Twin Otter while the airdrop was underway.

The flight by our plane to Korem was not an empty one. The pilot took two wounded soldiers and returned later with items such as butter oil and medical drugs, which were not suitable for airdrops. A Twin Otter could transport about one MT of cargo.

The drop ground, pick-up area, and immediate access road to the Secota airfield were in bad shape and had to be improved to not impair airdrop operations. The local authorities were requested to do something about it.

There was very little food in storage, but WVI expected a convoy of ten 4-wheel drive trucks from Korem the following day. Due to the poor roads, a round trip through Korem-Sekota-Korem (100 miles) lasted about four days. We surveyed warehouses and established requirements. Drugs were urgently needed. So was additional warehouse space. I knew we had a suitable tent in Addis and said it would be sent at the next opportunity. Particularly needed was ORS (oral rehydration salt) against diarrhea for children.

While we were investigating all this and visiting installations and houses, gunfire was constantly heard, sometimes a big bang from a mortar or a cannon. From Sekorta on top of this big hill, the fighting was across a valley on another ridge. I saw them fighting but could not tell which was which. The soldiers all looked alike and had the same type of guns. I think it was the famous Russian Kalashnikovs.

Later in the afternoon, the Belgian Transall aircraft came again. It was the first time I saw an airdrop from the ground. The plane was based in Asmara. On this flight, it carried fifteen MT of wheat in twenty-five kg bags on pallets and dropped it on two approaches. Quite a sight from the ground. (I have a good photo showing an airdrop!)

I knew the Ethiopian Air Force often assisted their ground troops and gave them air support. So I hoped this would not happen now: fighter planes appearing in the sky when the Belgian Air Force transporter was on a "mission of life" on a neighboring hill. But I am sure the Ethiopian Air Force knew of the airdrop being done this afternoon.

Our plane had to be here at 4:30 pm at the latest. This was a question of daylight. Except for Addis Ababa, there was no airport suitable for night landings. In Ethiopia, day and night are 12 hours a day, 12 hours night, 7 am to 7 pm, almost year-round.

(We had our own theory about the old British and their "sun-downer." It only worked because the sun sets year-round at seven pm in the tropics, give or take half an hour. There is a big difference between summer and winter in New York and Heidelberg. It would be challenging to have a drink at a regular time and call it a "sun-downer" given such different times.)

Before we left, I saw some soldiers carrying a young fellow to the ICRC station on a stretcher; blood was all over. I sympathized with these young lads; they were not soldiers for the Mengistu regime of their own will. Ethiopians, from their traditional background as well as from their religious past, were not communists.

We had many Ethiopian staff at the UN, for instance, my secretary. She had a fifteen-year-old son and was doing everything she could to take him out of the country, officially for education, in time before he was old enough to be drafted for the Ethiopian army.

The takeoff from the airstrip was a little scary but perhaps only for the passenger. However, we made it and were back in Addis just before dark.

SOUTH AFRICAN TASKFORCE

In August/September 1986, still assigned in Addis Ababa, Ethiopia, I got a call from Unicef headquarters in New York. They requested my participation in a "Logistics Taskforce" to examine the possibilities of an alternative shipment of Unicef supplies to the "Frontline States." South Africa had threatened to impose sanctions on these states.

Editor's note: The Frontline States (FLS) were a loose coalition of African countries from the 1960s to the early 1990s committed to ending apartheid and white minority rule in South Africa and Rhodesia. (Wikipedia.)

Despite all rhetoric against the apartheid regime in Pretoria, and largely unknown to most people in the West, import to most southern African countries, commercial and international aid supplies, was still done through the South African ports of Durban and Port Elisabeth.

In early 1986, South Africa threatened to close all their ports for shipments to the "Frontline States." The alternative ports: Mombasa, Dar es Salaam, Beira, and Moputo, were ill-prepared to receive and ship large tonnages of commercial and international aid cargo.

Unicef, which furnished all these states with essential quantities of project materials, drugs, and other supplies, wanted to find alternative routes for their imports.

For this purpose, a task force was created consisting of the HQ Shipping Officer, a senior Supply Officer, myself as a Logistics Officer, and local staff in the various locations. We visited the "Frontline States": Tanzania, Malawi, Zimbabwe, Mozambique, Botswana, Swaziland, Zambia, and Kenya. A fascinating month of travel in Southern Africa.

SIERRA LEONE

I went to Freetown, the capital of Sierra Leone, for a consultancy on program logistics at the request of the Unicef representative. The representative was a Korean lady. Her name was Mrs. Kim.

The ordinary people in Sierra Leone speak Creole or "Krio." It sounds a little like English and is undoubtedly derived from English.

When one listens carefully, one can understand the folks of Sierra Leone. For instance, the driver assigned to me, Kabia, "Mornin oh, sir" (good morning) "Ho yo do sir."

"Fine, thank you, and how are you?"

"smal, small sir."

In the market where I thought the fruits were expensive: "You nor go less." (No reduction.)

One day when I returned to the locked car, rain pouring, I asked a group of bystanders where my driver was.

"He go wet," meaning he went to take a pee.

I traveled by car throughout the country.

PORT OF ASSAB

Here is a rather amusing story that may come under the heading "Logistics." Location: Port of Assab. (Note: Assab is now, since independence from Ethiopia, an Eritrean port. At the time of this story, it was part of Ethiopia.)

In 1986, when I was posted in Ethiopia, I was on one of my weekly routine visits to the port to look after arriving relief supplies as well as checking offtake from the port by trucks. After finishing my other duties, I wandered around a little, accompanied by my driver, which I enjoyed.

There is always a lot to see in an African port, a lot of stuff, equipment of all kinds lying around, just left there for various reasons. On that day, when I wandered through the port and came to the older, no longer active section. I saw some steel containers, about 2.5 yards by 2.5 yards, half in shallow water and half on the shore. There were some markings on these containers. I observed the markings and thought they looked like Unicef shipping markings.

Sure enough, the containers bore barely readable markings that could only be a Unicef shipment. My driver climbed on one of the containers and opened the tidily closed and sealed hatch. There was some well-preserved equipment inside.

The hatch was closed again, and I took notes of all readable markings. We could not get any information on these containers, and the equipment inside, at the port.

Back in Addis Ababa, I sent a cable to our shipping officer, Ed Kenny, in HQ-NY and gave him all the information. The next day the reply came from New York.

This shipment had been reported lost some three or

four years ago. The equipment inside was for iodizing salt at the large seawater evaporation salt plant in Assab. Unicef's interest in salt plants was that salt produced from seawater had to be iodized to prevent goiter in children and adults.

These special floatable sealed steel containers were intended to be off-loaded from the ship off-shore and then floated to a landing site for unloading. Some of the ports in Africa are hopelessly congested. By using floatable containers, a vessel can reduce turnaround time significantly. In the case above, these containers floated away and were reported lost.

Meanwhile, the salt plant in Assab was still waiting and had no equipment to iodize their products. This machinery was finally delivered and installed at the plant.

1987

ZAIRE

In 1987, I had just retired from Unicef and lived in New York. Doris was working for the German Information Center. There was a call from Kinshasa via Unicef headquarters in NY, asking whether I would be interested in a consultancy on logistics in Zaire. Of course, I was ready and pleased to do something useful. Also, I was keen to see Central Africa again.

Unicef now had a large office in Kinshasa and was working on "development" as a priority. They were no longer trying to do something ad hoc in an impossible situation.

The Unicef Representative was Ludo Welffens, a young Belgian with nothing in common with his compatriots of the previous generation who had stayed on in Congo at independence. I knew Ludo well. We had been stationed together for years in the seventies in Abidjan, Ivory Coast.

I arrived at Kinshasa International Airport on the first of December with SABENA via Brussels. The old air connections to and in Africa were still the same. The Unicef driver who came to the airport took me to the Intercontinental. This beautiful hotel did not exist in the sixties. One thing international travelers to developing countries must be cautious about is not judging a country by hotels or fancy restaurants, which can only be used by some people.

Zaire was different, no doubt, since my last visit here. At least for people in the big cities, a certain prosperity could not be overlooked. In addition to Ludo Welffens, I met two other former colleagues, a Ugandan, Francis Kisinde, with whom I worked in the Kampala office in the sixties, and a Danish friend, Jorgen Andersen, who was stationed with me for years in headquarters in NY. One of the nice things about this international life is that you meet former colleagues wherever you go.

I was impressed when I met Francis again. He had really made a career in the organization. In Kampala, he was a locally employed clerk in Supply Section. This time, he was an International Program Officer administrating our important assisted education program in Zaire.

The present consultant contract required me to travel to the ports of Matadi and Boma on the South Atlantic and to Lubumbashi (formerly Elisabethville) in Shaba Province (formerly Katanga). Jorgen Andersen accompanied me on both trips. We went to Boma by car. It is about 370 miles South-West of Kinshasa, and the road was reasonably good.

We took a government official along on this trip. Training our government counterparts in program logistics management and creating awareness is essential. Boma could be used as a point of entry into the country for program supplies destined for western and central parts of Zaire, where surface transportation by road or river barges was possible. It was necessary, too, to keep close contact with shipping agents and freight forwarders at the port and in Kinshasa.

Eastern Zaire was different, hence our visit to Lubumbashi. This city, too, had changed very much. We stayed in a new Sheraton Hotel that had not existed in the sixties.

Program supplies came in from Durban or Port Elisabeth in South Africa then they traveled by rail north through Zimbabwe, Zambia, to Zaire. Another reliable route was from the port of Beira in Mozambique by rail to Harare/ Zimbabwe and by truck to Lubumbashi. At the time, this railroad was more efficient than the much shorter route by truck from the port of Mombassa/Kenya.

Circumstances changed, often depending on the political situation, port congestion, and security. For instance, Uganda, a transit country to Eastern Zaire, could, for security reasons, not always be used.

At this point, I may say that logistics in Africa

is no easy matter, particularly for landlocked countries. Governments often think they can do it, and urge us to do without commercial companies, consigning goods directly to a ministry.

That never works satisfactorily. This business needs a lot of experience, which only commercial companies have. Some shipping and forwarding companies have long traditions in the region. Sometimes, if political disturbances occur, they leave but later come back. In Zaire, practically all these companies are Belgian.

MADAGASCAR

Madagascar island is the fourth largest in the world, only 300 miles off the East African coast and divided by the Mozambique channel of the Indian Ocean from the African continent. From Europe or East Africa, the way to Madagascar is via Nairobi. As this was a former French colony, it is mainly Air France that flies to Antananarivo (Tananarive), the capital.

Another airline was Air Madagascar, with much technical and financial assistance from Air France, then Mauritius Airline, and, even under apartheid, the South African Airline. South Africa always maintained good relations with Madagascar. Nossi-Bé, a small island off Madagascar's Northern coast, had always been an El Dorado for white South African tourists. Particularly during apartheid, when they had nowhere else to go for vacation nearby.

Madagascar became independent from France in 1960 when many African nations gained independence from former colonial powers. Since then, the country has undergone several political changes. Eventually, in 1975, it became sort of "socialist." In a "Malagasy way of socialism," whatever that means.

In Madagascar, there are two distinct ethnic groups, Indo-Melanesians living mainly inland, on the high plateau, and Africans living along the coast and the south. Therefore, Antananarivo and other towns inland do not look like other African places. The main port on the Indian Ocean, Toamasina (Tamatave), on the other hand, looks like Mombassa in Kenya.

During my several visits to the island, road conditions in Madagascar were absolutely shocking. That includes the many bridges in the country. Hopefully, they have improved those in the meantime. I firmly believe that development starts with good roads so people can get together and trade goods.

If you want to locate places in the following story from an old atlas, you may have difficulty. The government has changed these names, the first achievement of socialism. I shall put the old ones in parentheses for what it is worth.

When I was stationed in Unicef Kampala, I visited Madagascar regularly. It belonged to the region I was responsible for providing advice on logistics. I was last there in April 1987. I had just retired from Unicef and was called back as a consultant to survey the logistics situation in our programs and develop a new strategy for the government and Unicef in the future.

My hotel was always the Colbert, situated in the middle of town in Antananarivo. I mentioned the old name "Tananarive," but everybody calls it, even today, "Tana." Abbreviations are frequently used on the island out of necessity. The proper names of people and places are often shortened because they are very long.

For example, while traveling by car in the county, you come to a village whose name is written on a banner or sign. Commonly there are thirty to thirty-five letters in a village's name. The principle seems to be: "The smaller the village, the more letters its name contains."

It's the same with people's names. There was a colleague in Unicef; his name was "Rakotoarivoni." Of course, for us, it was easy. We just called him "Rakoto." However, at home, the full name is spoken.

I met a government lady doctor, Dr. Ratsimbazafimahefa. Can you imagine if you met her and she introduced herself? I bet only a few Westerners would get the name right and be able to spell it too. But Malagasy people always volunteer to write the name down for you. (In Japan, they always hand you a business card. Not in Madagascar. I think they have no extra money to get cards printed.)

To my pleasant surprise, on my arrival in April 1987, I was met at the Antananarivo Airport by Ute Deseniss, a countrywoman of mine. Ute was a UN volunteer in Abidjan when we were there. Now she was our number one program officer responsible for all assisted health projects.

In my request for accommodation, I had expressively asked to be booked into the old Colbert Hotel, because I had always stayed there. Although there are more modern hotels now, I liked the old Colbert, it had an unusual atmosphere, which I enjoyed, besides it had good food. (I am conservative, in one way. I like to return to old places if I was satisfied on previous visits.)

Unicef assisted health services countrywide. The system now was that all our and the government's supplies for health services were shipped to the main port of Toamasina. From there, they were sent by an inefficient railroad to Antananarivo for no other reason than because the central government and its stores were there.

From the central store, supplies were again transported on trucks over the above-described bad roads to provincial capital towns, where distribution occurred. The idea now was to consolidate supplies into packages for provinces, to ship several packs (the volume for one district did not justify a container) in containers to Toamasina, break up the containers, and send the packages to smaller ports around the island. Most provinces had a port on the ocean.

This all sounds nice and logical, but it was not. If a system introduced by the previous colonial power had been followed, even after independence, for a hundred years or more, changing it is quite another matter. In most African countries, a central government in the capital wants to control everything. Madagascar is not an exception. Therefore goods are to be received in the main store, even if this doesn't make sense.

The French built a railroad in Madagascar from the main port to the capital. Tracks and rail wagons were in terrible condition, and the railroad was broken and inefficient. The government has few motor vehicles as an alternative transportation means.

Due to the shortage of transport, distribution from central government stores to the local stores was inefficient. Drugs were often kept in the main store past the expiration date. Health services in the provinces were chronically short of medicines and other clinical supplies. Children, for which Unicef has its mandate, suffered.

My mission in April 1987 was to find a better system of direct shipment to the provincial ports. The government was interested, even willing to improve matters. Therefore I had to travel to those ports and capitals. A government logistics counterpart accompanied me on these journeys.

MADAGASCAR II

The first field trip on this mission was to Toamasina (formerly Tamatave), the principal port city, some two hundred and thirty miles from "Tana" (Antananarivo). With me were: my Malagasy counterpart, Monsieur Randriamirado, a Unicef Program Officer from Tana, and the Unicef driver. We rode in a Toyota Landcruiser.

It had been more than ten years since I had been on this road, and I must say, there was some improvement. Still, it took seven hours to cover the distance. Despite the poor road and the time one has to spend on it, the flora and fauna are magnificent and not typically "African."

Driving from Tana to the coast, the road descends by almost two thousand meters and leads through a rainforest. There is no big game, like elephants and giraffes, but many smaller animals: lemurs (primates), snakes, chameleons, geckos, alligators, crocodiles, lizards, and what have you. And, of course, birds, the most exotic and colorful birds I had ever seen. In its fauna and flora, Madagascar developed quite differently than the African mainland, so close to the island.

In Toamasina, we went to the Hotel de Poste, a charming hotel. It had first-class cuisine and all kinds of fresh seafood. We had dinner and a drink or two.

Then I met a countryman of mine: Siegfried Henning was his name. His story is somber, and although it finished more than five years later, I will write it down now.

Siegfried was only about twenty-six years of age when I met him. He had visited Madagascar many times and intimately knew the country, particularly its fauna. He knew about all these snakes, chameleons, geckos, alligators, turtles, crocodiles, lizards, etc. Herpetology was his big hobby, but he was an amateur and spent his own money to travel this far.

By profession, Siegfried was a baker. He had a good job with a manufacturer of bakery products, meaning yeast, cake powder, etc. He was an experimental baker, trying out the products before marketing. One would not normally expect a person earning money as a baker to be a herpetologist. Although I know little about snakes and lizards, he impressed me with his knowledge. On this evening in Toamasina, he told me a lot about these species in Madagascar.

During my stay in Madagascar, I met him again in Ansiranana (Diego-Suarez) and later in Tana, where he also stayed in the Colbert. Wherever we met, we had interesting conversations. I told him of a UN colleague with similar interests in lizards who lived in one of the buildings in Waterside. This fellow (Noberto Muller) has a large terrarium in his studio apartment.

In Madagascar, Siegfried and I became good friends. One day he came to New York, and I introduced him to Noberto Muller. They had many common interests in their hobby and kept in close contact. Siegfried also wrote several articles in various publications.

Being a known amateur herpetologist and with his knowledge of Madagascar in general, he was asked by a German university in 1993 to participate in a Madagascar expedition. This scientific expedition obtained a license to export various specimens to Germany for further studies.

This group of six scientists was conducting their research at night in a national park north of Tana, with the full approval of the government of Madagascar. They were suddenly shot at by ignorant guards who followed the principle (often done in Africa): "Shoot first and ask questions later."

It was a terrible mix-up. I read the report of a survivor later. At the end of this incident, Siegfried Henning was dead, along with two of the scientists, and two more were seriously wounded.

MADAGASCAR III

The morning after my long talk with Siegfried Henning about snakes and reptiles, my counterpart, who accompanied me from Antananarivo (Tana) and I, engaged in "routine matters." That means visits to the port, inspecting sheds, and Unicef supplies awaiting forwarding to the Central Medical Stores in Antananarivo (Tana).

Then we met with the Toamasina Provincial Medical Officer to check the distribution of drugs and medical supplies. He confirmed that all supplies are shipped by rail to Tana's Central Medical Store first. On requisition, the supplies for the Province of Toamasina are, with significant delay, returned for distribution. It had always been done this way.

I wanted to see one of the out-post health centers and the roads which lead to it. The doctor suggested Fenoarivo, forty miles away. That trip was a memorable one.

About fifteen bridges cross over numerous small rivers that flow through the delta into the ocean. The bridges were built alright; some even looked solid. However, there was no proper surface on which a vehicle could safely cross.

This vital coastal road, including new bridge structures, was constructed about twenty years earlier. However, before a surface could be laid on the bridges, the government ran out of money or lost interest in this construction project, so the bridges were never completed.

The population helped themselves by laying planks and stripes of sheet metal on the beams of the bridge structure. Even trucks crossed these primitive makeshift bridges. After we crossed the first bridge with a makeshift surface, I was truly scared and crossed the following bridges on foot.

My fears were not unreasonable. Beneath almost all

of the bridges, I saw vehicles lying roofs up in the water. Although it was not a long drop, the rivers were infested by alligators and similar animals. Anyhow, we made it to and from Fenoarivo. The brave driver got the Landcruiser over all these dangerous bridges.

On this mission in 1987, I visited many more places in Madagascar. I saw the country's beauty as well as the poverty of its people. My contacts with the men and women engaged in our projects and joint efforts to improve the population's lives were an eye-opener about realities in the developing world.

One may recall that in the mid-eighties, the whole world spoke about AIDS. For a long time, developing countries did not know or did not want to know that AIDS was a problem in their countries. Most of them, including Madagascar, denied that they had AIDS cases at all. If there were isolated cases, these had been brought in by foreigners.

On that mission in 1987 to Madagascar, we talked with local staff during a coffee break in the Unicef office. I think I brought up the subject of AIDS (In French, it is called "SIDA"). I might have even provocatively said: "How about AIDS in Madagascar?"

A Malagasy secretary, from whom one could expect a certain level of education, told me honestly: "We can not get this disease here because we are an island!"

Uganda was one of the first countries to admit that they had a massive AIDS problem and to ask international organizations for help. Uganda was and still is the country most hit by AIDS in Africa.

1988

INDIA

I have been to India several times. The longest stay was in 1988. I spent two months on a logistics and procurement consulting mission in the Unicef Office in New Delhi. Even though I had mainly been assigned to Africa, Indians and their way of doing things were quite familiar. From the beginning of my international life, I had Indian colleagues and always appreciated their helpful, friendly discourse.

There were many Indians and Pakistanis in East and South Africa. They were generally just called "Asians." Referring to them this way did not do justice to the Indians or the Pakistanis. Yet, something makes me think: In India and in Pakistan, the various ethnic groups, Hindu, Shia Muslim, Sunni Muslim, and Sikh, have endless trouble and conflicts between themselves, often with fatal outcomes. The "Asians" in East and South Africa seem to live peacefully together, they blend very well, and one does not distinguish between the various nationalities and/or ethnic groups. By the way, Mahatma Gandhi was raised and educated in South Africa.

Back to my story, the British have a saying about Indian ways: "There is a wrong way, there is a right way, and there is an "Indian way." This is not meant to be a racist remark; it is instead meant to be a positive, friendly observation.

India has nearly one billion people. One-fifth of the world's population. This fact cannot be ignored. It would be wrong if I claimed to be an expert on India, but I have made some observations. I worked with Indians in foreign countries where they were colleagues and also in India. The Unicef office employs some 200 (90%) local Indian staff of various ethnic and religious groups.

Furthermore, I dealt with government officials and business people when procuring. I know there is a high rate of illiterate people, particularly women. But I also know the average Indian fortunate enough to attend school is well-educated.

My dealings were with educated men and women. There is nothing that India cannot manufacture. Admittedly they copy a lot and do not take it too seriously when worldwide patents and copyrights are involved. Industrial goods manufactured in India are for the local market. They are often crude and unrefined.

Take, for instance, the "Jeep." In the fifties, a corporation called Mahindra & Mahindra (M&M) got a license from Jeep US to construct various models of their production line. So M&M started to build the J-5 and J-6 according to technical standards that existed at that time in the USA. Unicef, which supplied many vehicles for rural health and education projects, decided not to import Jeeps any longer but instead buy locally, thus helping the local economy and avoiding delivering vehicles that were not serviceable in India due to incompatible spare parts. Unicef was the number one customer of M&M.

The Transport Officer of the Delhi Office kept close contact with the Jeep manufacturer. Now one would think a company like M&M would do something to improve their vehicles year-by-year and satisfy customers. Not M&M; their Jeeps got worse every year. We threatened to discontinue buying M&M Jeeps. They promised to improve but did not do so. For years M&M had no competitors in the four-wheel drive market in India.

Finally, in the early eighties, Japan came into the country and had their little SUZUKI 4×4 locally built in India. Only then did M&M wake up and do something to improve the quality of their vehicles.

The local industry could offer almost anything that was needed for Unicef-assisted programs. There was a countrywide "Extended Program on Immunization" (EPI).

As I have described in an earlier installment, the different immunization vaccines must be refrigerated until they are applied or injected. So naturally, in a big country like India, vaccination centers must be equipped with an enormous quantity of refrigerators. We had to go out on a bidding process for the required refrigerators. Bidding is a challenging thing in India. In particular, previous suppliers think they have a right to continue supplying, regardless of the price.

There are more than twenty states in India, and many states with important industries are reluctant to accept equipment manufactured in others. In addition, as far as refrigerators are concerned, there is little or no electricity in many states in rural areas. That is to say, the power is not steady but could be as low as 80 Volts and then range up to 250 Volts. Given such a power surge, electric appliances can be damaged. We had to supply voltage stabilizers, which were almost as expensive as the fridge.

When the bidding was done for competitive procurement, normally, samples were requested. Often the examples provided were OK. However, the delivered items were a different matter. Many suppliers knew we had insufficient staff to do proper quality control everywhere.

Unicef and the government of India did a lot in the way of information and communication with the population. Consequently, a lot of printing was required. Supplying suitable print material was challenging.

There are many different languages in the country. Even where the primary language is spoken, there are regional differences. The script employed in many languages and dialects is called "Sanskrit," a language in itself, but also the characters used in other languages. For instance, words written in Sanskrit in Bombay (West India) do not necessarily mean the same thing in Calcutta (East India).

This means you need "local" printers. A low bid for posters is not helpful if the language/script is not understood in other parts of the country. A simple item like a vaccination registration card that had to be available in health centers throughout the country created great difficulties because of language diversity. One could not just write things in English.

Although English is widely understood and spoken in towns, our information material had to be understood by the rural population, who did not speak English and were only semi-literate. Because of the masses of print material needed for populous India, little mistakes were never "little" and always involved many thousands of dollars.

We had a specialist in the office as a consultant in this printing field. He was, of course, an Indian national. No other nationality could have filled such a position. He was a busy man. Great importance in India is given to health education.

As mentioned above, many rural Indians, particularly women, are, at best, semi-literate. So posters and pamphlets had to take this fact into account.

Posters printed on paper were quickly done and worked. However, they did not last too long. Some suppliers offered to print posters on thin sheet metal, which is much more durable. The price was OK.

However, there was a problem. Indians discovered that the thin sheet metal was an excellent material for hut roofs. The idea is good, of course, but the execution did not fulfill the purpose of health education. Sheet-metal material was discontinued.

One weekend, I visited the Taj Mahal, one of the great man-made monuments in marble, well known to people worldwide. I participated in a local tour. Indians visit the Taj Mahal for tourist or other reasons and behave as we foreigners do.

I always used to think that it was constructed as a palace. It was not. It is a mausoleum on the banks of the Jumna River, built by the Mogul emperor Shah Jahan in memory of his beloved wife. She died in childbirth. An impressive complex of Islamic construction art. Frankly, I like the skyline of the Taj from a distance more than the actual mausoleum.

Agra, where the Taj Mahal is situated, is just sixty miles from New Delhi. Nevertheless, it takes time for any vehicle, particularly for a local bus, to travel this distance. Although a main road, it is narrow. There are often people standing on this road. When a tourist bus approaches, they are in no hurry to clear it. There are also countless animals, mainly cows, on the road. They do not move out of the way, either. Sometimes the driver has to stop the bus, get out, and gently guide a cow from the road. It is definitely very folkloric.

In conclusion, this vast populous country, with its contrast of poor and rich, of well-educated and illiterate people, of high tech to great simplicity, is truly fascinating. I have not had the experience of being posted for years in India as some of my colleagues were, so I am not an expert on this country. I may have seen many things superficially or totally wrong.

1989

KAMIKAZE BANANA

I oversaw an emergency project in Burundi for three months, starting in January 1989. The Unicef Office for Burundi is in Bujumbura, the capital. I lived there while I worked on the project. Local disturbances had taken place between Hutus and Tuzis five months earlier, so the United Nations set up an emergency resettlement operation.

The places where the disturbances had happened were about three hours to the north. They were called Kirundu, Ntega, and Marangara. There were other villages affected in between. I divided my time between Kirundu and Bujumbura. I spent two days each week in the area of operation in Kirundu and the rest in Bujumbura.

Bujumbura is a lovely city on Lake Tanganyika. At a relatively low altitude, this lake is situated in the great African Rift Valley, which runs north-south from Ethiopia to East Africa. The road to Kirundu leads up the mountains and begins just outside the city, a very steep climb with countless bends for about twenty-five km.

On the road up the first time, I was shocked when a bicycle came toward us, cutting corners. I thought the rider must have lost his brakes or, worse, his mind. The driver of my Land Cruiser just laughed and explained that this was a "Kamikaze Banana."

He explained that boys and young men of fourteen to twenty pushed their bicycles up the hills to the banana-growing fields. They buy trunks of Bananas for FBU 400 (about US $2.60) and resell them at the market in Bujumbura for FBU 1,200 ($7.80)

Unbelievably, they load up to four trunks of bananas on the backs of their bicycles. They make three to five trips daily from the hills down to Bujumbura.

My driver said their bicycles had no brakes, which I did not believe. However, the speed they rode down the hilly road was scary.

When we returned one evening from Kirundu and came down that hill, we saw a group of youngsters pushing their bicycles up for the first "Kamikaze Banana" trip in the morning to Bujumbura.

BURUNDI – FEAR

In February 1989, I was on a special Mission in Burundi. Some five months earlier, one of these periodic slaughters between Hutus and Tuzis, common in Rwanda and neighboring Burundi, had happened. This time, some five thousand Hutus were killed by Tuzis in several villages of the border area in Burundi. Many Hutus fled over the border to Rwanda.

Heads of state from Zaire (now again Congo), Rwanda, and Burundi met and agreed that the refugees could and should return to Burundi. Their security was supposedly guaranteed.

The UN, notably Unicef and the UNHCR, were to facilitate the return of the refugees and help with resettlement in their original villages. I spent three months in Burundi overseeing Unicef's involvement in this project. During this time, I lived in Bujumbura, the capital of Burundi. But, I traveled weekly to Kirundo, where resettlement, including essential services, was provided.

At this time, I wrote a little story in my diary in German. It may be titled "nightly trip to Kigozi" or just "fear":

At lunchtime one day, I went to lunch at a mission guesthouse called "Maison d'Accueil de Kigozi." The mission guesthouse, "Maison d'Accueil," was a good place to stay. There was nothing suitable in Kirundu. I planned to book a room for that night.

My Burundi driver was with me. He drove us to the mission. There was not a problem, as he knew how to get there. As I wanted to return by myself in the evening, I tried to memorize the details of the way: two times to the left, right, left, after that right, through the hedges, and then left again. I also remembered a little airfield for small aircraft where I had to keep to the right. After lunch, we returned to Kirundu.

That evening I drove alone in the Land Rover, which was adventurous. The distance from Kirundu to Kigozi is only ten km. The bush trail is rough, and there is only one signpost a short distance before the mission guesthouse. I would not be honest if I did not admit I had a funny feeling in my stomach. I was outright scared.

I had driven this trail before, but never alone and not at night. Finding the right way in the African bush, away from the main roads, is difficult even in the daytime. One has to have a sense of direction. African drivers have it.

Another thing, when you are being driven, you do not pay too much attention to little details on the road. It was already dark when I left for Kigozi. OK, two times left......oh, was this the trail or the entrance to a kraal? No, it was right. It was the road; go on....or was I wrong? At night, it looked so different. Shouldn't there already be the branching off to the right? Am I still on the right trail? Where is the airfield? Everything was dark. Of course, this airfield was not lit up at all.

I remembered that some months ago, five thousand Hutus were killed with machetes right here.

Someone appeared in the headlights of the Land Rover. Should I ask for directions? No, of course not. The fellow would not speak French in the first place. Never stop and get out of the car. You are too vulnerable outside the Land Rover. I decided to go on for another five minutes, and if the crossroad did not show up, I would return.

Of course, I knew perfectly well that finding the way back would be just as tricky. Suddenly there was the crossroad.....yes, I now remember these were the hedges. Go on, I encouraged myself. Then came the best moment of the evening. The one and only signpost on the road: "Maison d'Accueil de Kigozi."

I withstood the urge to stop, get out of the vehicle

and kiss the ground. From here on, it was easy. Only one more mile to drive. I recognized the trail. The lake was to my right. Through the open window, I heard the grunting of the hippopotamuses. Finally, the lights of the mission building.

Shortly after that, I was sitting on the terrace of the mission with a cold beer. Two colleagues from UNHCR were already there. The African night with all the sounds was lovely. Nice relaxing from the heat of the day. We had a good meal that evening. The sisters were great cooks. I told nobody about the scary moments I had earlier on the trail from Kirundo to Kigozi.

AFGHANISTAN III

My third visit to Afghanistan in October 1989 was a memorable one. I was retired from Unicef and living in Germany when the call came, asking whether I would be interested in going on a four-week mission to Afghanistan. The proposal was a three-member team, under the leadership of Ed Kenny, Emergency Coordinator in Unicef Copenhagen, for "The purpose of assessing the current supply and logistics situation in Afghanistan, finding new supply lines, points of entry, and warehousing of emergency as well as regular program supplies."

This was to my liking, so I accepted immediately. My status was "consultant," a contract was set up, and an entry visa and other travel arrangements were organized.

On October 22nd, 1989, I departed on a Lufthansa plane from Frankfurt via Kuwait to Dubai in the Persian Gulf. In the Ramadan Hotel, I met Ed Kenny. He had come earlier and contacted freight forwarders. Dubai was in our plan as a staging point for supplies to be airlifted to landlocked Afghanistan.

The following day we left with Afghan Airlines "ARIANA" for Kabul. The Russian Tupolev plane was packed, mostly with Indians going to Delhi via Kabul. They discovered connecting through Kabul was cheaper than a direct flight to Delhi. There were seldom foreign passengers to Kabul. Afghans could not travel, so they sold tickets on a "supply and demand" basis. The connecting flight from Kabul to Delhi was also done by Ariana. Our journey to Afghanistan was less than three hours. As we passed over Kabul, I recognized the city from a high altitude. Then suddenly, the plane started spiraling in very narrow arcs toward the runway. I was scared because I had never experienced such an approach.

Later I learned that they had to fly this way because of the Mujahideen in the mountains surrounding Kabul. Flying at high altitudes is safe. Rebel ground-to-air missiles could not reach the plane. Also, within a limited circle around the airport, it was safe. We were told that the Mujahideen were not after the Ariana planes, but who knows when they might change their minds. So we had our first impression of Kabul under siege.

We were met by a driver at the airport. He brought us to the Unicef office. The office was surrounded by sandbags stacked two meters high to protect against rocket attacks from the Mujahideen.

After a briefing in the office, we were taken to a house Unicef kept as a guesthouse. There were also sandbags around the guesthouse. It had several rooms, quite comfortable, and an Afghan servant kept it clean. He also prepared tea and other simple things, which was convenient. We had to go out for proper meals, usually to the UN Club.

In October 1989, the situation in Kabul was quite tricky. Of course, we had a mission, and that was not to "safe" Afghanistan. We represented the UN Children Fund and tried to find, together with other UN agencies, the most practical ways and routes to bring emergency supplies to Kabul so the endangered population sector could get over the winter. Many mothers and children were highly vulnerable, and they were our concern.

When the Soviets left some months earlier, President Najibullah and a significant part of his army survived. Reason enough for the Mujahideen not to give up fighting. Kabul was still under siege.

One might think that no food could be left in a town under rocket fire and siege for so many years. (First, when the Russians were still in town, and after that, when the Russian-installed president continued to rule the country). However, there were food and other goods but at exorbitant prices.

Ordinary people, especially the vulnerable groups of mothers (many widows) and children, could not afford them.

The private sector transport brought supplies on roads closed to the government or "official" transportation. The Salang Pass connected Kabul with the north of the country. This was the traditional supply route for the capital. Mujahideen could close this road at will, but commercial truckers had an arrangement with them. By giving them part of the cargo or paying them off, they were allowed to pass. Anyhow these commercial trucks kept Kabul supplied.

Although the Russians had gone, the military machinery of Afghanistan was still provided with hardware by the USSR. Huge military transport planes were landing and taking off all the time from Kabul airport. They were the target of rebel missiles, but planes could defend themselves. They could not climb as fast as passenger planes did. Their defense was to fire "heat flares" from the aircraft, which distracted heat-seeking missiles. Watching these planes take off with these bright flares behind them was pretty interesting. Often at night, we heard rockets or other shells hit the town, some closer, some further away.

We intended to visit the Northern towns of Mazar-i-Sharif and the USSR border towns of Heiraton and Termez to investigate the supply route via Tashkent in the Soviet Union. We planned to visit these towns and Herat in the country's west together. However, for four days, the Kabul airport was under severe rocket fire by the Mujahideen, which prevented our flight from taking off.

Now we had a time problem, so we decided to split up. Ed Kenny went with a colleague to Mazar-i-Sharif, and I went directly to Herat. On the fifth day, the rebel fire on the airport stopped. Ariana announced they would fly, and we had to be at the airport by eight am. How they knew there would be no rockets this day is incomprehensible to me.

Ed and I left together because Mazar-i-Sharif was in the same direction as Herat. We were relieved when our Soviet

YAK-40 airplane finally gained altitude and was out of the firing range of the missiles. I wished I could have visited Mazar-i-Sharif, the famous trading and religious center. Unfortunately, I saw it only from the air and the airport.

My flight continued over the spectacular panorama of the Hindukush Mountains to Herat. There was one colleague from the Kabul office, Arne Roswall of Sweden, with me. At the airport, Dr. Farid, the Provincial Medical Officer, received us. He drove us to the hotel. One disappointment was that the hotel was so full I had to share a room with two other UN colleagues, but it was a large room. Arne was an amateur radio operator and never traveled anywhere without his radio. The first thing he did when we reached the hotel was to set up the radio. That was good to have.

One thing about our flight to Herat that I should mention was the interim stop in Mazar-i-Sharif. The runway was under repair. Big construction machines were in action. Our Russian YAK-40 airplane, with three turbofans mounted in the rear, demonstrated its "off-runway capability." It landed parallel to the runway in the desert, causing a big cloud of dust. While on the ground, I had a chance to talk to the Afghan captain. He was talkative and told me that the YAK-40 can land almost anywhere, so the desert landing we had just made was nothing special. I remember he gave me a beautiful, delicious pomegranate. They grow in abundance on this northern plain.

As mentioned, Dr. Faried, the Provincial Medical Officer, collected us at the airport. He accompanied us all the days we were in Herat. His office was in the main hospital. There he also had a small store. We found a stock of Unicef-provided medical supplies and vaccines for preventive and curative mother and child care. He introduced us to his staff. A lady doctor in his team appeared competent and helpful in assessing realistic requirements. I was impressed by Dr. Faried's professional people, who did an excellent job under challenging circumstances.

After we were taken to the hotel, Arne set up his radio in our room. The room had four beds. So far, we were only three staying in it. A young fellow climbed on a nearby tree, fastened the antenna cable, led it to the balcony, and into our room. With this arrangement, reception to the UN-Radio in Kabul was excellent.

Arriving with us was a British TV team from "ETN-TV," two men and one lady reporter. She was young and good-looking, but she also showed it by wearing tight jeans and an equally tight t-shirt. Her name was Elena Panell. Her outfit may not have stirred much excitement in London or New York. Still, the effect on Allah's warriors in Herat must have been similar to a Coca-Cola billboard in the desert.

The first night, she came to our room asking to stay with us because the hotel guards were harassing her. So for the remaining days, we were four in the room. But we also advised her to adapt her dress to Afghan surroundings; for a European woman, that did not necessarily mean wearing a Chadari or completely covering her face.

The town of Herat is surrounded by high mountains in a broad valley on the big Harirud River. It is the capital town of the province by the same name. Located in the northwest of the country, only seventy miles from the Iranian border. The distance to Mashhad is about 350 miles. For centuries the route from Mashhad to Herat was the traditional way to bring goods to the northwest of Afghanistan.

Herat is also situated on an ancient road that swings in a large half-circle to the south and connects the big centers of Farah, Kandahar, Ghazni, and Kabul. This old road is now a broad modern highway, built and financed mainly by US engineers and US money in the fifties.

The road was still being used by private-sector transport companies. They did so on a similar arrangement as the Salang Pass to the north. The truckers had an understanding with the Mujahideen. "Official" transport could not use the road. Several factions of warlords absolutely controlled it and closed or opened it at will.

My recommendation was evident as soon as I realized the situation: Firstly, we should use the traditional Iranian route via Mashhad to import relief supplies to the Western part of Afghanistan. Secondly, supplies were to be consolidated, stored in Herat, and shipped by commercial trucks to Farah and Kandahar. Thirdly, we needed to work with other UN Organizations to make logistics more rational.

So my contacts were mainly with commercial trucking companies. These meetings were very positive. However, using commercial transport meant we needed somebody in Herat to contract for transportation whenever needed.

Several transport companies were in the province, but contracting had to be done competitively. The UN sister organizations World Food Program (WFP) and UNHCR were in the same situation and came to the same conclusions. WFP was expecting a substantial amount of food aid.

The various UN Agencies in Kabul discussed setting up a joint UN sub-office in Herat. Coincidentally there were other colleagues from sister organizations in Herat. Together we were able to rent suitable warehousing and office space for the proposed UN sub-office.

As is customary, we called on the governor's office for a courtesy visit. He was quite a nice man and was said to be equally respected by government supporters and the Mujahideen. He was very friendly to us and supported setting up a UN sub-office in Herat.

Back in Germany, some weeks later, I heard that the governor was killed in renewed fighting in Herat. I felt sorry for the man.

Herat was partly destroyed by heavy fighting between government troops and Mujahideen over the years. Like Kabul, food was available in the bazaars, but prices were not affordable for ordinary people, say mothers and children. That was the same throughout Afghanistan. Western Afghanistan had a general shortage of drugs, vaccines, and medical supplies.

Part of this was covered by the Red Cross (ICRC). But, also Unicef planned to send medical supplies and supplementary baby food for the sector mother and children. Again as so often in similar situations, I got the feeling that warlords, including the responsible people in the government, bought and brought any amount of military hardware into the country. Still, they relied entirely on international aid organizations for food and medical supplies for their population.

On our second evening in town, we were invited to a government guest house for a festive evening, some 1000 returning refugees from Iran intended to celebrate. They had left their villages years ago and fled to Iran, where they had found refuge from being drafted into the army and consequently from fighting. Under a general amnesty, they now returned to their villages.

When the organizers were told that a TV team was in town, they invited foreigners from the hotel and showed us to good places in the first row. There were some one thousand five hundred people in the hall, all men. Elena Panell, our female TV reporter, was the only woman. She was now much more modestly dressed. Still, I think she was brave to be there. Of course, there was no alcohol being served, yet, the men were chanting and dancing. After some time, the crowd became so excited I got claustrophobia and had to leave, although it was very folkloric.

The following day we intended to return to Kabul. Still, in Afghanistan, these things are always “Inshallah” (If god wills it). Because of the shelling of the Kabul airport by the Mujahideen, Ariana could not fly. Their YAK-40 came two days later. I had time to spend and bought a small but charming Persian rug. There were reasonable prices for these items in Herat.

Finally, back in Kabul, we wound up the mission and

made our recommendation. We found and opened supply lines that were used for years. My colleague Ed Kenny was posted in Kabul for some time, and logistics in all our projects there functioned well.

It is known to the reader that religious fanatics, the "Taliban," have now taken over almost all of Afghanistan. The first thing they did when they conquered Kabul was hang President Najibullah.

As I am writing this, up in the north, in Mazar-i-Sharif, Afghans still resist the Taliban today. It does seem that the Taliban succeeded in suppressing most of the country. One does not hear these days of Mujahideen attacks on Kabul or other cities.

However, when I hear of the Taliban's fanatic implementation of what they think are "Islamic rules" or the "Sharia," I am really concerned. Especially with how they treat and restrict women. Women are not to be seen publicly; they are not allowed to go to schools and universities or be employed anywhere.

I think of Dr. Faried's medical team, of the lady doctor I met in the hospital in Herat. I can only feel deep sorrow for the Afghan people who have suffered more than twenty years of civil war and religious fanatics.

1990

CONDOMS

During a visit to Uganda in 1990, I wrote my report on a computer in a small room in the Unicef office in Kampala. There were several cartons stored in that room. During a coffee break, when some secretaries were present, I asked what was in the cartons.

It was an air-shipment of condoms awaiting delivery to the Central Medical Store for distribution in a health project.

One secretary spoke of her doubts about the usefulness of condoms in Uganda. She said most women knew that their husbands were not faithful. Nevertheless, they could not ask their spouse to use a condom when he commits adultery or with his wife. It would not be "culturally" acceptable. It would be impossible for a woman to make such a request. She was speaking of couples in an urban situation.

In rural areas, among lesser educated people, and in a village environment, our secretaries thought condom use was even more unthinkable. No African would buy condoms. Besides, there were no pharmacies around. No organization or government health center could distribute enough condoms. And again, given a village environment, how would you dispose of used condoms?

This coffee break was some ten years ago in the Kampala office. This country, Uganda, was hit so severely by AIDS that practically no family was spared. Thousands of orphans roam around towns, homeless. Many carry the Aids virus themselves and live on the streets until they die. It might well be that many of the more educated urban people cast cultural reasons aside and are now sensible enough to use these life savers.

JIU-MISSION ON LOGISTICS

Following a request by the Unicef Board in 1990, the Executive Office asked the UN Joint Inspection Unit (JIU) in Geneva to survey Unicef's logistics operation. The aim of this was to find out whether the substantial financial engagement by Unicef, particularly in the provision of motor vehicles to assisted governments, was necessary and justified.

The JIU is not a Unicef institution but an inspection office for all United Nations organizations. It comprises eight to ten "inspectors" from member states and their support staff. The JIU has no knowledge of logistics in developing countries. Usually, their inspection activities are about financial matters.

Therefore the JIU required an independent logistics expert, not a Unicef staff member, who could accompany the inspector and work with him on this task. They could only do the job if they found such a person.

It was not easy to find an "independent" logistics expert; those are rare indeed. Nevertheless, someone (a clever person) in management thought, wait a moment, there is Horst Ruttinger, a perfectly qualified person to act as a consultant to JIU. Horst is not a Unicef staff member. Yes, he was one, but he'd been retired for three years. On the other hand, he knew the Unicef logistics operation intimately.

So he was proposed by management to the JIU and accepted. I did not know of these preliminaries and negotiations. On the contrary, I was enjoying a leisurely springtime in Heidelberg. This romantic town on the Neckar River is particularly charming in the spring.

This idyll was interrupted by a telephone call, which Doris took. She handed me the receiver, saying, "A guy from Geneva wants to talk to you." The "guy" was Mr. A. Nolte, the

Executive Secretary of JIU. I had never dealt with him before.

He proposed a consultancy for several months with JIU involving travels to developing countries. If accepted, I should meet the inspector, Mr. Schumm, at the Unicef Supply Division in Copenhagen on May 17th for a "first contact" with Unicef officials and to develop a strategy for the proposed mission. (Having a "first contact" with former colleagues I had worked with for a long time sounded strange to me.)

That, of course, was something for me. Frankly, I was not the person, and still too young, to enjoy a leisurely spring idyll in Heidelberg.

On May 17th, I traveled to Copenhagen, Denmark, and met the inspector who was charged with carrying out this survey. It so happened that Mr. Schumm was a countryman of mine: German. In my long career with the UN, I did not often work with another German. Mr. Schumm brought Mr. Michael Njume-Ebong, his Assistant in Geneva, along for this meeting in Copenhagen. Michael was a national from Cameroon, so while he knew nothing much about logistics, he knew Africa.

A lot had to be discussed with the Unicef colleagues and prepared. Firstly we agreed on a questionnaire to be sent to some twenty field offices, requesting descriptions of problems and proposed answers to their most burning and pertinent logistics problems.

Then we decided on the field offices that should be visited by the team. This was regarded as very important. Mr. Schumm was a very experienced inspector, but his experience in logistics and field environments was limited. This was not necessarily a disadvantage. We "old hands" in the field often had "tunnel vision," meaning we always saw things the same way and often thought we knew the exact solution for each issue. It turned out that an outsider, one who can think logically about a problem and ask: "Why should it be done that way?" was a good thing. Mr. Schumm had the talent to ask that "why" question at the most appropriate moment. Initially, I was irritated, but later I learned to value his "why."

We decided to travel in one long journey to the following Unicef Country Offices during the proposed mission: Mali, Ivory Coast, Congo, Brazzaville, Angola, Ethiopia, Kenya, Uganda,
India and Pakistan. As a consultant to the JIU, I contributed a lot to this list of countries to be visited because I knew the situations in each were typical in their own ways for program logistics.

Later we had to shorten the list of countries. The inspector preferred to work more thoroughly in particular countries and visit the interior rural areas. He thought seeing more countries would not enlighten him more. So we canceled Congo, Angola, and Pakistan. Still, the number of countries to be visited was impressive. It promised to be an exciting trip.

For me, it was a sentimental journey. I had been to the countries we were visiting before. I had lived with my family in Uganda and Ivory Coast for years. For a trip like this, preparations have to be made. Field Offices must be advised of the visits, visas obtained, airline and hotel booked, and shots taken against various tropical diseases.

JIU – MISSION ON LOGISTICS II

The preparations lasted throughout the summer. I was home, but phone calls from Geneva and Copenhagen came daily. The first questionnaires came back from field offices. They were copied to me, and we began analyzing them. The UN in Geneva arranged for airline and hotel bookings and obtained the required visas. Finally, in August, everything was set for departure.

On a Sunday, August 19th, Mr. Schumm departed from Geneva. I flew out of Frankfurt. We arrived at Charles De Gaulle Airport in Paris within half an hour of each other and met in the UTA departure lounge. Your choices were limited when flying from Europe to francophone West Africa. UTA, a French airline, flew to all destinations in West Africa where French was spoken. Then there was Air Afrique, an airline of ten African French-speaking countries that cooperated more or less well together.

Air Afrique received technical assistance from UTA. So much so that UTA pilots often flew Air Afrique planes. In addition, maintenance of their aircraft was done by UTA. That was reassuring for passengers. On the surface, Air Afrique was an example of African cooperation. However, it was and still is not a viable business as an American airline works. Air Afrique loses lots of money. It's mainly for the national prestige of the participating countries. But UTA and Air Afrique successfully prevented any other airline from flying to West Africa.

At 11 AM, our UTA flight left Paris for Bamako; we were on our way to an exciting journey and mission. After a 5-hour flight, we arrived in the capital city of Mali. It felt good to get out of the plane and be again on African soil, yet it was hot and dry.

Like many African capital cities, Bamako airport had a new terminal building. That was part of the prestige game. After independence from the colonial power, most of the countries had new terminals constructed.

They were often bigger than needed and constructed for air conditioning without the ability to open a window. After a short while, the air conditioning machines were no longer functioning, or there wasn't money to run the A/C. As a result, it became very uncomfortable inside the terminal building, where one could not even open a window.

There are only two or three daily flights in a place like Mali. Running air-conditioning in the excessive terminal building for these few flights and passengers is not economical. I still remember old fashion airport buildings in African capitals: Nairobi, Kampala, Lome, and even Bamako. Those were open and airy, comfortable, and looked "African." They were torn down and replaced by modern, unsuitable structures.

An arriving plane from Paris always stirs up a big commotion at Bamako airport. Returning Africans are met not by a person but by the whole tribe. Immigration, health, and custom control are elaborate and take time. Then it takes time to get one's luggage. Porters fight for your suitcase. Taxi drivers do not just accept if you tell them you are being picked up; they still bother you for a fare. And it was hot, very hot, and sticky inside the building.

As an active UN official, Mr. Schumm had a diplomatic passport; however, as a UN pensioner, I just had my German one. But there was very little difference in our treatment anyhow. It took him as long as it took me to get through the hassle. Mr. Schumm had never been to Mali before. Finally, we were outside and met Seidu, one of the drivers from the Unicef Office.

Seidu knew me from previous visits; his joy at seeing me again was genuine. He took care of our baggage, and we drove fifteen kilometers to Bamako. We were booked in the L'Amité Hotel on the Niger River, a little outside the center of town. It was a Sunday afternoon, and there was not much to do but enjoy the pool and, later, the hotel bar.

There is a story about L'Amité (Friendship) in Bamako. The building structure made its stamp on the otherwise flat skyline of Bamako. It had been there for years, and I believe it was the only building with an elevator.

In the wake of French colonialism that ended in 1960, a socialist government under Mouatibou Kaita emerged. This was overturned by the military in 1968. Later, in 1979, the republic peacefully returned to civilian rule. During the socialist époque, fierce competition existed between the Western World and the Eastern Block. Each tried with special favors and assistance to get developing countries on their side. Some African leaders, of course, tried to play one side off against the other.

After independence in 1960, Mali was on the Eastern USSR side. The USSR proposed one of their special favors, something to be seen from far away, the construction of the huge hotel, the L'Amité. Before the hotel was done, when it was just a shell, Mouatibou Kaita was ousted by the military.

The new government turned away from the East and had no interest in a USSR project. Hence, the shell of this tallest building in Bamako stood there unused for many years. Mali had neither knowledge, money, tourists, nor business travelers to run such a large hotel.

Otherwise, Bamako had lousy small hotels. I had tried them all. I was pleased to leave the place each time.

After 1979, when Mali became a civilian government, business began flourishing, and tourists discovered the place. A French hotel chain took over the shell of the L'Amité. They completed the structure and furnished it nicely. It is now run as a first-class hotel. It had excellent French cuisine and a year-round outside pool and bar when we stayed there. So our first day back in Africa was not what one could term a hardship mission.

Work started the following morning. A driver collected us for a drive to the office on the other side of the Niger River over a small bridge always congested by traffic. At least ten colleagues knew me, either local staff from previous visits or international colleagues from elsewhere who had now been posted in Bamako. The Unicef Representative was Alan Everest. We met and worked together in Phnom Penh, Cambodia. There was a big hello of welcome.

Mr. Schumm was a little irritated. He was the high-ranking JIU inspector and Chief of Mission, and I was only a consultant. But I could not help that I was popular with the staff, many of whom I had known for a long time.

Actually, it was not a problem. Later, Mr. Schumm was amused when we visited other African offices; the welcome was always the same. It may have relieved him and convinced him that I was the right consultant and knew my business and Africa.

There is also a story about Alan Everest; he is British-born and raised in India. All his ancestors were in the Royal Indian Army or the civil administration in India when it was part of the British Empire. His great-grandfather was the famous Sir George Everest (1790-1866), the English surveyor who surveyed, measured, and placed the highest mountain on earth on the map: Mount Everest (29028 ft). This British colleague spoke fluent French, a prerequisite to be appointed Unicef Representative in a francophone country.

Mr. Schumm and I worked well together. When we were alone, we talked in German. But he spoke fluent French, which was essential in West Africa, and English. He was a very sharp observer. I wrote it earlier but repeat it now again: I learned that to be a good inspector, you do not have to be an expert as long as your mind works logically.

The JIU mission had just begun, so several more stories will follow.

JIU – MISSION ON LOGISTICS III

Mali is one of the LDC (Least Developed Countries) as defined by the United Nations. In the mid-eighties, Mali was struck by one of its regularly recurring droughts. During our mission, the country had not yet returned to normal, meaning food still had to be provided by the international community to the most affected areas.

Unicef was less involved in food distribution this time. Its priority had changed to a countrywide immunization program called EPI (Expanded Program on Immunization). In addition, they provided regular assistance to the government in programs on child development. These were extensive activities that required mobility in that vast country.

Climatic and road conditions were only acceptable in the Southern part of Mali, about one-quarter of the territory. The rest is in the Sahelian zone, where roads are shocking and the climate unbearable. During the last five to six years, the drought reduced livestock and the population's income.

Unicef created a Logistics Base in Bamako under the technical supervision of a Swiss logistics specialist, Heinz Rieben, for the necessary mobility in assisted programs. This base, with its storage facilities and technical services for maintaining cars, jeeps, and trucks, was essential for health programs in Mali.

The problem was that although Unicef set up the base, trained local technicians and warehouse personnel, and paid all the staff and running costs of vehicles, the Ministry of Health showed no inclination to engage in this project and take it over. The idea was that Unicef would assist the government in building up infrastructure and running health services but not do it for them.

We had numerous working meetings with Unicef officials, government officials, and other UN people, notably with UNDP (United Nations Development Program) colleagues. Alan Everest also suggested a field trip on good and bad roads to see some of the activities to the North of Bamako.

We traveled in a Toyota Landcruiser. The trip lasted the whole day and was very tiring. It was informative for Inspector Schumm. He experienced local conditions and could see the difficulties the local office was up against. As far as UNDP was concerned, the inspector's interest was also to see how UNDP and Unicef cooperated. Should they do more in this respect, and how could this inter-agency relationship be improved?

After several days of work in Mali, we left Bamako for Abidjan, just an hour and a half flight in an Air Afrique airliner. The reception at the airport and in the office by the driver and former Unicef friends was as cordial as in Bamako. I was among this Regional West Africa Office's staff for seven years. Needless to say, I was well known to everyone except those colleagues who had only recently been posted in Abidjan.

The Regional Director at the time of our visit was Stan Adotevi. A national of Togo, he hadn't been in this position when I was in the Ivory Coast. Nevertheless, I knew him from missions to Burkina Faso, where he had been the Unicef Representative in an earlier posting. The Abidjan office, being a regional office for all countries in West Africa, was a good place for the inspector to get information with a regional scope.

Stan Adotevi, too, was a good source. He had many years of experience, first in his government (Togo) and later in Unicef. In Unicef, he served through the ranks from program officer to country representative and finally to his position as a regional director. Another advantage is that he is an African with an inside view of things.

Abidjan is a very sophisticated town. Its many hotels are Western standard, its restaurants are outstanding (which does not mean you couldn't still get an upset stomach if you were not careful.), and government officials and business people were well educated. They call it "The Paris of Africa." I always liked the city, and so did my family. This time, Mr. Schumm and I stayed at the Hotel Tiama, which had the advantage of being in the middle of town. The office and other places are easily reached by foot.

I have written about Abidjan in previous installments and do not want to be repetitive here. But I want to recount one little story.

In her New York office, Doris had a colleague, Evita Resch. In the US, Evita met a young man. His name was Rolf. He, too, came from Germany. They got married in upstate NY. We (Doris, Susanne, and I) were at their super wedding party in the spring of 1989.

Not long after that, Evita was transferred by the Foreign Office in Bonn to the German Embassy in Abidjan. Her newlywed husband Rolf followed her without having a job in this African country. By the time of our JIU-mission stop-over in Abidjan, they had been in the Ivory Coast for about one year.

I gave her a call at the embassy. She was obviously pleased and came over to the hotel for a chat. Her office was only a few blocks away from the Tiama. We agreed to get together the following evening for dinner. Of course, her Rolf and Mr. Schumm would come. Evita said they knew a first-class new place past the port area of Treichville, a little outside the city.

It was already dark when they collected us from the hotel the following evening. In a good mood and with high expectations for good food, we went toward Treichville in search of the new restaurant. We drove for about twenty minutes to where they thought the restaurant was.

However, it was not there. Either it was out of business, or Evita did not remember where it was. Both our hosts were a bit embarrassed that they were obviously lost. Where to go by then? It was about nine pm.

From my years in Abidjan, I remembered an authentic

family restaurant, an Italian place: "Pizzeria du Sorrento," not far from where we were. This absolutely charming place featured about fifteen open straw huts, "paillots," around a brick pizza oven. A lovely ambiance.

The proprietor remembered me and greeted us warmly. He seated us in his best paillote. We had pizza, red wine, and an excellent conversation under a clear, warm African sky. Evita and her husband jokingly said I should come to Abidjan more often to show them places to go. That evening, I was the one who was successful in finding the right place.

* * *

We only stayed three days in Abidjan before heading to Addis Ababa. There was no need to make a field trip within the Ivory Coast.

There was no direct air link from the Ivorian to the Ethiopian capital, so we left the Abidjan airport, "Port Bouet," in the afternoon on an Air Afrique flight for Lome, the capital of Togo. This flight was just 45 minutes in the air.

In Lome, we stayed overnight in one of the French-chain hotels called "Sofitel"; First class! The following day we took Ethiopian Airlines to Addis Ababa. There are few cross-continent air connections in Africa, and Ethiopian Airlines is the only airline flying East-West-East. This situation has not changed during the last forty years. There are plenty of North-South and European connections, but only a few routes by EA cross-continent.

* * *

Ethiopian Airlines was created in the fifties when the country was under the reign of Emperor Haile Selassie. At that time, it was technically and financially assisted by TWA. TWA trained all their pilot, cabin crew, and other staff. Ethiopian Airlines planes are now flown by national pilots. It is an excellent airline with a Western standard.

Even during the socialist time, when everything else went down the drain, Ethiopian Airlines kept its high standard. I may have written this before. (Am I repeating myself?) Ethiopian people are disciplined and sometimes called: "The Prussians of Africa!" I am much more critical of Air Afrique. Malicious people call it (in French) "Air Tragique." Over half the passengers on an Air Afrique flight often have complimentary tickets.

One day I wanted to fly from Lome by Air Afrique to some destination; I can't remember where. When I arrived at the airport, the check-in counters were crowded with African passengers. Modest as I am, I went to the end of the very disorderly line. I thought: *this flight seems to be hopelessly overbooked. I will never make it.*

When I had almost given up hope, a nice African lady asked me: "Are you a paying passenger?" Of course, I was. I had never seen a free ticket. She shouted something in her local language, and I was escorted to the front of the line and in no time had checked in. The plane was only partly occupied. The people waiting at the counter were all "petit fréres" (little brothers) of Air Afriques functionaries with free tickets but low priorities.

* * *

Our flight to Addis Ababa took the whole day, with some stops. We had comfortable seats, good service, and friendly people. The plane was not crowded at all. Flying under these conditions in daylight over the vastness of Africa is very mystic and exciting.

JIU-MISSION ON LOGISTICS IV

We arrived at Addis Ababa Airport in the evening. It was already dark. The Unicef driver collected us and drove us to the Addis-Hilton in town. The driver was Gebreselassie Haile. He had been my driver many times during my Addis time.

I greeted him: "Tanastali," (how are you) in Amharic. He was pleased to see us and flattered because I had not forgotten his language. (Amharic is only one of several Ethiopian languages. It is spoken in the Shoa province around Addis Area. Emperor Haile Selassie was of the Amharic tribe.)

The Addis-Hilton I knew very well. When I was stationed in Ethiopia, there was a severe housing shortage. Being posted without my family, I had no priority in getting an apartment. So I stayed in the Addis Hilton for nine months. Some ninety percent of the hotel staff knew me. (I have always been a generous tipper.) So again, this evening was a bit of a "homecoming." By now, my traveling companion Mr. Schumm was making jokes about my popularity in Africa.

Ethiopia had changed drastically since I left it three and a half years earlier. The government had renounced Marxist communism, and Mengistu left the country for exile in Zimbabwe. There was the sense of a new era about to dawn.

Also, there were changes in the Unicef office. Paul Ignatieff, a Canadian, was the new Representative; Bashige Bashizi, a Congolese, was his second in command. I knew both, but I had had more to do with Bashizi in the past.

After our questionnaire reached them in May, they had extensively looked into their logistics operation themselves and had already made improvements. They were, in any case, ready to answer all of Mr. Schumm's questions. That is what one likes on a survey mission. With such positive attitudes, results can be achieved. In this respect, we had some positive and some negative experiences.

Addis Ababa is located at a high altitude. From about 7500 ft at the airport to around 8000 ft at the University College grounds. Around the outskirts, it has several hot springs, where hot water dashes from the earth's center. One of these hot springs is in the garden of the Addis-Hilton and feeds their outside swimming pool. It is a great pleasure to dip into the pool's warm water in the early morning while the outside temperature is relatively cool. It sets you up for the day. I suggested that Mr. Schumm come to the pool before breakfast and before we met people at the office, and he took my advice.

Addis Ababa is an important place as far as the United Nations is concerned. It is the seat of the Economic Commission for Africa (ECA), one of five similar offices in five regions worldwide. The European Union also has a regional office in Addis called FED.

We had meetings set up with several officials of those international organizations. These were valuable contacts because one could get background socioeconomic information on present-day Africa. Mr. Schumm was particularly interested in this subject because only by considering the socioeconomic conditions could one realistically judge what governments could contribute on their side in a joint (government/Unicef) program.

My mission companion knew his way around ECA much better than I did. Although Unicef's offices were in the ECA compound in Addis Ababa, I never had anything to do with those guys from the UN. I only met some of them casually in the joint cafeteria. But they all knew and highly regarded the Joint Inspection Unit in Geneva, and many knew Mr. Schumm personally.

The hospitality of colleagues and their families on a trip like the one which brought us to Addis Ababa is pleasant. But there were rules too. I was always conscious of this. You were usually expected to re-invite on a one-to-one basis. However, in an organization such as Unicef, where people knew each other well, one also knew which of your colleagues didn't reciprocate.

Doris and I could not return generous invitations in all cases, but we did whenever we had a chance to do so. When we were in New York, we had plenty of opportunities to invite visiting colleagues from field offices where I, or we both, had been guests.

During our four-day stay in Addis Ababa, we could not possibly accept all the invitations from colleagues and friends. Paul Ignatieff and his charming wife invited several colleagues from the office and us for dinner. This is how you get to know your colleagues and their wives and families. So, the outsider to Unicef, Mr. Schumm, also got to meet a bit of the "Unicef family."

As I mentioned above, I did not know Paul Ignatieff too well. Still, I knew one fascinating story of his life with Unicef, which he could tell during this dinner party. I did not have to ask him twice. He agreed to recount the story:

I knew of the story because in May 1975, when I was stationed in Abidjan, I was invited to attend the annual two-week Unicef Board Meeting in New York for the first time. Some field staff members were invited to participate in this meeting, a sensible thing for management to do.

One morning of the board meeting at one of the big conference rooms in the UN Secretariat Building, we were about halfway through the session, discussing a program from Africa. The door opened, and Paul Ignatieff came in. As soon as the delegates and staff present knew who he was, they all stood up and applauded him. It turned out that Paul had just flown in from Bangkok. He was the last Unicef Representative in Cambodia when on April 17th, 1975, the Khmer Rouge invaded Phnom Penh. He was an eyewitness to the brutal expulsion of all civilians from the capital by Pol Pot's Khmer Rouge.

The day before the invasion, Americans and high Cambodian government officials were evacuated by helicopters from the US embassy ground. This did not apply to UN employees, other expatriate people, and, of course, not to local (Cambodian) staff of UN/Unicef offices. Most of them fled to the French embassy ground in Phnom Penh. The situation was particularly tragic for the locals. Some took refuge with their families.

After days of being practically imprisoned at the French embassy compound, they tried to negotiate with the Khmer Rouge for passage, including for local UN staff. They tried everything: issuing them French passports, performing "emergency marriages," etc., to no avail.

All the Cambodian-born people had to remain. Paul and other Unicef expatriate colleagues were driven in a closely watched convoy to the Thai border. They had to leave them all behind. None of the Cambodian colleagues survived the incredible hatred of the Khmer Rouge. Paul was very emotional when he told the board in May 1975 an eyewitness account of these events.

* * *

This stay of mine as a consultant to Inspector Schumm in Ethiopia ended on September 6th, when we departed for Entebbe, Uganda. I have never returned to Ethiopia since, but my heart is still there. Anyone who reads what I have written in this book could not fail to see my affection for Ethiopia and its people. I still think of those days and miss them.

For some reason, Mr. Schumm and I were seated in first class on Ethiopian Airways when we traveled to Entebbe on that Thursday afternoon, September 6th, 1990. It might have been that someone who knew Mr. Schumm in ECA hinted to someone in Ethiopian Airways that there was a VIP booked on this flight.

But there was another unusual happening on this day. Contrary to schedule, the plane flew directly to Entebbe instead of taking the usual flightpath first to Nairobi, then from there to Entebbe. We were told only halfway to Nairobi that the route had been altered. The reason: An African President, I have forgotten which, was expected for a state visit to Kenya. Therefore the airspace over Nairobi was off-limits and closed to other air traffic. Nothing unusual. It happens all the time in Africa.

So we were in Entebbe two hours ahead of schedule. The first problem was getting our baggage out of the plane. I had to crawl into the plane's hull and point out our bags to a porter. The second problem was that the driver, who was supposed to collect us, was not at the airport, because nobody expected us so early. There was no way to call the driver. Cellular phones were unknown in Africa then.

We went to the airport bar and had a beer to pass the time. The airport is in Entebbe, which is twenty miles away from Kampala. The latter is now the capital of Uganda. Entebbe was the capital in colonial times.

JIU-MISSION ON LOGISTICS V

Let me make a correction here. It is important because we do not want to be caught saying something wrong that would discredit an otherwise good story. I wrote that when we visited, the government of Ethiopia had renounced Marxist-communism and that Mengistu had left the country.

That was not entirely correct. The government renounced communism, all right, in early 1990. This was in the wake of the collapse of the USSR. Mengistu tried to become "democratic," but it did not work. The people didn't trust him. Then in May 1991, he resigned from the presidency and left the country eight months after our JIU mission to Addis Ababa.

Back to Uganda. Our landing in Entebbe brought back memories. As a passenger, I often flew in over Lake Victoria. The passengers would wait until the wheels touched down on the tarmac, which began only a few meters from the water. There was always a sigh of relief from everyone on board when that thump was heard.

Not so this time. We landed on the new runway at a ninety-degree angle from the historic old landing strip. As we came in, we saw the old runway and the airport building I knew so well. This former civilian facility was now used by the air force. This place became somewhat famous when Israeli troops raided Entebbe in July 1976 and rescued 103 hostages seized by Arab and German terrorists. They could not recover one Israeli lady, as she was sick. Her name was Dora Bloch. Two days earlier, the terrorists let her go to a hospital for treatment. After the raid, Idi Amin was so angry that he ordered her killed at the hospital.

The Israeli knew that part of the old airport well. In the sixties, when we lived in Kampala, they had an excellent relationship with Uganda. They trained their army and also the Ugandan air force. On the occasions of military parades, Ugandan Jets flew low over the parade grounds, releasing flares in the colors of the Ugandan flag. This required skillful flying. They were so low that one could see the faces of the pilots. We always speculated that these planes were not piloted by Ugandans but by Israelis.

After some commotion with our luggage (see my last story), we were driven by a Unicef driver to the Sheraton Hotel in Kampala. That used to be the Apollo Hotel, named after the first Prime Minister Obote's middle name. When we lived in Kampala, we took the kids to the Apollo Hotel swimming pool on weekends.

In the Unicef Office, we met the Representative, Sally Fegan, a lady from Ireland. Again a warm welcome. I think I mentioned before that Unicef has more female staff in higher, and management, positions than other UN organizations. Unicef's Executive Director is a lady. But at the time, when Sally became the Representative in Uganda, Carol Bellamy was not yet with the organization.

In a nutshell, Sally's main problem with implementing programs was inefficient government project personnel. They were not motivated because of minimal, insufficient wages. There was a severe shortage of transportation and, therefore, impaired mobility. Like in Mali, Unicef was compelled to create a logistics unit, including warehouses and vehicle maintenance facilities. Unicef had to appoint an international manager for this unit and pay all the Ugandan staff. This activity should actually have been a government responsibility. One of the problems was security: frequent burglaries and armed robberies. Unicef project materials, drugs, and spare parts were the targets of the burglars.

On the human side, Uganda was, and I think still is, the African country most affected by AIDS. Three of the local staff, one a female colleague, who served in the office when I was there, had died of AIDS. When one hears that 1000 people died of AIDS, one thinks: "Poor people," but it hits you differently when it happens to people you know.

When some fifteen to twenty years ago, AIDS became known in Africa, Uganda was the first county to admit they had an AIDS problem and ask the international community for help. For national prestige, other countries denied for years that AIDS was a problem in their countries, and some still do so today.

Now, something unforeseen happened to our mission: Mr. Schumm fell sick. Apparently, something he ate did not agree with his constitution. He had a violent diarrhea run, a fever, and felt lousy. So he panicked. Remember, he was not an "old African" as I was. He wanted to fly straight back to Geneva. The office made inquiries and found a seat on an airliner to Paris, so Mr. Schumm left two days after we arrived.

We agreed that I should continue the Uganda mission and go to Kenya. He would join me again in India. So here I was, being "the JIU Mission." I continued taking information and drafted a report on the findings. I felt very much at home in Uganda. The Ugandans are intelligent, usually well-educated people. They got into disrepute because of that "nut" Idi Amin. Because this man was crazy, the whole world thought Ugandans were crazy.

I have another example, and that is Syria. I believe that individual Syrians are the nicest and kindest Arabs. We lived there for four years. We also lived in other Arab countries and can judge. For instance, Lebanese are usually very arrogant. Not so Syrians. (I hope that I do not sound racist!) But admittedly, the Syrian government and its policy during the last thirty years, including shielding terrorists, made the world conclude that Syrians must be horrible people.

It so happened that a Unicef station wagon from the office, with a driver, had to go to Nairobi to collect something from the Regional Office. I cannot remember what they needed to get, but it seemed advisable to bring it to Uganda by car rather than by air.

Although I had an air ticket to Nairobi, it was a perfect opportunity to travel with that Unicef car on the road to Nairobi, a trip I had taken several times before on business but also in a strictly private capacity in my own car with the family. It was 450 miles from Kampala, 3700 ft altitude, to Nairobi, 5500 ft altitude across the equator, which at this point is at an altitude of 9000 ft.

We left early Sunday morning with a long road ahead of us. You must travel overland in a car to get a good feeling for Africa. Some younger folks do it in a public bus. For this, I was already a little too old ten years ago.

After fifty miles, a two-hour drive, we reached Jinja, the second-biggest town in Uganda. The road leads through African villages and little towns, tea plantations, and some miles through the middle of a rainforest. The villages are busy places. They usually have a market in their center, which is even more active, where farmers offer their goods and small live animals.

At the beginning of my time in Africa, I was indignant to see how they treated chickens. Well, not only in Africa. Chickens are bound together on their legs and carried miles on a stick in front and back of the carrier, head down in bunches of twenty or more. As one sees this picture for years, one gets used to it. Of course, they have no refrigeration and have to carry animals live.

Jinja is an industrial town known for Owens Falls, where the Nile dashes out of Lake Victoria. The place is also known for its large textile factory, producing colorful cloth. This is by no means a poor land. Women in Uganda have very beautiful colored dresses with wide puffed sleeves. The fact that men often walk around with partly torn shirts or holes in their trousers and shoes is by no means an indication of poverty. This fashion is what makes an African peasant feel comfortable. The shortage of food and medical care is real poverty, the signs of which are more difficult to detect when one drives by on the highway.

At Tororo, we left Uganda and entered Kenya, then Eldoret, 6900 ft high. This place was famous for its "boarding schools." During the colonial time, the British settlers sent their kids to Eldoret for schooling. We stayed at this altitude and even climbed a little higher on a beautiful road with a good surface, mountains, and forest to the left and right of the road. Then the equator, of course, a reason to stop for a moment and leave the car. Oh, it was cold outside. The blue sky over us did nothing to make it any warmer. What a difference when one visits the equator near Kampala.

We had had enough of the mountains and the cold of high altitude. So we followed the road down into the rift valley to Nakuru, then to Naivasha, and finally to Nairobi. The trip took us the entire day. Near the equator, daylight is about twelve hours from dusk to dawn. The driver, Joseph Mugarra, did an excellent job. I mentioned in other places that African drivers are good. Well, not all. Applicants have to be selected well, from many, for an opening.

A room was booked for me at the InterContinental, which has excellent Western standards. Needless to say, my driver, Joseph, did not stay in the InterContinental. This is not meant to be snobbish, but first, he would not have felt comfortable there, and second, he stayed with friends. It is how drivers save a bit on their travel allowance.

So I was back in beautiful Nairobi.

JIU-MISSION ON LOGISTICS, VI

How should I describe Nairobi? It is difficult. Nairobi is a huge city, one of the biggest in Africa. There is Nairobi, as seen by tourists: comfortable climate, excellent hotels, restaurants, and touring/excursion services to game parks. English is spoken by anyone with whom the average tourist may come into contact. Security, such as muggings, is a little bit of a problem. Tourists are warned, but some ignore warnings and suddenly find themselves robbed of money and passport (It never happened to me). The situation is similar in New York and other large cities worldwide.

Secondly, there is the Nairobi for expatriate residents and business people. This includes old "Africans" like me. Still among the expatriate residents are the old settlers from colonial times. Many of those old settlers have taken Kenyan citizenship. Not all of them are happy with their decision. Then there are, particularly in the larger towns of Kenya, "Asians," meaning Indians and Pakistanis. Most of them are Kenyan citizens and are in commerce. Asians are "a well-to-do minority" with all the problems such hard-working commercial people face. (Including, often, envy.)

Those visiting Kenya on business meet tourists at the hotel, but that is about all. They go to restaurants and see their business partner's shops. People like me have contact with officials from the UN and the government. We know what is really going on in the country.

There are certain bars in Nairobi where you do not see tourists. They can be interesting meeting places to have a drink before lunch or dinner. I remember the most famous of those in the old days was the bar in the New Stanley Hotel. It was, but is no longer, strictly for men. I remember this bar from the sixties. Going there by eleven am, one would meet all the important people one might like to meet. For instance, the Permanent Secretary of the Ministry of Health. Getting an appointment to meet with him in his office at the ministry was difficult, but you could meet him at the Stanley Bar.

Then, of course, in a "big family," like the UN/Unicef community in Nairobi, there are always friends who live in Nairobi. There are headquarters and regional offices of many of the sister organizations. Many colleagues asked us to come to their houses as visitors. There you meet their families, spouses, and kids, and then you really hear what is happening. International life is not all pleasure. One of the big problems is schooling for children. You can imagine, if a tourist on the one hand, or a Unicef traveler on the other, both returned from a week-long visit to Nairobi, each would have a different story to tell.

To return to the JIU mission: With Mr. Schumm sick, it was now reduced to just one person, me. I was collected by a driver in the morning and went to the office. The first person I met was Mary Racelis, the Regional Director. I wrote previously that Unicef employs many female staff in high positions; Mary was one of them. We were old friends. Mary even speaks my language. She was married to a German-speaking Swiss for years but is now divorced. Mary, a highly American-educated (several PHDs) woman, comes from the Philippines, so she was from a developing country herself.

Perhaps this shouldn't be in this book, but I write it here to better explain the "Unicef family." Unicef has a "Global Staff Association" (GSA). I would not like to call it a "union." It is a necessary body that keeps the dialog between all staff (field and headquarters alike) and management open. In New York, Mary was chairperson of the GSA for two years. I was the first vice chairperson. We had to deal with and discuss routine management personnel problems, salaries, leave, etc. But for a global working staff, the conditions at a duty station are much more important. There are what are referred to as hardship duty stations. Nairobi is not called a "hardship" station.

For example: what would happen when a drilling rig operator in a Unicef-assisted water project, searching for drinking water in the Nubian desert, gets addicted to alcohol. That person needs help. Management alone cannot or will not do it. So the GSA assumes an Ombuds Function and helps the man get a new posting in a more sociable place or get into an alcohol withdrawal program. Particularly with field staff, there are often situations where they or their families need help. For these problems, the Global Staff Association was helpful.

After meeting the Regional Director (Mary Racelis), I made inquiries. I met with colleagues from Unicef and several government officials to obtain information that we, the JIU, needed to conclude this mission successfully.

After one more installment about the JIU mission, I shall write the promised summary of our findings on the state of "logistics in Unicef programs." As I have written extensively about Kenya, I shall not write more about this country now.

On Saturday, a week after I arrived in Nairobi, I left on Air India in a Boeing 747 for New Delhi via Bombay. This was a tiring flight. It lasted the whole night, landing on Sunday at eleven AM in New Delhi. It is not bad at all to arrive on a Sunday. With time and climate changes giving me the well-known "jet lag," resting a whole afternoon was necessary to be fit again.

JIU-MISSION ON LOGISTICS – INDIA

A brief review of what had happened already during this mission: The UN-Joint Inspection Unit (JIU) was charged with looking into Unicef's program logistics. I was hired as a consultant to the inspector to advise him on technical details and peculiarities of Unicef's work.

Inspector Schumm, with whom I traveled to Mali, Ivory Coast, Ethiopia, and Uganda, fell sick in Kampala/Uganda. He flew back to Geneva for treatment. I continued the mission alone through Uganda and Kenya. Mr. Schumm intended to rejoin me in India.

* * *

From Nairobi, I traveled on Air India to New Delhi, arriving on a Sunday morning. I had in mind to sleep in the afternoon to recover from a night flight and jet lag. This is not what happened.

I was taken by a driver to the Ashoka Hotel in New Delhi, where I checked in. I had barely gotten to my room when I received a call. My colleague, Mogens Munk, from the Delhi office, was in the lobby and wanted to welcome me to India. We were old friends, so I went down at once.

After a big hello, we went to the bar where, over an Indian beer, he gave me the latest news. Firstly he told me that Mr. Schumm from Geneva would not be coming to India to continue the mission. Instead, he had sent the JIU Research Officer, Mr. Michael Njume Ebong. (I mentioned him previously. Michael was from Cameroon.) He had already arrived that morning and was staying in the same hotel.

Secondly, all three of us (Mogens Munck, Njume Ebong, and I) were to fly the following morning (Monday) to Pune in the State of Maharashtra because that was where we could see activities about what we were investigating. That gave me very little time to recover from the jet lag. However, this mission was not intended to be a pleasure trip.

Let me write a bit about my friend Mogens Munk. He is Danish, and his name is not uncommon in Denmark. India, with a population of more than one billion people, has a very large Unicef country office. Mogens was the Logistics Officer, a position only the larger offices had on staff.

India, a federal republic, had twenty-five states at the time. Maharashtra is one of them. Pune is the state capital. Services for the population, such as health and education, are a state responsibility, not a federal one. (I believe this is the same in the United States.) This being the case, Unicef Delhi had dealings with all these states regarding assisted programs. Hence our field trip to Pune to get first-hand information on logistics.

We traveled in an Indian Airliner. The trip is about two and one-half hours. We were booked in the "Blue Diamond Hotel." Accommodation in India's provinces is not as comfortable as in Delhi.

We contacted government officials of the Ministry of Health. We got a good picture of the magnitude of their logistics operation in delivering health services to all the people in this vast state. As in many other countries, mobility is the most critical part of modern health services.

Unicef's first priority, and, in fact, its mandate, is looking after mothers and children. Preventive medicine saves more lives than curative medicine. Therefore state-wide vaccination campaigns and outreach to rural areas' services are the first priorities. (As I had written before, this also applies to other countries.) Such campaigns depend on the cold chain to keep vaccines potent and suitable vehicles to bring them to the vaccination centers.

Maharashtra did a good job of keeping vehicles in good running condition. The Ministry had a garage and a system of preventive vehicle maintenance. A vehicle's life is like a human life. If you take good care of yourself, eat healthy food, have the necessary shots, and regularly see a doctor, you will likely live long. If you treat a vehicle well and have regular preventive maintenance performed, it will likely last a long time.

We remained in Pune for two days. I think our newcomer Michael Njume Ebong, escorted by two "old hands" (Mogens and myself), got a good feel for a logistics operation in an Indian province. Our Air India flight was delayed by two hours, so we returned to our hotel only shortly before midnight.

The following morning we went to the Unicef office. We were received by the Representative, another of Unicef's successful ladies: Eimi Watanabe from Japan. She, too, had been to headquarters in New York, and I knew her well. She gave us, and particularly Michael, information on logistics problem areas in the whole of India.

Although Mr. Schumm was still the responsible inspector for this mission on logistics, his research person Michael was the one who had to write the draft report on it and therefore took a keen interest in all the details of the matter.

One particular thing in India was that all the motor vehicles provided by Unicef for assisted programs were locally manufactured Jeeps. The manufacturer of these Indian Jeeps was Mahindra and Mahindra LTD of Bombay. In the early sixties, they got a manufacturing license for the J-5 and J-6 from Willys Jeep, USA. So Mahindra and Mahindra had built these early sixty models with very little change for all these years.

So we decided to provide only locally manufactured Jeeps. Unicef was the biggest customer of Mahindra and Mahindra LTD. The good news about this was that we did not need to provide spare parts; they were easily obtainable in the whole country. The bad news was that Mahindra jeeps, although they had been built for a long time, got a bit worse in quality each year. It was a big job for Mogens to check if the Jeeps in each delivery were up to the ordered specifications.

We met with a vice chairman of Mahindra and Mahindra LTD, who came from Bombay to Delhi to meet us. He thought our visit to India would be a good opportunity. He believed we had something to say about purchasing vehicles worldwide. We did not; that was not part of our mission. His company wanted to extend business with Unicef and export jeeps to neighboring countries.

He was, supposedly, unaware that vehicles delivered in India give rise to complaints about quality and missing parts. This was a chance for us to express our dissatisfaction. He probably thought it had been a mistake, and a waste of time, to fly over from Bombay to meet us.

Michael Njume Ebong from Cameroun, a UN official from a developing country (Cameroun) and not a logistics expert, had quite an interesting time in India. Mogens and I did our best to explain what was done and what could go wrong in big operations.

Four days later, on Friday, I returned to Germany. Except for giving my written input in the inspector's report, which I could do from home, the long JIU mission on logistics, in which I was not the leading actor but rather an advisor and consultant, was successfully concluded.

JIU – SUMMARY

There was, of course, a valid reason for the request made early in 1990 by the Unicef Executive Board to the UN-Joint Inspection Unit in Geneva (JIU) to critically examine logistics with a focus on the provision by Unicef of motor vehicles.

There was a more than ninety percent increase in program transport expenditures from US $23 million in 1984 to $42 million in 1989. This expenditure rise was linked to programming because the programs' emphases have changed to outreach strategies requiring more mobility.

Back in 1974, the "basic services for children" approach was adopted. In 1978, at a conference in Alma Ata, the board endorsed the "Primary Health Care" (PHC) strategy emphasizing district-focused or community-based activities.

But then, in the early eighties, Unicef "shifted into 4th gear," as the newly appointed (1980) Executive Director James Grant (USA) used to say. Measures were introduced aiming to drastically reduce child mortality rates worldwide through the PHC approach. This led to the adoption by Unicef of a "Child Survival and Development" (CSD) strategy. This strategy involved several "simple" but sometimes "not so simple" measures for achieving its ambitious target.

For this approach, a new acronym was created: "GOBI," each letter standing for a basic program: "G" for growth and weight monitoring in young children; "O" for oral rehydration therapy (ORT), a simple method of replacing life-sustaining fluids lost in diarrhea; "B" was for breast-feeding (slogan: breast is best!).

Why? More and more mothers from developing countries switched to bottle-feeding their babies with formula products from Nestlé and other multi-million-dollar corporations, believing that formula was better for their child than their mother's milk.

Finally, the "I" was for "immunization" against childhood diseases. The "Expanded Program on Immunization" was, from the logistics point of view, the "not so simple" element of the GOBI programs. The World Health Assembly, including Unicef, declared an ambitious goal of "Universal Child Immunization" by 1990. Pursuing this objective, especially at an accelerated pace as envisaged in the Unicef medium-term plan 1987-1991, implied increased supplies, vehicular transport, and logistics management. The three are interdependent.

Now all this came at a time when countries had less money to run their affairs. The original idea of the Unicef/government partnership was that Unicef would provide program materials for which foreign currencies had to be spent, and governments would pay for local costs. In the case of vehicles, back in the sixties and early seventies, Unicef furnished, for example, a Land Rover, and the government paid the local costs for its operation, including the driver's wages. As governments became increasingly unable, or in some cases unwilling, to pay their share of the program costs, the cost-sharing principle was gradually abandoned. Unicef was required to pay more and more local costs too.

It took some time, even among Unicef colleagues, to realize that as the government's transportation fleets (not just those vehicles provided by Unicef) increased, actual transport availability in assisted programs decreased and became unsatisfactory. This was because many trucks and cars fell into disrepair and were unavailable for service in programs. Often all that was missing was a small part. No money was available to purchase spare parts. Our government counterparts insatiably requested more from Unicef. But they ignored the high operating costs, and their budget contained no provisions for running additional vehicles.

I prepared a chart of operating expenses for all the countries, giving the actual fuel, maintenance, labor, spare part, etc., costs in a table for the different types of vehicles. These costs depended on local conditions, notably fuel costs. By and large, one could say that the average operating cost of a vehicle is about one-third of its purchase price.

For instance, a Land Rover was about $18,000 for Unicef. Running this Land Rover would cost the local government about $6,000. Ten Land Rovers in a program were not unusual. Consequently, their running costs were $60,000, which many countries could not sustain. The result was that program vehicles were underused because of a shortage of fuel money and became prematurely unserviceable because of poor maintenance.

The JIU mission to Africa and India clearly brought to light and convinced the inspector that mobility in assisted programs and Unicef's provided transport equipment was vital. Unicef had to take on local costs for efficiency's sake, initially the government's responsibility. Providing vehicles that the governments could not afford to run made no sense.

In my work and travels in Africa and elsewhere, I advocated a policy of "fewer vehicles in better, more reliable condition, attainable through better maintenance is equal to more availability of transport in Unicef-assisted programs" for years. We saw the first positive example on our JIU field mission in Mali. I have written in my story, "JIU – Mission on Logistics III," about the "Logistics Base" that Unicef set up in Bamako/Mali.

Having agreed that Unicef has to get more involved in local services and consequently bear local costs, it made sense not to do this independently from governments. Their involvement must be insisted upon for various reasons. One critical reason was "capacity building."

Vehicle maintenance is a critical issue. Developing the ministry's maintenance facilities is more logical and economical for a fleet of vehicles, such as in health programs, as commercial garages can not be used. They are too expensive. We called these ministerial facilities "Transport and Equipment Maintenance Organizations," or TEMOs.

Unicef could provide garage equipment, spare parts, and replacement tires for such facilities. We even offered experts to work for some time to help set up and train the technical staff. This sounds very simple and logical, but it was not that easy. The primary constraint was management and, in particular, personal.

I have high regard for the technical skill that Africans and Asians possess. I had written about this in previous stories. For instance, Ethiopian private truck owners still operate pre-WW-II Fiat trucks for which they manufacture spare parts, as those are no longer available for purchase. Indian mechanics are highly skilled. They can repair anything: old cars, locomotives, and airplanes, which we Westerners have forgotten how to fix. Mechanics in our countries only replace defective parts in a vehicle; they repair them.

Now the 100 million dollar question: "Why do TEMOs not work, or are at best inefficient?" The answer is that mechanics in government garages are not motivated at all. Their wages are meager. The salaries of government officials in developing countries are, in general, low. It is because of this that there is corruption everywhere.

A high government official can not live on what they officially earn. Therefore he/she gets money "on the side" through corruption. A government driver can always make some money on the side by taking passengers. Although that was not permitted, who can check a driver in the African bush? A government mechanic has very little chance to earn money on the side. What he makes in a government TEMO is too little to live. Mechanics in commercial workshops earn ten times the amount of a government one and, in return, perform good work.

Good mechanics are in short supply in developing countries. If one is good, he will never join a government outfit. Such rare skill is valued in commercial, expensive garages. Franchise holders of Mercedes, BMW, AUDI, Peugeot, and others maintain excellent servicing and repair facilities, and their technicians are highly qualified.

Unicef had tried to arrange with governments to get good technical and management personnel by supplementing their government wages. The money did not even reach the technician concerned if such supplements were paid through government channels.

So it had to be paid directly to the worker who, because of this, regarded himself as a Unicef employee. This was a situation that Unicef wanted to avoid. Further, when the payment of the supplement was over, after an agreed time, the governments would not pick up the tab. They would again start paying a low wage, and the inefficiency returned. It was and still is an almost insolvable situation.

These were the logistics problems in program implementation as they were found and confirmed by the inspector on this JIU mission, in which I participated as a consultant. The inspector wrote a 42-page report on his findings, essentially the same as those I had reported after past field visits. It has been years now that I am no longer in the business, but of course, I have contacts with Unicef and know that these problems still exist today. They seem to be the characteristics of "underdeveloped nations" and will surely be this way for a long time.

EPI AND LOGISTICS

Although the World Health Assembly created the Expanded Program on Immunization (EPI) in the seventies, massive immunization programs only got underway in the early eighties. That was when the target of "universal child immunization by 1990" was adopted. With this target, major donor countries became ready to provide the enormous financial resources necessary for EPI.

These programs did not stand isolated on their own but were part of a strategy for primary health care. The EPI and the 1990 target of universal child immunization required a massive effort to build an infrastructure. That infrastructure required cold chains for vaccines, vaccine supply, shipment to the respective countries, distribution, and training of vaccinators and other staff along the whole chain. Logistics was a significant component of the EPI, considering that universal coverage meant vaccinating children in remote rural areas. The task was very challenging.

I was in charge of the Field Logistic Unit in the headquarters Supply Division in New York. (I was not responsible for vaccine procurement). The American Heritage Dictionary defines logistics as "the procurement, distribution, maintenance, and replacement of materiel and personnel." In Unicef's terms, it meant: the right project material for the right price, in the right quantity and quality, at the right time, in the right place to be received and handled by qualified people with timely reorder of stock. (For example, sending an electric refrigerator to a site without electricity is useless.)

When the World Health Assembly declared that universal child immunization would happen by 1990, the manufacturers had difficulty supplying the massive amount of various vaccines (polio, DPT, measles, etc.) that were suddenly in demand. They had to develop the methods of refrigerated packing and flying out vaccines with major airlines. Country officials were sometimes reluctant to accept shipments of vaccines that "appeared not to be fresh" or otherwise spoiled.

For instance, the USSR at that time also manufactured vaccines, and there was no reason (or justification) for Unicef to reject vaccines from this member state and donor. However, their packing and appearance were often extremely bleak compared to packages in nice Styrofoam boxes from Western manufacturers.

Post-Emperor Socialist Ethiopia was a great friend of the Soviet Union. Nevertheless, in one instance, I was called to inspect and see a large shipment that the Ministry of Health (MoH) rejected, claiming the medicine was inferior. The packages were partly torn, the labels were in Russian, and there was no knowing whether it was still effective. Western vaccine shipments had a color indicator applied, which proved that the cold chain had always been maintained.

Shipments at main airports in developing countries had to be organized. Under no circumstances could the cold chain be interrupted. The MoH in capital cities usually had refrigerator equipment. But it was not uncommon that such equipment, even in capital locations, did not function satisfactorily.

Another thing was power supply: usually available in a country's capital, it was pretty different in local and regional sites. Electricity was unreliable. Even when it was present, there were fluctuations from about 140 to 280 volts, ruining refrigerators quickly. We had to develop stabilizers and uninterrupted power supply systems with the manufacturers.

That was often done in India, where Unicef purchased large quantities of locally manufactured refrigerators for the EPI. In Africa, however, standard refrigerators for rural areas were powered by kerosene or, in some instances, bottled gas. Those were quite effective if properly serviced. The wick was crucial; kept in good order, it would always maintain a clean burning flame. Clean fuel (kerosene) was of utmost importance.

Kerosene and bottled gas availability in rural areas was always a problem; supplies were often interrupted. Kerosene was used by the local people for household fuel. Therefore kerosene provided to run the EPI refrigerators was a big temptation. Sometimes stolen quantities of kerosene were replaced by water, which, of course, was no longer usable for the refrigerators. Keeping beer in an EPI refrigerator was not allowed, but to my thinking was not a big crime. On the contrary, I thought it was an incentive to keep the refrigerator functioning.

The refrigerators had to maintain the vaccine temperature and freeze the water-filled elements of cool boxes, the last link in the cold chain. These cool boxes (the same as we take out for a picnic) were then transported in utility cars or on a motorcycle or a bicycle to where the shots were given.

Solar-powered refrigeration equipment was another option. In Africa, where sunshine is plentiful, it would seem logical to use solar power. There were, however, some drawbacks. Solar Units were still expensive, about $4,000 to $5,000 per unit.

They are getting cheaper now. The system we used was the photo-voltaic type. Panels of photocells were mounted on a roof. During the day/sun, these panels charge a large car battery, which powers the refrigerator. Proper maintenance of the panels and the battery is essential.

In the Sahelian Region of the Republic of Chad, the EPI team used two camels, one to transport a solar unit and battery, the other to carry a mobile refrigerator, to provide cooling for vaccinations in remote desert areas. At the time, it went through the press with sensational pictures. I think it was more a publicity stunt than a genuinely helpful innovation.

1991

ZAIRE II

The last time I visited Zaire was in 1991. Maria Diamani, a Greek national, was the new Unicef Representative. (Unicef has a good record of employing women in higher management positions. The organization, after all, is about mothers and children.)

I knew Maria well. Two years earlier, I worked for her in Burundi when she was in charge of that country. Now she called me back to active work out of leisurely retirement in Germany (In 1990, Doris and I moved from New York to Heidelberg). The assignment was to provide consultation on program logistics and inland transportation from ports of entry to Zaire's interior.

The situation in Unicef is constantly changing. Security needs change, but also the focus of international assistance changes. For Unicef, the focus was now on programs in Kasai Province, the center of the enormous country of Zaire. In the last few years, Unicef set up sub-offices in various towns. These sub-offices in Zaire would now be included in a computer-based monitoring system for greater efficiency.

On March 9th, 1991, I landed at Kinshasa International Airport in Ndjili. I was taken by a Unicef driver to the Intercontinental Hotel. One of the first people I met in the lobby was Helene.

I was speechless and really astounded. Helene was my secretary in New York until I left there five years earlier. I had always been very grateful to Helene because, for years, she turned reports and letters drafted by me into readable English. "Helene, what on earth are you doing in Zaire?" I greeted her.

It turned out Helene had become a wizard on the part

of Unicef's computer system, which pertained to ordering, procurement, shipment, and monitoring program supplies, a huge task in the organization's activities. She had come to Zaire for two months to train staff on the software.

Helene was a native-born New Yorker. As far as I knew, she had never traveled outside the USA, certainly never to a developing country. Helene and many of her headquarters colleagues were confronted daily with talk, phone calls, and writing from and about foreign countries, but this was all theoretical. They had not been to or seen these countries. It was also Maria Diamanti's idea that a staff member like Helene should have field experience. She thought it would make her work in New York more efficient.

One time when I returned to NY from an African field trip, Helene asked me, "Aren't you afraid for your health when you travel in those counties?" Now she was in the midst of Africa herself.

One of my first activities on this mission was to travel to the Atlantic coast. Unicef had a small port office in Boma. As this office needed to monitor all landed supplies and send shipping reports back, it had to have the new computer program installed on the computer.

I suggested to Maria that Helene come with me to Boma, where she could load the software and train the office staff. At first, Maria was a little suspicious of my suggestion. Jokingly she asked me: "Are you her lover?" But in the end, she thought it a good idea for Helene to travel with me and not by herself.

We went with a Unicef driver in a Toyota Landcruiser. Four years ago, I traveled these 370 miles (See a previous chapter!). In the meantime, the road had gotten worse. It took the whole day. Helene will remember her first day in the African bush. At the halfway point is a town called Thysville, where we stopped for a bite to eat and something to drink.

Now comes a story that should perhaps not go into the book, but it happened: I sat in front with the driver, and Helene sat in the rear. After driving for some time, I looked into the rearview mirror and felt something was bothering Helene. I asked, "Are you alright?" She said, "Yes."

After some time, I looked again and saw that Helene clearly had a problem. I insisted that if she were not well, she must tell me.

To make a long story short, Helene had to go to a "bathroom." There was no bathroom and not likely to be one before we'd driven another two or more hours. Usually, that is not a problem for experienced male or female "Africans." I asked the driver to stop.

Helene did not think this was an easy matter. She thought of snakes she had heard of and "natives" who might turn up out of the bush. I calmed her down and assured her that the driver and I would remain in the car, looking straight ahead. No snakes would attack if she didn't go too off the road.

We arrived in Boma at dusk. The hotel was not too bad. When we arrived, there was electricity, and we checked into our respective rooms. A little later, Helene knocked on my door. She was frightened. She told me there were creatures in her room. It turned out the "creatures" were harmless geckos. I told her they were good to have in the room, they caught mosquitoes, and they would never attack a person. I do not know whether she believed me.

While we were eating dinner, the electricity suddenly failed and did not come back on the whole night. It was hot and not comfortable. Helene told me the next day that she had a candle burning most of the night. She did not enjoy staying there with those geckos on the wall.

The following day the electricity worked again, so Helene could work and demonstrate the computer software. I spent the whole day working at the port, in warehouses, and contacting commercial freight forwarders.

The good news was that we had air conditioning again for dinner and during the night. Helene slept much better this second night. The following day we drove back to Kinshasa with the mission completed.

* * *

Mbuji Mayi was another field trip I had to do. The Kasai Province consists of two sub-provinces, Kasai-Occidental (West), whose capital is Kananga, and Kassai-Oriental (East), with Mbuji Mayi as its principal town. I flew there in a Boeing 727 of a commercial "airline" called SCIBA. They have only one aircraft. They shuttle back and forth between Mbuji Mayi and Kinshasa.

I stayed in a small but good hotel called Mkumbi-Kumbi (I wish I would recall what the name means). The food and bed were excellent. Mbuji Maji is by no means a poor African village. On the contrary, it is a wealthy mining town. But there are also poor people there. I have seen them.

Unicef has a sub-office in Mbuji Maji. Barbara, a Belgian lady, was in charge of the five employees. Helene could not travel there, so I loaded the new computer program and instructed the staff. But that was a sideline. I was mainly concerned with logistics and warehousing. One thing was clear, Boma's Atlantic port was not the right place to import supplies. It was better to ship those in containers from the east coast via Zambia and Lubumbashi into the Kasai Province. One of my recommendations.

Union Minière, a multi-global corporation, mines diamonds from one of the richest diamond deposits in the world. This corporation employs thousands of people. They are, by African standards, well-paid and cared for. There is a housing project for the miners.

Apart from the mining corporation, individuals can prospect for diamonds in well-marked areas. Citizens of Zaire can get a "claim" by paying a certain fee and, like in the American old-west, prospect for diamonds. Some are more, others less fortunate.

In the market in the center of Mbuji Maji, there is a street where Zaire citizens (Citoyen and Citoyenne) can sell and buy diamonds. I walked through this street and was approached by several dealers, they told me they could not sell the stones to me in the market, but they could come to my hotel, no problem. These are raw diamonds. They just look like a stone. I would not know what to do with them. Diamonds are smuggled all over Africa. This must be big business. Unfortunately, I do not understand anything about it. The cutting of diamonds is mainly done in Holland and in South Africa, so I was told. I liked Mbuji Maji in the center of Africa. I could live there.

You read "Citoyen and Citoyenne" above, which I must explain. After the French Revolution towards the close of the 18th century, the French didn't title themselves "Monsieur" et "Madame" any longer, but Citoyen and Citoyenne. Zaire is essentially French-speaking. In addition, there are four or five other significant languages (Lingala, Swahili, Kikongo, Tshiluba) and many tribal languages.

After the dictator Mobutu took over in the early sixties, he changed the names of towns and rivers. He also made people with Christian names (For instance, Joseph: Mobuto's name) adopt an African name. At the same time, "Monsieur et Madame" was changed to "Citoyen (male) and Citoyenne (female)" by order of Mobutu.

Not very respectfully; we ridiculed this a little and called each other by this title. Occasionally I would say Citoyenne Maria to our representative, and she would call me Citoyen Horst. But there is more behind it. Before the fall of the Iron Curtain, several African countries tried to go the socialist/communist way. For instance, Mali, Guinea/Conakry, Angola, Ethiopia, etc. They addressed each other with "comrade." This was compulsory among nationals, but some called us foreigners "comrade" as well.

OK, so what? Zaire was the opposite of socialistic/communistic. Mobutu and Zaire were truly capitalistic. That was appreciated by the big corporations and by Belgium and USA. In short, by anyone who had money invested in that mineral-rich country.

The problem has always been the Eastern provinces:

Haute-Zaire, Kivu, and Shaba, too far from Kinshasa and with no roads, as I wrote in the chapter called "Congo." They were not controllable from the faraway capital. Ethnic differences are also a reason why these provinces are difficult to rule. Uganda, Burundi, and Rwanda are very much closer.

Some three years ago, the East rebelled. Uganda and Rwanda assisted the rebels by having "volunteer troops" in Eastern Congo. The rebels' leader was Laurent-Désirè Kabila, a military man by background. He successfully invaded the west, conquered Kinshasa, and made Mobutu leave the country. Mobutu died from cancer shortly after that.

Kabila is now president of the country, which he renamed back to its original name, "Congo." Kabila turned out to be a very ruthless president. He is hardly different from his predecessor. So his old friends in the East turned against him. With the help of Rwanda and Uganda, the eastern rebels are now attacking Kabila. The provinces of Haute-Zaire and Kivu are under rebel control. However, they could not take mineral-rich Shaba as neighboring Zimbabwe and Zambia came to the help of Kabila.

As to recent developments, I just heard a few days ago that they had a peace conference in Lusaka between Congo, Zimbabwe, Zambia, Uganda, and Rwanda, and representatives of the rebels. Allegedly, they negotiated a ceasefire and agreed further that all foreign troops must leave the Congo. That would be fine and good for the country and its people. I am skeptical, however.

1992

CAMBODIA

Eleven years later! How much a town and country can change in a relatively short time. It was an almost sentimental homecoming when I landed again in January 1992 at PNP International Airport, this time in a commercial airliner. I arrived to take a three-month assignment in Cambodia, as it was called again.

I acted as the Unicef Supply/Logistics Officer during these three months. The previous colleague was gone, and the new one, already selected for this position, was not free from his old job. So I, a retired person, filled the gap for three months. Now engaged in large development programs, Unicef had a big office in a new building.

The old Samaki Hotel was now called the "Royal Hotel," its former pre-communist name. I could not believe my eyes; the Royal was completely renovated with an excellent dining room and edible food. The old maitre d' recognized and embraced me.

PNP also had a new 4-star hotel, the "Cambodia Hotel," managed by a Singaporean management company. This hotel compared well with other international hotels in the Far East. It was full of tourists on excursions to the magnificent Angkor Wat ruins in the North of Cambodia.

The town was full of shops. One could find anything to buy locally. There were many excellent restaurants in town. As in other Asian countries, most shops had Chinese owners. Local markets, not just in PNP, were full of merchandise. There was plenty of oriental food.

There were many new houses, and Unicef colleagues now lived in apartments. Cambodian landlords were happy to find international (UN) people to rent their new homes. I compared, of course, with my first stay in the city twelve years ago. Again I must say "despite the politicians," the country was relatively prosperous.

Politically Cambodia was in a mess. The country had had civil disturbances and warfare for the last twelve years. The remaining Khmer Rouge and other political factions fought for influence and power.

A peace agreement was brokered in 1991 in Paris between the various factions, including the Khmer Rouge. In this agreement, hosted by the United Nations, it was decided that Cambodia be placed for two years under the administration of the UN. The main objective was to prepare the country for free and independent elections.

A UN Organization, "UNTAC," was created for this purpose. Its chief was a Japanese, Yasushi Akashi. There were twenty-two thousand blue-helmeted peacekeepers from many nations in the country. Finally, the elections were held, and the peacekeepers left again. But Cambodia being Cambodia, it was still, or is again, a political mess.

However, this did not concern me much during my three-month stay in PNP. I believe in the creativity of the Khmer population "despite the politicians." The most repeated phrase by Cambodians is: "No problem." Not just a saying; this is their attitude.

One of the best restaurants in town was called "No Problem!" Why? In Asia, it is common to get an upset stomach when eating in a restaurant, particularly uncooked food like salad. The "No Problem! Restaurant" in PNP guarantees that whatever you eat there, you will have no problem.

It was nice to see the bustling life in the streets of PNP. There were cars on the roads, but not very many. The means of transportation for the average Cambodian family was a motor-scooter. In my country, such two-wheelers are made for one, or at most, two riders. Readers may not believe it, but I have seen families of up to eight people (two adults and their children) on motor-scooters trucking along the main roads in PNP. On a

Sunday or a holiday, they file up and down the big boulevards four to five scooters side by side.

Another means of transportation in town is the "Cyclo-Taxi," a pedal-powered three-wheeled "rickshaw." Cyclos were introduced by the French in the thirties. Intended for two passengers, families with six or seven members were sometimes transported. The poor cyclist, pedaling away with this load, never complains.

One other change I want to mention. In 1980 and again in 1981, I was in the East German GDR Embassy. Firstly on business, as they were donors, but also one time for a cocktail party. In 1992 I went to the same building, this time to visit the Federal German Ambassador. The only Germany left had taken over. Communist East Germany no longer existed.

1993

CALLED OUT OF RETIREMENT

In 1993 I was once again called out of retirement by Unicef on a logistics consultancy for OLS (Operation Lifeline Sudan). I have written a story titled "OLS" (See below). I was based in Nairobi. Our base camp and warehouses were in Lokishokio on the border with Sudan.

At this time, I often flew from Nairobi north over the Great Rift Valley to Loki (as it was called for short). Most of the time, I flew in a small Cessna provided by an NGO organization. The trip lasted 3 1/2 hours. Almost the whole distance was over the Rift Valley.

That was a long flight in the Cessna, always full to capacity. The small plane's advantage was that it flew relatively low, clearing some of the volcanos, of which the rift features many, only by a few meters. I recognized many of the roads in the valley I had traveled before by car. Flying over it in a Cessna brought back memories and was truly unforgettable. I have no words to describe the splendor of this landscape.

OLS

OLS stands for "Operation Lifeline Sudan." This is a UN operation with several UN agencies and international NGOs (Non-Governmental Organizations) participating. The ICRC (International Committee of the Red Cross) is also involved. This project is a massive effort to save the people of Southern Sudan from starvation.

There are (still are) two OLS headquarters, one in Nairobi, Kenya, and the other in Khartoum, Sudan. Unicef and the WHP (World Food Programme) are the main actors in OLS.

Sudan is the largest country in Africa. Their civil war has been ongoing for about thirty years, and the end is still not in sight. Sometimes fighting is more intense. Sometimes, it is quieter. It has been fierce for years recently, bringing immense suffering to the population.

To many people's thinking, this war is between Muslims of the North and the Christians of southern Sudan. This is a straightforward but incorrect assumption. The people of the North are Arabs and Muslims. The people in the South are of the African race with a variety of religious beliefs, Christians as well as animists. There are also Muslims in the South; for instance, Idi Amin, Uganda's former dictator/president. His people came from southern Sudan and were Muslims.

The southern freedom fighters are divided into factions and often fight each other. Their "leaders," also called "warlords," are not fighting on the front. No, usually, they sit in Nairobi in comfortable villas and "direct" the war in the relative security of the Kenyan capital.

The international efforts to "save" the poor people of southern Sudan are tremendous. I believe that measured by population and beneficiaries, more international donor money is poured into southern Sudan than any other developing country. While the fighting continues, no real development work can be done. Former costly development projects of the seventies and eighties in southern Sudan (The regions of Wau and Juba) were not maintained and are no longer functioning. Again, personally speaking, I suspect that the warlords are using donor help, chiefly food aid, in their war strategies.

In 1993 I served as a logistics consultant for OLS-Unicef and was based in Nairobi. Most international donor help to southern Sudan is provided from the South via the Kenyan border. The OLS base camp, including food storage facilities, is in a northern Kenyan town called Lokichokio.

Lokichokio is called "Loki," for short. It's one of the least inviting places on earth. It's situated in the Rift Valley. The town is desert-like and on the edge of the Lotagipi Swamps.

The camp consists of large warehouse tents (Rubb-Hall) for storing food and other emergency supplies. In addition, there are tents and "dooguls" (round huts with straw roofs) for personnel. One large tent is a mess hall where meals are served to the many international people living in Loki.

The road from the Kenyan coast is long, and the last four hundred km are in deplorable condition. There is a rainy period when trucks can not pass at all. Generally, the OLS chartered Kenyan commercial truckers are as tough as their roads. Thanks to them, Loki warehouses are well stocked.

The shipments onward to the needy people in southern Sudan are more problematic. For years this had to be done by costly air transportation. The logistics core of Lokishokio is the airstrip from which large planes start and land with emergency aid. They land at even worse airstrips in Southern Sudan to deliver this aid to the population. The runway in Loki is not tarred but has a graveled surface.

The transport planes working out of this airstrip are chartered by the UN-OLS from commercial companies. The biggest is the four-engine Hercules C-140. Another big transport plane is the Canadian de Havilland Buffalo. We even had exotic planes, like a DC3 with two turboprop engines, altered in South Africa, flying for us for some time. One has to have high regard for the brave pilots who fly these skies, sometimes even get shot at, and land on these improvised airstrips.

For this assignment at OLS-Unicef, I needed to visit the supply base at the Sudanese border several times. A chartered six-seater Cessna flew there three times a week, flying personnel to Lokishokio.

At the end of April 1993, I took this flight. The weather forecast said we would have rain. The good thing about this journey in a small Cessna is you fly low over the most beautiful areas in Africa and see the great richness of the country, its wildlife, landscape, mountains, lakes, and forests. The not-so-good part is flying low in the weather, not above the clouds. The ride can be very bumpy and sometimes even scary. It takes a long time, three and a half hours, from Nairobi to Lokishokio.

Before takeoff from the Wilson Airport in Nairobi, we met the pilot, Eddy Watt, a Scott. He instructed us on what to do in an emergency. He showed us the place in the aircraft where the survival kit, including drinking water, is kept. "In case I'm not with you anymore." Well, that was scary.

We took off to the north. Mount Kenya was visible on the right side of the aircraft. It's the second-highest peak in East Africa, with a snow-covered summit. Then along the Rift Valley: Naivasha and Nakuru, with their lake clearly visible. The last big lake before we flew over the desert was Lake Baringo.

We saw a black wall in front of us two hours out of Nairobi. It got bigger and bigger. No doubt, this meant we were hitting bad weather. The pilot saw no chance to fly around the clouds. He said he would try to reach Lodwar, a big airfield with a long tarred runway half an hour flying short of Loki.

Well, we made it, and shortly after we landed, a big storm swept over the airfield. An hour later, we tried again and took off. But it was no-go; the heavy rain, and the violent bumps, made us turn back to Lodwar. While in the air, Eddy Watt contacted Loki by radio, explaining our situation.

We went into the little town of Lodwar and found a restaurant where we could have a simple meal. After this, Eddy announced that he had to fly back to Nairobi. Even though the weather had improved, he had to reach Nairobi during daylight, as his plane was not equipped for night flights. A final radio contact with Loki was made. They promised to send an aircraft to collect us.

After a long wait, a plane appeared on the horizon. It was a turboprop Cessna Caravan piloted by a lady, Shawna McKeever, from Canada. She flew us safely to our final destination.

The runway in Loki was graveled and OK for the landing. The plane's parking place, however, was very muddy. The camp leader, Predja, who collected us, arrived with a pair of rubber boots for each of us. He then explained that a tremendous storm had swept over Lokichogio. Thank god they could move all the perishable food inside the tents, and nothing was spoiled.

PREDJA

He was the manager of the OLS base camp in Lokichogio. Predja is his last name, and his friends only knew this one. He once told me his first name was too hard to pronounce, so he did not use it. Predja was a Yugoslav from Belgrade and was married to Brigitte from Switzerland. They met in Afghanistan, where Predja worked for Unicef and Brigitte for the ICRC (International Committee of the Red Cross). They have a son, who was eleven months old at the time of my visit to Loki. I first met Predja in Afghanistan, where I had been on a logistics consultancy some years earlier. I had not met Brigitte before.

After we arrived in Lokichogio, Predja assigned me a very good tent. It was quite comfortable with a camp bed, table, and chair. A generator was operated until ten PM, so the tent had electric light. Although it had been raining all day, the tent's heat and humidity were still high. That improved in the evening. Being in the desert, the night became quite chill.

Apart from the tents, the camp had some solidly-built "dooguls" (phonetic spelling!). In the African tradition, a doogul has mud walls, is round, and has a straw roof. Those in Loki for international civil servants were made of bricks. They were round-shaped but were much more comfortable inside than an African hut. Predja lived in one of the dooguls. The tents were more for temporary staff and visitors like me.

After settling in my tent, it was evening, and there was no more work to be done. I went to see Predja and his family for a sundowner. It is always nice to meet an old friend, even in the middle of nowhere, like Lokichogio. So we had a nice talk.

Predja was very proud of Niklas, his eleven-month-old son. He could walk around with some help and was pleased visitors were in the house. We went to the mess tent together at about eight PM and had dinner. There were no longer clouds, and it was a lovely evening. The restaurant manager had moved the chairs and tables outside. We sat under a beautiful sky full of stars and listened to all the typical sounds of an evening outdoors in Africa.

Later, we had a few more drinks in Predja's doogul, then I went to my tent and managed to find the bed, although there was no more electric light.

In a camp like this, it is essential to have a torchlight. As one can imagine, there are no individual bathrooms in each tent. Having had a few drinks, I had to use the bathroom in the middle of the night. Now I needed the torchlight, not to find the latrine, that was no problem with all the stars and moonlight. No, it is important to carefully examine your shoes before you put them on. Scorpions tend to hide in your shoes at night in this desert environment. They are dangerously poisonous.

Otherwise, I slept well and was ready for hard work when I woke up. There were improvised showers. African employees heated water over an open fire. The hot water was now in altered oil barrels up on scaffolding. The shower stalls were made of bamboo mats, a perfect shower in this environment.

Lokichogio was, of course, not a holiday camp. A day of hard work lay ahead. In the morning hours, the place was full of young people. They had cups of coffee from the restaurant tent and were ready to depart for their work inside Sudan. The airplanes were loaded to capacity in the early morning with emergency aid, mainly food.

Personnel of the WFP (World Food Programme) and NGOs now boarded the planes to fly to little airstrips inside Sudan where distribution was being done. Most of these international helpers flew to the distribution centers in the morning and returned in the evening. It was not safe for foreigners to stay in southern Sudan. All the personnel returned to the OLS camp in Loki for the night. In the morning, they flew in again with a cargo plane.

In addition, there was a de Havilland Twin Otter for transporting small cargo and personnel to their project sites and back in the evening. All of this was and still is a costly operation.

Nevertheless, how much aid went daily to this hostile land was impressive. It was being distributed to needy people, often at great risk to the courageous young volunteers from the NGOs. There was and still is no road transport possible over the border.

I did not fly inside Sudan. My mission concerned logistics matters, the upkeep of adequate supply levels, food storage, and other emergency supplies. A significant problem was the availability of A1 Jet fuel for the aircraft, including the big Hercules and the de Havilland Buffalo, which daily shuttled several flights of aid, fully loaded, to the small airstrips for distribution.

All fuel had to be purchased at the coast some 1000 miles away and transported by commercial trucking companies to Lokichogio. Strict inventory control had to be applied. The inventory was kept at a low level. Nevertheless, the supply line from the coast and/or Nairobi to Loki was long. Particularly during the rainy season, adverse weather conditions often resulted in trucks being stuck for days before they arrived at the base camp.

The emergency items were all in demand and valued by the local population. This northern part of Kenya was not an affluent region, they knew what was being shuttled over the border, and many could not understand why nothing went to them. Therefore there was jealousy, and the temptation was great. We had to investigate missing items from an education project on this mission. These simple items intended for schools for Sudanese children had disappeared, and it was no longer possible to establish how this had happened.

Predja, his wife Brigitte, and I were invited for dinner in

the ICRC camp in the evening. The Red Cross had its own camp on the other side of the village. They used the same airstrip as the UN; otherwise, their mission differed. They had a small hospital where soldiers wounded in the fighting in Sudan were treated. I met a German doctor who was serving with the ICRC. Here again, a memorable night under the stars of an African sky with simple food and good conversation.

Predja was a Serbian Yugoslav. During my visit to Lokichogio, the Bosnian war was happening. We discussed the war and who might be at fault. He is by no means a friend of Milosevic, but he is still Serbian. I know that he must suffer now with a more fierce war, bombs falling on his hometown and the whole world against Milosevic and the Serbians.

The afternoon of the following day, I traveled back to Nairobi in a de Havilland Twin Otter. This aircraft is much more comfortable and faster than the Cessna I arrived on. After two hours of flight, we landed at Nairobi Wilson Airport. It was an exciting mission to Loki, where so much of the action for the Southern Sudan Operation was taking place.

1994

KHARTOUM, SUDAN

In January 1994, I was called again out of leisurely retirement. This time, the Unicef Representative in Sudan asked me to come on a mission to Khartoum and survey the logistics situation. That included the operation of OLS' northern sector. The southern provinces of Sudan are internationally recognized as part of the country. However, the South is hardly accessible to the authorities in Khartoum. Except for some bigger towns, like Juba and Malakal, Khartoum cannot control the southern rural areas. Even today, these places are firmly in the hands of the rebels.

Sudan is Africa's largest country. Khartoum is its capital on the river Nile. Actually, there are two Niles that join together just outside the capital. The Blue Nile comes down from Lake Tana high up in the Mountains of Ethiopia; the White Nile comes from Lake Victoria in East Africa.

It is quite a sight from an airplane to see where these rivers join. The Blue Nile is really blue. The waters of the White Nile are more a dirty brown. For some miles after the rivers meet, the blue and brown blend together like paint being mixed. Gradually, however, the blue fades away. The Nile just looks murky after that.

Khartoum is on the East side of the Nile. Across the river on the West side is Omdurman. Both, together, are just one big metropolitan city with a significant historical background. Sudan was jointly ruled by Egypt and Britain; they suffered a bitter defeat when in 1885, Mohammed Ahmed, alias Mahdi overrun Khartoum/Omdurman. During this battle, the famous British General Gordon was killed.

Contrary to the world's (Western) opinion, I found Sudanese people to be very friendly, with genuine oriental hospitality towards foreigners. The present regime in Khartoum and their support of terrorists is different.

Basically, Unicef was engaged in two different kinds of programs in Sudan. In collaboration with the government of Sudan, Unicef's assistance sector was mainly in health services that benefited mothers and children. Within this scope were a vaccination project and a project to provide more potable water in rural areas. The latter means the drilling of water wells and the installation of hand pumps. The second program in which Unicef is still active is "OLS," Northern Sector, together with other UN organizations, particularly with the WFP (World Food Programme).

For both programs, substantial supplies were necessary. Most of the items arrived in Port Sudan on the Red Sea. I visited this port in an Air Sudan Airbus from Khartoum for my mission. The flying time was just about one and one-half hours. There was a small office there to manage the large quantities of Unicef cargo that arrived in Port Sudan. My Sudanese colleague showed me around and explained the operation.

Port Sudan is a typical Arab town. Although there is everything there that tourists are looking for, the sea, beaches, warm climate, and the relative proximity to Europe, there were no tourists but only a few business people in town.

I met two Australian sheep farmers at the hotel, which was quite comfortable. They regularly came to the country to buy live sheep for export to the land "Down Under." I had quite an interesting discussion with the two gentlemen at dinner. Selecting the right sheep for Australian conditions from big herds seems to be a tough job. Bargaining with Sudanese herdsmen for a fair price must be equally challenging.

Given the vast country, the poor road conditions, and the unreliable performance of the national airline, Unicef, and other major international Organizations operating in Sudan, had their own aircraft. Most organizations accept cargo and passengers of others on a reciprocal basis.

Our plane was a De Havilland Twin Otter. It had been in operation for many years, and I had flown in it during previous visits to Sudan. It is the only permanent aircraft that Unicef owns. When air transportation is required elsewhere, it is hired on a case-by-case basis.

Consequently, Franz, its pilot, is the only staff member with this profession, which is sometimes a problem for Administration. How do you rate his duties, salary-wise, when there is no benchmark category in the organization?

Anyhow, Franz, a countryman of mine, having flown in the country for some twenty-five years, is very knowledgeable about conditions in Sudan. He knows all the possible landing sites, fuel availability, people in the business, and, most importantly, weather conditions. Sandstorms, which occur at certain times of the year, are no small matter for such a light aircraft.

Our Twin Otter is painted white and bears large UN/Unicef markings. Despite this, it has been shot at several times, even by ground-to-air missiles, in rebel-held Southern Sudan. Jokingly, staff in the office refer to his air operation as "Air Franz," not to be mistaken with the French Airline "Air France."

On my mission, I used "Air Franz" for a trip to Malakal, one of the southern centers held by government troops but entirely surrounded by rebels. Unicef maintains an outpost there, a tough job for colleagues. There are many refugees, mainly women and children, in this town.

As we approached to land, Franz pointed out where the rebels usually hide and where anti-aircraft fire may come from. Perhaps he only wanted to scare me. Normally, the rebels did not shoot at UN planes. They knew their own women and children in the enclosed city depended on our emergency aid.

Malakal is on the Nile, and the bulk of food and medical supplies came on river barges as part of the OLS-northern sector. Both forces, government as well as the rebels, can attack these barges, but this does not happen. They respect international help.

Off-loading in Malakal ranges from easy in the wet season, to very difficult in the dry season, depending on the river's water level. The river banks are steep. Carrying a fifty kg bag up to street level is no easy matter.

I had some experience with this from the Mekong River in Cambodia, where we had conveyor belts. Not in Malakal. An additional handicap was that, because of the frontline situation, UN agencies were not allowed to operate their own radio system but depended on government radio communication. On the day of my visit, radio reception was practically nil.

Within the framework of OLS, the Northern Sector, there were many little places where the population suffered because of the civil war. They depended on food and medical supplies from somebody. From the government, they could expect nothing. The roads to many centers were not only poor but also insecure. The Unicef-only aircraft, piloted by Franz, did a formidable job flying to the most remote places and landing on almost any stretch of flat surface.

As the plane had a limited loading capacity, which always included the weight of the fuel for the return flight, it was necessary to have gas transported by trucks and stored in forward positions so that flying time could be kept to a minimum.

The barges that supplied the population with food and medical needs along the river were from Kosti, about 170 miles South of Khartoum. We teamed up with WFP in hiring the necessary river crafts, barges, and tugboats for this purpose. Kosti had sufficient warehouse space and was well-equipped to be an OLS staging area.

Logistics can always be improved and made more efficient and rational. The situation changes and must be reviewed frequently, particularly in a civil war, when conditions and access routes change often. My logistics mission to Sudan in January/February 1994 was gratifying, and I think it resulted in many improvements.

1999

LASSA FEVER

That brings me to a story that happened just a few days ago here in Germany. My family and I were not overly concerned about catching a disease when we lived in the Middle East and Africa. Apart from one malaria case our oldest daughter Renate developed in Kampala, we were never sick with a tropical disease.

More than immunity, which doctors would be skeptical about anyway if one lives and travels in the tropics for a long time, one gains a certain behavioral knowledge. There are things you never do, knowing what can happen. For instance, one would not eat raw vegetables, salad, or lettuce away from home, even in a good restaurant. One would not eat local stuff in a marketplace, even if this food is sometimes tempting and one is curious how it may taste. Swimming in a river or lake is equally dangerous.

In a previous story, I wrote that Peace Corps volunteers, in particular, thought it would be expected from them that they behave more natively than the natives.

Now to tell this case of a young German art student. It has occupied the front pages of the newspapers for days. A twenty-three-year-old female student was with her class, escorted by a teacher in Ghana, and the Ivory Coast, to study original African art.

This student was sick with a high fever on her return from Africa. Her brother, who picked her up in Frankfurt, took her directly from the airport to a hospital. She told the attending physicians that she had just returned from Africa. They treated her for malaria, but she got sicker and sicker.

Then the press got hold of the story. Finally, she was flown by helicopter to a special clinic for tropical diseases.

They diagnosed her with a viral infection called "Lassa fever" (German spelling), a rare but deadly disease. She had a new aggressive strain of the virus. The press reported on her condition daily. It went from bad to worse.

The health authorities tried to contact anyone who may have had contact with her, particularly anyone in the airplane when she flew from Africa to Frankfurt, for fear that others may have been infected by the virus. No one else seems to have been infected.

Because of the coverage on TV and in the papers, the whole country prayed for her recovery. Particularly when it became known that her father died of cancer in another hospital while she was battling the "Lassa fever." Alas, in vain, she died seven days after her return from Africa.

Doris and I now ask ourselves: did we live in such a dangerous environment for so many years and downplay the possibility of getting seriously ill? Were we too careless? Did we adapt properly to local conditions, or were we just lucky?

I suspect that Africa has become a more dangerous place to live in recently. Health infrastructures have definitely deteriorated. There is now AIDS, which was not known in our times; increasing cases of tuberculosis; deadly malaria resistant to standard "quinine" treatment and other health problems.

On the other hand, the population is growing fast, too fast, in certain countries such as Kenya.
Perhaps it is nature's equalizer.

LOST PEOPLE

In the last days of December 1999, something happened in West Africa that I did not think possible. A coup d'etat in the Ivory Coast. It started with a mutiny of soldiers in the capital city of Abidjan, apparently over not receiving their pay. It escalated and resulted in the toppling of President Bedie from power and the dissolving of Parliament by the military. President Bedie called loyal troops in vain for help and had to leave the country.

The Ivory Coast was a shining example of African democracy, the pride of all the Ivorians, and France, its previous colonial power. When President Felix Houphouet Boigny was alive, France always favored the Ivory Coast and provided extraordinary aid. With Houphouet Boigny dead, the same chaotic conditions in many other African countries seem to have taken over.

The whole continent is in a crisis. Economies are in shambles, countries are indebted up to their ears, and families and entire villages are devastated by AIDS. Western industrialized nations do not seem to care anymore about African countries. Eastern nations have their own problems and do not care either. During the "good old days," when the West and East confronted each other in a cold war, African countries were courted from both sides. No more. They seem to be a lost people now.

COMPUTERS AND Y2K AND AFRICA

Just a day before Christmas, with all the Season Greetings dispatched to friends and relatives (a few by e-mail), I find time to sit down in front of my computer screen and resume writing about the story of my life.

Here in Germany, as elsewhere, the talk in these last days of this century is about the Y2K phenomenon. All the sectors: water, gas, electricity, hospitals, etc., of our municipality are releasing statements. They say they are certain services will continue, and life will go on as usual.

Nevertheless, employees and technicians will stand by during New Year's Eve in case something goes wrong. Local newspapers are full of stories and speculations related to the millennium bug. There are conmen taking advantage of the uncertainty and hysteria. Is that all a gimmick? We shall know in a few days.

On December 29th, 1999, we went to a Bavarian resort hotel for a grandiose Millennium Party. We were at dinner at a table with a Bavarian couple. All of a sudden, the lights went out. Nobody was prepared for this. Was Y2K already sending a message? We had lots of fun and jokes about the lights being off. It took some time until the hotel staff brought candles and matches to all tables. Later the manageress told us they were all prepared for a blackout on New Year's Eve but did not at all expect the lights to go off two days earlier.

Afterthought: The new millennium came, and nothing happened in the developed or underdeveloped world alike! What was all the fuss about Y2K? A gimmick? Or was it that people were prepared, and companies and organizations checked and adjusted their computers and software, thus preventing a major breakdown of systems? Nobody seems to know.

EDITOR'S AFTERWORD

Considering his lifelong work with Unicef and other charitable organizations, I believe it can be honestly said, more than for many of us, that Horst left the world a better place than when he entered it. I'll close with a poem I wrote and read at Horst's memorial service in Heidelberg in 2020:

Für Horst:
There's a hole in the world, a gap,
where a person used to be.
A person with ideas, feelings.
A person with uniquenesses.
There's a hole in the world,
that can never be filled.
It can be replaced; it will be.
But, not filled. Not in the same way.
There's a hole in the world.

Printed in France by Amazon
Brétigny-sur-Orge, FR

21478460R00233